Fight
for
Democracy

Fight
for
Democracy

Fight
for
Democracy

The ANC and the Media in South Africa

GLENDA DANIELS

WITS UNIVERSITY PRESS

Published in South Africa by:

Wits University Press
1 Jan Smuts Avenue
Johannesburg

www.witspress.co.za

First published 2012

ISBN 978-1-86814-568-3

Edited by Monica Seeber
Cover design and layout by Hothouse South Africa
Printed and bound by Creda Communications

CONTENTS

Dedication

This book is dedicated to journalists

ACKNOWLEDGMENTS

This book came out of two processes: first, my passionate attachment to press freedom and then the indulgence of this attachment in a huge task – a thesis on the role of the media in a democracy, unraveling the politics between the media, the state and the ANC. The essence of that thesis has been distilled in this book. I thank my supervisor, Professor Sheila Meintjes, for her consistent encouragement, her warm support, and for creating and generously hosting in her home in Norwood – for about a year, in 2009 – a wonderful group. We called ourselves the Politics and Media Discussion Group.

This group met once a month and we took turns to present papers. We debated issues related to media and democracy while eating croissants and muffins from fine china. The group consisted of the Wits Journalism veterans, Professor Anton Harber, Professor Franz Kruger and Lesley Cowling; the head of the School of Communications at the University of Johannesburg, Professor Nathalie Hyde-Clarke; the Open Society Initiative of Southern Africa media and ICT manager, Dr Dumisani Moyo; the Save Public Broadcaster Campaign coordinator, Kate Skinner; Professor Jane Duncan from Rhodes University; Sheila and me.

I am indebted to and respectful of my MA supervisor Peter Hudson for introducing me to the world of political philosophy. He was generous with his time, his ideas, his reading and commenting and his lending of books. My interest in political philosophy began with him in my undergraduate years at Wits in the 1980s. His intellectual rigour was such an inspiration that I returned to do an MA with him in 2006. It was a great experience, learning with some life experience behind one.

To the colleagues who gave their time enthusiastically to be interviewed, to put across the point of view of journalism, particularly Mondli Makhanya, Justice Malala, Abdul Milazi, Hopewell Radebe and Rehana Rossouw – thank you. But there were also many others who I interviewed who gave their time generously.

I acknowledge the Swiss-South Africa Joint Research Programme (SSAJRP) for its financial support in the last two years of the PhD. My research was located within the SSAJRP 'Safeguarding Democracy: Contests of Memory and Heritage' project. It was a great interdisciplinary opportunity for all of us in the team to share ideas related to democracy, memory, history and philosophy with our Swiss partners at Basel University. I also received the National Research Foundation prestigious scholarship for three years, 2008-2010, for which I am grateful.

I would also like to mention two important organisations in my recent development. First is the M&G Centre for Investigative Journalism (amaBhungane, or dung beetles, who dig up dirt) where I spent just over a year, 2011-2012, as advocacy coordinator, before I joined Wits Journalism. AmaB afforded me a good opportunity to learn about access to information problems, the Protection of State Information Bill (Secrecy Bill) and to write a fair number of comment and analysis pieces about it. During that period I also served on the Right2Know national and regional structures and so personally witnessed and experienced the impact that civil society pressure and activism can bring to bear upon draconian impediments to democracy, such as the Secrecy Bill. The May 2012 proposed amendments by the ANC, or partial backing down from the draconian nature of the bill, were a testament to the success story of civil society formation, coalitions, and activism – even though the State Security Agency rejected these amendments in June 2012. A personal boon from R2K activism has been the media freedom friendships I formed with Kate Skinner and Julie Reid.

For diligent reading and commenting thank you to my friend Heidi Brooks. To the Wits University Press team, Veronica Klipp, Roshan Cader, Melanie Pequeux – what a treat to work with you. And copy editor Monica Seeber, from whom I have learned such a lot in a short space of time, especially how to be unsentimental about deleting material that's not necessary, for instance, deep philosophy that can often do more confounding than illuminating – thank you. Hothouse South Africa, especially Lisa Platt, did a creative job in translating words into visuals for the design and layout.

To my friends Penny, Tendayi, Amber and Diane your support continues to inspire. It is good also to have a large family who encourage academe, too many to mention all by name but especially Reynaud, Julian, Desiree, Vivienne and Allan. Last, but most importantly, thank you to dear Nigel for your optimistic disposition, wise counsel and consistent encouragement to fight to maintain a free press, freedom of expression and access to information. Now Alex and Ash follow that example and lend the same kind of support to the same issues.

PREFACE

I undertook this work from the position of a practicing journalist. It is a work of advocacy that grew out of my 2010 PhD thesis in the Department of Political Studies, University of the Witwatersrand. I have also added my own experiences from time to time. The particular standpoint *ab initio* is in support of a press free from party political interference and control. I have always worked in the print media, and therefore I do not, and cannot, hide under an impossible cloak of detachment and objectivity. My position is that journalism makes a contribution to the deepening of democracy in South Africa and my focus is on the print media's role of public watchdog, holding power to account.

This book also examines the view that journalism in this country is shabby, unfair and irresponsible and therefore it needs a statutory media appeals tribunal. It challenges the Protection of State Information Bill (known as the 'Secrecy Bill') under which journalists would suffer severe penalties including jail sentences for being in possession of a classified document. In addition, disclosures of classified information to reveal criminal activity will be criminalised. Further deliberations on the Bill were postponed to September 2012.

The ANC's lead in a noble fight in exile, and inside the country, for liberation towards a democratic South Africa, can hardly be disputed. However, the irony is that the fight had to be strategically undertaken from exile, largely in secret, because of the nature of the organisation and its military component, and because it was banned inside the country. In this analysis of the relationship between the ANC and the media in South Africa, I've drawn a picture of highly contentious politics in the ANC vis-à-vis its support for the Secrecy Bill and a statutory media appeals tribunal (notwithstanding some backing down in 2012), a portrait of an organisation virtually turning against its own project of developing a radical democracy. We should also note the new General Intelligence Bill, which consolidates and centralises the power of a security regime in the making, giving more to the State Security Agency (although this bill has not been dealt with in this book).

Why was the ANC seemingly becoming anti-democratic? Was it because large sections within it believe that the Constitution, punting freedom of information, free speech and media, was a series of compromises which many regret today, hence talk of a 'second transition' in the 'National Democratic Revolution'?

Significant developments regarding the media appeals tribunal and the Secrecy Bill took place in 2012. In addition, a court date was set (October 2012) for the lawsuit against Zapiro by President Jacob Zuma for the 'Lady Justice' or 'rape of justice' cartoon, with an emphasis on the matter of the president's 'dignity' – the same discourse as is evident in the reasons for establishing a statutory media appeals tribunal. There were four big developments to do with print regulation, all confusingly tripping over each other. First, starting in January 2011, the Press Council of South Africa held public hearings around the country, to hear what people felt about the press. The subsequent new Press Code was formulated with more stringent criteria for ethical journalism. Second, in July 2011, the South African National Editors' Forum (Sanef) and Print Media South Africa launched the Press Freedom Commission (PFC) to examine different systems of regulation around the world, and to hear via oral and written submissions what South Africans had to say about press freedom. Third, in September 2011 Parliament held an indaba into diversity and trans-formation in the print media, at which ownership, transformation and diver-sity were all collapsed and conflated into one convoluted bundle. The event signalled the start of the imposition of the media appeals tribunal, which would ultimately see the media controlled by political commissars. However, by June 2012, a media charter became the flavour of the month according to the Parliament communication committee. Fourth, the PFC held public hearings in January 2012, at which the ANC's secretary general, Gwede Mantashe, the head of communications, Jessie Duarte, and the spokesperson, Jackson Mthembu, made passionate appeals for a statutory media appeals tribunal. In their argu-ment such a body would ensure that the media made fewer mistakes, would be more 'accountable' and would observe individuals' right to 'dignity', referring to an aspect of the Constitution which jostles alongside freedom of expres-sion. They did this with a new twist: they argued for 'independent' regulation by a body, which must be statutory, like many Chapter nine institutions (state institutions set up to safeguard constitutional democracy, established in terms of chapter 9 of the Constitution) in a 'parliamentary oversight' process. The contradiction at best, and obfuscation at worst, about 'independent' but statu-tory was not lost on many of us who attended the hearings and made submis-sions too (I made a submission on behalf of the M&G Centre for Investigative Journalism, amaBhungane, on why self-regulation was the best system for print media). In a nutshell, it appeared that the ANC wants the media to ultimately report to Parliament, where the majority of members are ANC. Then, in an interesting turn of events, on 25 April 2012 the PFC announced its review of regulation of the press: 'independent co-regulation' which, on the face of it, appeared to be a political compromise for what the ANC desired. The ANC said that it 'welcomed' the PFC report and that it was 'a step in the right direction'. The report said that there were 'perceptions' in the public mind that self-regulation did not work, and that the system favoured journalists. In fact, this is an ANC bias and the most recent statistics of the ombudsman's rulings over the past three years, 2009-2012, showed that the majority of rulings, about sixty per cent, went against the press and in favour of the complainant.

As we head towards the ANC's elective conference in Mangaung in December 2012, the control of the media could still be on the ruling party's list of priorities. The argument in this book takes its cue from the Declaration of Principles on Freedom of Expression by the African Commission on Human and Peoples' rights: 'Effective self-regulation is the best system for promoting high standards in the media'. If a statutory body to control the media were to be introduced in South Africa it would signify significant closures for freedom of expression, media freedom and therefore democracy, as has occurred in a number of African countries after colonialism. However, the idea of a media appeals tribunal seems to be in abeyance now, with the acceptance of the PFC report, although it can only be completely off the table if the conference in December 2012 rescinds the Polokwane 2007 resolution to investigate it.

And if the Secrecy Bill was passed in the unamended form it would create a fearful and secretive society, one that hides corruption from scrutiny. Whistle-blowers would think twice before handing over documents for exposure or publication. The average citizen's access to information would shrink. A tame media would censor itself, while bold journalists would go to jail. There wouldn't be less corruption but you would read less about it.

The Secrecy Bill has been a huge drama in public life over the past two years. After numerous postponements the Bill was passed by the National Assembly on 22 November 2011, with 229 yes votes, 107 no votes, and two abstentions. It was then referred to the National Council of Provinces (NCOP), the second tier of parliament, for further consultations, public hearings and submissions. The NCOP conducted hearings around the country in the first few months of 2012. The bill has to be passed by the council before it proceeds to the president for gazetting. The public participation process threw up some surprises for the ANC. Citizens from the Cape Flats, for instance, questioned the ANC about service delivery and asked pointed questions about what the party wanted to hide. Forewarned by this attack, the ANC in the Eastern Cape bussed in supporters and the NCOP tried a new tactic. Every time anyone said 'Secrecy Bill' he or she was shot down, and told to address the issue and, further, not to mention service delivery. Reports from participants in the Eastern Cape hearings, as well as in many of the other provinces thereafter, questioned why the government was prioritising the Bill at this time. Given this mixed bag, it was rather perplexing when Parliament issued a statement: '2 February 2012: Bill gets resounding approval' and a careful reading of the statement does not explain why the hearings were considered a resounding success. The Right2Know campaign made other findings. Many people do not know the implications of the Bill, but when they do, they state unequivocally that they want less secrecy in society, not more. They want a free flow of information so that they can make informed decisions about their lives. In March 2012, a further postponement was announced, and only seventeen of the 263 written submissions were approved for presentation to the parliamentary committee. The parliamentary committee heard oral submissions on 29 March 2012, and when it was Mark Weinberg from the Alternative Information Development Centre and the Right2Know's turn, he was ordered to stop, because he was making 'political statements' (*Sunday Times*: 1 April 2012). He was expelled after he submitted that there was a 'rise of conservative authoritarianism' and a 'rise of the securocrats' in the post-Polokwane dispensation. Weinberg said his ejection was more evidence of the 'undemocratic culture gripping our government'.

My argument is that the ANC is obsessed about the print media and its numerous uncoverings of corruption within the party's ranks. These exposés destroy the image the ANC would like to portray of itself as the noble liberation movement. It summoned two outrageously undemocratic 'solutions' to deal with the 'problem'. Under the guise of 'development', 'transformation', 'rights to dignity', and maybe even 'the second transition' there is something highly ideological and seriously political afoot: the desire for political control through curbs on access to information. This argument proceeds that the ANC does not want the party's internal divisions and problems hung out for the public to see; it does not want the inadequacy of service delivery exposed; and it finds the corruption within its ranks embarrassing.

Legislative curbs and muzzling would spell doom for democracy but nonetheless, alongside the gloomy picture there are civil society forces rallying against this authoritarianism creeping in to steal democracy. As Nic Dawes, editor of the *Mail & Guardian*, aptly wrote in his end-of-year freedom essay: 'It is a fragile creature, and new, but the ANC's fear and rage may be giving birth to a politics more threatening to its hegemony than any lurid caricatures of its paranoiac imagination' (*Mail & Guardian*: 23 December 2011-5 January 2012).

In its attempts to cover up its own failings, the ruling party uses obfuscation and some serious ideological social fantasies, and projects many of its internal problems onto a robust press. For this reason, I have employed psychoanalytical concepts such as hysteria, fantasy, gaze, surplus and excess to explain the issues in the various case studies that have occurred since the advent of democracy. While democracy is fragile, there are optimistic moments lying side by side with pessimistic moments. The ultimate point is that a critical and robust press plays a significant role in keeping the spaces open for the deepening of democracy and it must be left alone to do its job.

ABBREVIATIONS AND ACRONYMS

ANC	African National Congress
ANCYL	ANC Youth League
BEE	black economic empowerment
BDFM	*Business Day/Financial Mail*
Cosatu	Congress of South African Trade Unions
DA	Democratic Alliance
FBJ	Forum of Black Journalists
FXI	Freedom of Expression Institute
GEAR	Growth, Employment and Redistribution
Idasa	Institute for Democracy in South Africa
IPS	Inter Press Service News Agency
Misa	Media Institute of South Africa
MMA	Media Monitoring Africa
NCOP	National Council of Provinces
NAIL	New African Investments Limited
PFC	Press Freedom Commission
SABC	South African Broadcasting Corporation
SACP	South African Communist Party
SAHRC	South African Human Rights Commission
Sanef	South African National Editors' Forum
TAC	Treatment Action Campaign

1. INTRODUCTION

The ANC and the media post-apartheid

Gratitude for liberation should not mean unending gratitude to the leading movement in that process. It is very human to be caught in the seductive embrace of one's liberators, but it is irresponsible and shirking one's duty to continue to entrust the future of one's society solely to a party or parties associated with the liberation struggle.[1]

The role of the news media in South Africa's democracy presents a paradox, a historically created conundrum: the South African media finds itself subjected to the ruling party's desire for more unity and consensus in the country's fractured society. The desire of the ruling party, the African National Congress (ANC) would be met if there was a more supportive and loyal press but the press finds compliance with this desire out of kilter with its professional code of ethics, its role of holding power to account, loyalty to the citizenry, exposing abuses of power and being a 'watchdog' in the unfolding democracy. The historically created conundrum consists of the 'logic' that because the ANC led the liberation struggle and was democratically elected it deserves a more sympathetic press. But as Mamphela Ramphele has noted in the opening quotation to this chapter, it would be irresponsible to be 'caught in the embrace of one's liberators', and then arguably in support of a media independent from political control she averred that 'we must guard against the closing of the mind and inward turning of the gaze that leads to tyranny ... We need to know how open our society is so that we have a yardstick against which to measure South

Africa's progress in creating an open society.' Since 1994, prominent members of the ANC have, to varying degrees, conceptualised the media as an 'us and them', or in a matrix which positions the media as outside democracy. Yet the tensions are internal to, and inherent in, democracy itself.

This opening chapter provides an introduction which is thematically grounded in political philosophy. In their 1985 work *Hegemony and Socialist Strategy*, Ernesto Laclau and Chantal Mouffe argued that democracy is secured precisely through its resistance to realisation, a foundational point which has been accepted by the key political philosophical works of the three authors whose perspectives have guided this book: Slavoj Žižek, Judith Butler and Chantal Mouffe. Laclau and Mouffe stated that the different political spaces, and the plurality of such spaces, are part and parcel of the deepening of a democratic order. Within this multiplicity of open spaces there are contestations, changing meanings and constant flux. Difference, rather than unity of opinion, is therefore necessary in any democratic transition. Dissension should be accepted, and those who criticise should be viewed as legitimate adversaries rather than as enemies. This is how a radical democracy is generated, according to Mouffe in *The Democratic Paradox*. One of my central arguments is that the media is one such space or platform for a diversity of views but, even more importantly, it is a medium for the questioning of meaning in politics. Running through this book is the thread that journalists are not 'enemies of the people' or outsiders in a democracy. On the contrary, they play a critical and essential role in the deepening of democracy. Democracy, in this book, is a floating signifier, which denotes that it does not have full meaning (a 'signifier' is more than a mere sign but stands for, or represents, the subject – and a floating signifier, then, is a signifier with no fixed meaning).

The intersection between the independent media (that is, the news media – journalism, news reporting, analysis and political commentary) and democracy in an unrealised democracy is under scrutiny, the aim of which is to preserve the ideal of democracy, to ward off dissolution, and also hopefully to inform action or activism to halt the whittling away of the 'free' space of the media (by 'free', here, is meant relatively free, relatively autonomous and relatively independent, with the focus on relative freedom from political pressures and state interference).

The South African media professes to play a vital role in entrenching the articles of the Constitution, ensuring a transparent democracy which holds public officials accountable for their decisions and actions and exposes the abuse of power and corruption by ruling elites. The questions are to do with the concept of democracy and its realisation; the tension between the two constitutive dimensions of democracy; and the realisation of the popular will

– particularly pressing in South Africa with its history of apartheid racism, class divisions, growing poverty, unemployment, and failures of service delivery, especially to poor people.

According to Mouffe (2006: 974), in a 'radical pluralist democracy' the media can be gate-openers rather than gate-closers. Her model of democracy not only allows for theorising the increase of pluralism *within* journalism, but also allows for the increase of pluralism *through* journalism. In South Africa, as in many other parts of the world, the media does not exist as a fixed, homogeneous entity. Although organisational forums and non-governmental and academic bodies (such as the South African National Editors Forum (Sanef), the Forum for Black Journalists (FBJ), the Media Institute of Southern Africa (Misa), the Freedom of Expression Institute (FXI), Media Monitoring Africa, Institute for the Advancement of Journalism and Wits Journalism) enable representatives of the media to share ideas, debate professional issues and even outline codes of conduct, the media in South Africa does not share a collective or unitary identity.

Different forces drive editorial content, from the diverse theoretical platforms from which journalists operate to the different economic and political agendas of the media owners and managers. The South African media is fractured, open-ended and undecided in its nature. It is for this reason that I have chosen to use a radical democratic perspective, coupled with a blend of Žižekean psychoanalysis, which goes beyond the liberal democratic paradigm. In Žižek's conceptual analysis, especially in his 1989 work *The Sublime Object of Ideology*, a postmodern twist is that of the Master-Signifier. The Master-Signifier could be described as a 'quasi transcendental big other'. Through imaginary and symbolic identification we see ourselves in how we are seen by that 'big other'. But as there is no 'big other', the Master-Signifier is empty, a signifier that puts an end to the chain of meaning. As Kay (2003: 159) has stated, the idea that there is an other of the other is psychotic; this is why we need to discover that the big other does not exist, that it is 'merely an imposter ... lacking or inconsistent as a result of its deficient relation to the real.'

The question is, if the media is not independent and free to criticise, what is the intersection between democracy and an independent press? A critical question is, first, how the ANC 'sees' the media vis-à-vis democracy. (I refer here to the ANC's 'gaze', the lens of which one is part and which therefore prevents one from seeing from an objective distance – one's own view is subscribed in the content of one's gaze.) To use a personal example, my gaze, having worked all my adult life as a journalist, is inscribed in this book's gaze on the media.

A second question, pointed out by Mondli Makhanya, then editor of the *Sunday Times*, in a 2008 interview, is how, in contrast to the ANC's view, journalists view their role and seek not to be 'ideologically in tandem' with the ruling party. A third question follows, then, as to how attempts are made by the ruling bloc to unify society via foreclosures, and whether the media succumbs to the ideological interpellations[2] or 'turns' from the attempt at subjugation. Are the attempts to quilt or unify society via a *point de capiton,* a tight knot of meanings (Žižek, 1989: 95-100)[3] succeeding through the interpellations of the media? These are the key questions. While the book's focus is on the relationship of the ANC and the media vis-à-vis democracy in post-apartheid South Africa, I also discuss and trace the ANC's stance on the media prior to its becoming the ruling party. In 2010 three significant events took place which, it could be argued, highlighted the greatest tension in the democratic dispensation between the media and the ANC. The three events in 2010 that related to threatened closure of spaces for media freedom were: first, the desire of the ANC for a statutory media appeals tribunal became quite intense; second, the Protection of State Information Bill (dubbed the Secrecy Bill) which, in its 2010 form, would have created a secretive society and criminalised investigative journalism and whistle-blowers was on the table; and third, the arrest of the journalist Mzilikazi wa Afrika of the *Sunday Times* on 4 August 2010 for 'fraud and defeating the ends of justice' which raised concerns about state bullying (*The Times*: 5 August 2010). These events signified the unprogressive hegemonising of society by the ANC. The reaction of the media, according to the ANC, was 'hysterical' (used as a psychoanalytical concept signifying paranoia and obsession). In October 2010, the country dropped five places in the Reporters without Borders annual Press Freedom Index (*Mail & Guardian*: 22-28 October 2010), largely because of the behaviour of senior members of the ANC towards the press.

Let us turn to some of the main events in 2010 which signalled that press freedom was under serious threat from the ruling party and the state.

First, in July 2010 the ANC decided to revive the resolution from its 52nd National Policy Conference in Polokwane in December 2007 to investigate the establishment of a statutory media appeals tribunal to curb the excesses of a media that was, in the words of Julius Malema, leader of the ANC Youth League (ANCYL), 'a law unto itself'. In a discussion document, *Media Transformation, Ownership and Diversity,* produced in preparation for its National General Council in September 2010, the ANC argued that the self-regulatory system of the media (the Press Council, the ombudsman and the Press Appeals Panel, with the press code governing the system) had become self-serving. The media appeals tribunal could be constituted by members of parliament, nearly two-thirds of whom are ANC members, or could be chosen by MPs, and could be an appeals structure, probably with strong punitive powers. In support of the media appeals tribunal, Jacob Zuma said that human rights were trampled on by the media, that the media invaded people's privacy, and that the media 'must behave like everybody else'. He declared that ' ... this media that says it is the watchdog for democracy was not democratically elected' (*The Times*: 12 August 2010).

The aim of the media appeals tribunal, according to ANC spokesperson Jackson Mthembu, was to halt journalists' 'excesses and waywardness'. 'If you have to go to prison, let it be. If you pay millions for defamation, let it be. If journalists have to be fired because they don't contribute to the South Africa we want, let it be' (*Mail & Guardian*: 23-29 July 2010). Blade Nzimande, the general secretary of the South African Communist Party (SACP) who became the minister of higher education in 2009, supported the media appeals tribunal because 'if there is one serious threat to our democracy, it is a media that is accountable to itself ... we have no opposition other than the bourgeois media' (*The Times*: 2 August 2010). Siphiwe Nyanda, a former general in the South African National Defence Force who was to become minister of communications (although he was fired in 2010), also supported the media appeals tribunal after he had endured criticism in the press for 'high living': 'I do not understand how the purchase of cars and hotel stays amount to corruption. The media trivialises the matter by tagging as 'corruption' things done by politicians that they do not like' (*Sunday Times*: 1 August 2010). Julius Malema said: 'It is important that we need to fight this media which is ruling itself, the media which is now a law unto itself. These people, they can destroy the revolution. They think they are untouchable and they can write about anything they like ... that time has come to an end ... these people are dangerous' (*Sunday Times*: 8 August 2010).

The above rhetoric has several implications. First, it is argued in this book that all those quoted above – Mthembu, Nyanda, Zuma, Nzimande and Malema – use ideological interpellations against an independent media, labelling and positioning the media as outsiders to democracy. The discourse suggests closures in society, and the proposed interventions – a media appeals tribunal and the Protection of State Information Bill – signalled an ideological social fantasy of the ANC: that, through political control of the media, it could cover up its own inadequacies, its own fractious nature and the disunity of society itself. Here, 'fantasy' refers to the way antagonism is masked; in Žižekean philosophical discourse, ideology is used to mask antagonism, and a social fantasy refers to disguising antagonism by altering perceptions and interpretations of reality.

The second implication of the ANC's rhetoric is the attempted subjugation of the media via the Protection of State Information Bill. If enacted, in its present form its impact on the world of journalism would be severe: penalties for offences range from between three to twenty-five years in jail. Many stories would not be publishable. The Bill is draconian, a violation of media freedom and freedom of expression, one which would have had a chilling effect on the publication of matters of public interest and, further, one that would kill the free flow of information and transparency and finally, one which would not stand the test of constitutionality.[4] For the state law advisor, Enver Daniels, however, the Protection of State Information Bill was meant to 'balance' the Promotion of Access to Information Act of 2000. He argued that the reactions by the press and civil society groupings (including Sanef, Print Media SA, FXI), the Institute for Democracy in South Africa (Idasa), South African Human Rights Commission (SAHRC) and the ANC's own alliance partner, the Congress of South African Trade Unions (Cosatu)) which had made submissions to Parliament, were 'emotional and hysterical' (*The Star*: 28 July 2010).

A third implication of this increasing intimidation of the free press arises from the arrest on 4 August 2010 of a *Sunday Times* investigative journalist, Mzilikazi wa Afrika, outside his newspaper offices in Rosebank, Johannesburg. While Sanef was engaged in a meeting with journalists (of whom I was one) to discuss the attempts at muzzling the media, the chairperson, Mondli Makhanya, asked what the commotion was outside. A few of us ran out and witnessed Wa Afrika being roughly handled by seven plain-clothes policeman who were escorting him to an awaiting police vehicle. The police said he was being arrested for 'fraud' and 'defeating the ends of justice' (*Mail & Guardian*: 13-19 August).[5] It subsequently emerged that the ANC was unhappy about the exposures of divisions and fractures in the party's leadership in Mpumalanga and the arrest was part of a strategy to stop Wa Afrika from his investigative reporting. The incident had a surreal quality about it, reminiscent of the dark old days of apartheid.

The deepening of South Africa's democracy will depend upon acceptance and tolerance by the ANC and the government of media scrutiny of its performance. Pallo Jordan, who is a member of the ANC National Executive Committee (NEC) and chairperson of the NEC subcommittee on communication, and has always been regarded as one of the organisation's intellectuals, made this point too. He wrote that in the spirit of the Constitution the value we place on a free independent and outspoken press in democratic South Africa cannot be overstated, and he asserted that:'The ANC has not and shall not wilt under criticism or close scrutiny' (*The Times*: 20 August 2010). He also wrote that his argument was within the tradition of the ANC itself: 'The ANC has a long track record of commitment to media freedom. In defending a free media, we are defending the ANC's own rich heritage ... ' (*ANC Today*: 20-26 August 2010).

However, a mere month later, Jordan did an about-turn. He announced at a press conference after the ANC's National General Council (NGC) on 24 September 2010 that the media appeals tribunal, which the organisation had resolved to take forward, was an indication of the 'ANC's commitment to press freedom' (*Sunday Independent*: 24 October 2010), and that the media did not reflect the transition to democracy. 'When you read our print media you never get a sense that this country is moving from an authoritarian state to democracy.' He became even less a champion of an independent press and an open society when he later stated that 'there is no country that has no secrets. The purpose of the Bill is to protect the secrets of this country' (*Mail & Guardian*: 29 October - 4 November 2010).

The ANC as an organisation is not ideologically united, nor had it been left unscarred by the reports of the scandals of corruption exposed in the print media. Could this be why its leaders, including Zuma, Nyanda, Malema, Nzimande and Mthembu, wanted a media appeals tribunal, which aimed ultimately at political control of the media? The graphic on the next page by artist John McCann (*Mail & Guardian*: 20-26 August 2010) showed the exposures of corruption in the print media by the above leaders: 'Nyanda's five-star hotel binge'; 'Blade's [Nzimande] high life'; 'Zuma for sale'; 'Malema's new tax dodge'; and 'ANC leader's jailhouse rock', referring to a story about Mthembu's drinking and driving.

But what are the problems with the media and the self-regulation system? Many other critics of the media, such as Lumko Mtimde (*ANC Today*: 30 July-5 August 2010) and Essop Pahad (speech delivered to Wits University Colloquium on 'Media Freedom and Regulation'. University of the Witwatersrand, Johannesburg. 15 September 2010), have argued that the existing self-regulatory system did not give sufficient protection to those whose rights to dignity (also protected in the Constitution) have been violated; that the Press Council was toothless as it did not levy fines while the corrections and apologies are not commensurate in size and placement to the damage done by the offending article; and the Press Council is composed mainly of former journalists.

Franz Kruger said at the colloquium on the media and self-regulation that some of the arguments from critics of the media needed to be considered and there should be more self-examination by journalists. 'Some house-cleaning needs to happen and journalists need to be more careful'. Some of the issues raised in this respect included: the view that leaks should be handled with more care as journalists were vulnerable to manipulation; apologies were not commensurate with mistakes made; there should be a clearer distinction between reporting and commenting; and that there were far too many headlines which do not reflect the actual text of the story. These criticisms pointed out by Kruger and others at the event showed that the media was not above criticism and that there was a need for greater self-examination of the way in which it operated.

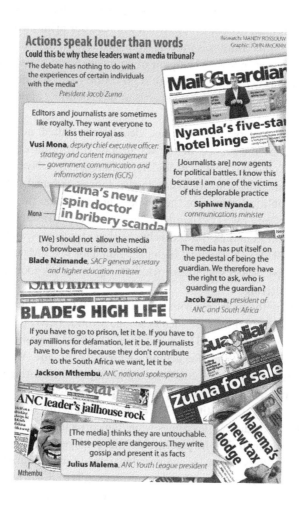

In support of a free press

The aim of this book is to unravel the politics of the independent media and the ANC through looking at specific case studies after apartheid, theorising trends, contradictions and splits, observations and reflections, and to produce findings about the intersection between the independent media and democracy. My aim is to limit the focus to particular examples of political interference. While I am aware of arguments from its detractors about the media's commercial imperatives and how they impact, my main focus is on the ANC and the media.

By combining Mouffe's conception of a radical democracy with Butler's theories of power and subjection (wherein concepts such as 'reflexive turn', 'subjectivisation', 'passionate attachments' and 'resignifications' are applied, together with the Žižekean conceptual tools of Master-Signifier and social fantasy), a discussion, reflection and analysis of events regarding the media and the ANC since 1994 ensues. In addition, I examine what 'turn' journalists made in response to subjectivisation, or subjugation, that had already taken place and what this means for democracy in South Africa. Were these reflexive turns, as in turns against themselves, or were they resignifications and a break from the past, as in loyalties to the ANC because it was the liberation party which freed South Africa from colonial and racist oppression? (Resignification here means to not reiterate oppressive norms of the past; to detach oneself from past signifiers – resignification is a form of resistance, as in not acknowledging the name-calling.)

I use several specific examples, or 'case studies', in as many different chapters, to investigate the expectations of the ANC regarding the media and how the ANC imagines the media, as well as how the media itself defines its role. I then proceed to explore how the independence of the media is under threat.

It must also be said at the outset that I use the terms 'the ANC' and 'the media' in an affirmative deconstructive way – that is, I use the terms and interrogate them at the same time. When I write 'the ANC' I do not mean that the ANC is one ideological entity. I constantly attempt to show various strands of the ANC through its various discourses, and to capture the ambiguities, nuances and ambivalences within the organisation. In the same way, 'the media' is not a monolithic bloc, and this too is shown in the different issues analysed in the different chapters. The theoretical concepts used will be discussed in the forthcoming sections of this chapter, and will be further elucidated in the rest of the book.

The fundamental reason for writing this book is to preserve the free press from political interference as there have been several interjections in discourse since the advent of democracy which show that there are threats. In South Africa's less than 20-year-old democracy, the ANC's perspective is that the media's role needs to be clarified, contained, and directed toward the project of nation-building and transformation as it has defined these processes. Thus the ANC sees itself as engineering democracy, a democracy that is transitional, in a society which remains unequal along racial and class lines.[6] Should the media in fact be free and independent from political interference? Or should its primary function be to enhance 'nation-building', development, and democracy in the manner defined by the former liberation movement? For many journalists, the latter would be a conflation with party political interests, and the national interest should be de-linked from party politics. Should the media take on the role of civic watchdog, forming part of the system of checks and balances on the misuse of political power and ensuring accountability for the actions of those in power, as is its role in conventional democratic states of the West? Should it simply be a mirror of the society in which it operates, reflecting the opinions of the ruling elite in a particular society? Or should journalists embrace the role of organic intellectuals, as did Gramsci?

The growing mistrust and miscommunication between the government on the one hand, and editors and journalists, on the other, since 1994 in South Africa led to a major indaba in June 2001 between the Cabinet and Sanef. The president at the time, Thabo Mbeki, remarked then that there was a need for interaction, dialogue and a process of engagement 'so that we understand each other better'. 'What is this national interest?' Mbeki asked. It was interesting that Mbeki acknowledged that the term 'national interest' was a 'troublesome one', as we all come from 'different angles, different histories and therefore respond in different ways' (Mbeki 2001). What he did not add was that we all seem to have different understandings, not merely of what the 'national interest' is, but also of what 'democracy' is and of what a 'free media' means. This is the crux of the matter in this book, hence one of the key conceptualisations: democracy is a 'floating signifier' (open-ended in respect of its meaning).

One of the significant reasons for this book was to make a contribution such that journalists and the ANC, with their plurality of views, begin to understand one another better. Thus I offer a two-way gaze: the media on the ANC's interventions and the ANC on the media's interventions. Both appear to talk past each other in the way they understand press freedom, the role of the press and what the national interest is. In my understanding, it is in the national interest to expose abuse of power and corruption. This book shows how democracy is a free floating signifier in the eyes of journalists, but how the ruling tripartite alliance, primarily the ANC and the SACP, attempt to make its meaning rigid.

A postmodern, psychoanalytic approach to South African politics is apposite, for its usage shows how impossible it is to predict the twists and turns that democracy is taking and may continue to take, with the only *a priori* understanding being that the future path is undecided and unpredictable. As Anthony Giddens theorised, 'Postmodernity is characterised by the fact that nothing can be known with any certainty' (1990: 46). This lack of certainty describes the position in South Africa, post apartheid.

The idea of the politics of renewal, resignifications, critical intervention and the slipping and sliding nature of this kind of democracy provides a series of concepts that assist in analysing the reality of what is happening in the South African case. For example, the concept of resignifications is elucidated in how a populist left-wing coalition, which defeated Mbeki and brought Zuma to power, then itself began unravelling as alliances changed. Using the theories of Laclau from *On Populist Reason*, I have highlighted how democracy in South Africa is characterised by contingency. Through the examples of 'Babygate' and the Budget speech by Finance Minister Pravin Gordhan, I show how easily alliances can become unsettled, especially if heterogeneous demands are crystallised in one popular figure. In this case, demands were crystallised in the figure and the name 'Zuma' – a name which was beginning to prove an 'empty signifier' for the left.

Some useful concepts

Radical pluralism, agonism

This work is set within a radical democratic political framework through which I deploy and adapt Mouffe's works, particularly *The Democratic Paradox* (2000) and *On the Political: Thinking in Action* (2006), which grew from her earlier groundbreaking and seminal work with Laclau, *Hegemony and Socialist Strategy* (1985). Mouffe (1999) argued that within the rational consensualist model of democracy you become an enemy if you do not follow the rules of the game. In a radical democracy you can be conceptualised as a legitimate adversary. This research shows that in South Africa many journalists' voices do not follow the rules of the game, that is to say the ANC's game, or the voice of authority that attempts to interpellate.

In this argument for the importance of the plurality of political spaces, there is a distinction between legitimate adversaries. I show that the ANC sees voices in South Africa that are critical as 'enemy' rather than 'adversary'. It would prefer unity with the press, which, in its view, would create social harmony and cover up the flaws of the unfolding democracy. It would prefer to fix the meaning, or tie it in a knot via the terms 'developmental journalism' and 'transformation', to the past liberation role of the ANC. In the book, *The Challenge of Carl Schmitt* (1999), Mouffe dissected Schmitt's argument for political unity, arguing instead that antagonisms do not disappear even with consensus. Schmitt feared the loss of common premises and consequent destruction of political unity and his thesis on consensus politics appears to have resonance with the views of the ANC on the media, as given voice by all three democratic presidents of the country, Nelson Mandela, Thabo Mbeki and Jacob Zuma. I argue, and show, that there is no unity in the media itself: it is not a fixed, definable, single ideological entity with a totalised identity, in the same way that Mouffe argued that society does not exist as a clearly defined single entity.

Enemies of the people, the gaze and social fantasy

Žižek's works *The Sublime Object of Ideology* (1989), *The Ticklish Subject* (2000a), *Interrogating the Real* (2006a), *How to Read Lacan* (2006b) and *The Indivisible Remainder* (2007), contain important theoretical foundations for this book's conceptual, analytical approach. These texts are used to explain the analytical concepts constitutive of the theoretical framework and have been applied to this analysis. Particularly pertinent is *The Sublime Object of Ideology* because Žižek's concepts of social fantasy, loyalty and the symbolic 'big other' seem to speak directly to the current tension between the South African press and the ruling party. Equally, his concepts of 'enemies of the nation', 'the gaze', '*point de capiton*' the 'rigid designator' and '*Che Vuoi*', are all apt in my examination of how the ANC, through its desire for a 'development journalism', actually aims at unifying society through an unprogressive hegemony around its own ideological structuring principles.

Che Vuoi

One of the most significant Žižekean concepts is the question that causes hysteria: *Che Vuoi* (1989: 87), meaning 'what do you want?' More than this, it means 'what are you really aiming at?' 'You're telling me that, but what do you want with it, what are you aiming at?' It is experienced by the subject as an unbearable anxiety. In this book, both the media as subject, and the ANC as the subject of the media, experience anxiety. There is a split between demand and desire and this is what defines the hysterical subject (*op cit*: 111). This application is pertinent for the ANC's hailing of the media as 'hysterical'. Hence, the psychoanalytical theoretical works and analyses of Žižek have been important. *Interrogating the Real* (2006a) provided some of the key concepts I have used in my analysis, such as the Master-Signifier, object, subject and social fantasy. Similarly, *The Ticklish Subject* (2000) gives examples of what 'surplus' and 'excess' mean, which is pertinent to my analysis of the ANC's reaction to the *Sunday Times* exposé of the former minister of health and the chapter on the discourse of the ANC on the media. By 'surplus', Žižek means what is attached to the object, more than the object itself. Herein lies the fantasy. Žižek is a devout Lacanian. For Lacan, himself a devout believer in psychoanalysis and a Freudian, the fantasy is a sort of magnet which will attract those memories to itself which suit it. According to Leader and Groves (1995: 128), 'If you have only a few memories from your childhood you could ask yourself why you remember only those elements and not others'.

Žižek discussed the concept of the 'unconscious social fantasy' using the example of racism against Jews. In Nazi Germany anti-Semitism became a paranoid construction and 'the Jew' became a fetish and a social symptom. The 'surplus' and the 'excess' (something more seen in the object than the object itself, something that the object stands for) were evidenced in the discourse to describe the features of the Jew – greedy, sly, profiteer, corrupt (1989: 125) – who was then constructed as the 'other' and thus could not, by virtue of that identity and that difference, be part of society and must be expelled – indeed erased completely. I show how the media has become, in the discourse of the ANC, a paranoid construction, with a surplus and excess attached to it, labelled negatively to the point of a social fantasy: threat to democracy, anti-transformation, racist and enemies of the people.

According to Kay (2003: 163), by fantasy, Žižek does not mean that which is opposed to reality: 'on the contrary, it is what structures that which we call reality, and determines the contours of desire. Likewise it is not escapist; rather it is shot through with the traumatic enjoyment which it helps to repress; thus fantasy shields us from the Real and transmits it.' Two other Žižekean concepts used in this book are that of 'the rigid designator' and 'the gaze'. In explaining the rigid designator, Žižek says it aims at what the object represents and when this becomes exaggerated it produces a signifying operation.

The term 'gaze' is used by Žižek in the sense of the gap that it creates. He gives the example of the gap in Brueghel's paintings of idyllic scenes of peasant life, country festivity, reapers during midday rest, and so on. These paintings were removed from reality and any real plebeian attitude. 'Their gaze is the external gaze of the aristocracy upon the peasants' idyll, not the gaze of the peasants themselves upon their life'. In attempting to explain this conceptualisation of 'the gaze', Kay sees it as an object attached to the scopic drive. It is an imaginary construct but it has a strong attachment to the Real. For Žižek, she stresses: 'the gaze does not involve my looking but my being looked *at*'. For the ANC, the media's reaction to the proposals to curb its freedom is hysterical.[7] Yet, actually, both parties are hysterical, with the ANC being more hysterical than journalists.

On political subjection

Butler's theories in *The Psychic Life of Power: Theories in Subjection* (1997) contain important theoretical positions which I have drawn on to understand the attempts to subject, or subjugate, critical media voices in South Africa through the idea of interpellation and, even more importantly, to reflect on what reflexive turns were made towards the voices of power, and why. I have used Butler's concepts of 'passionate attachments', 'reflexive turns' and 'resignifications' to show how subjects can become attached to subjection and how an unpredictable turn can show resignifications or, if you like, detaching from past signifiers to permit liberation from the past. In his seminal work, *The Ideological State Apparatuses* (1984), Louis Althusser's central thesis was that all ideology hails, or interpellates, concrete individuals as concrete subjects.

But ideology and hegemony cannot be conflated, for ideology 'plays a crucial role in the construction of hegemony', according to Torfing, whose book *New Theories of Discourse* provides a comprehensive coverage of the theories of Laclau, Mouffe, Butler and Žižek, as well as the philosophical debates and differences between them. Eagleton (1991) noted that we might define hegemony as a whole range of practical strategies by which a dominant power elicits consent to its rule and from which it legitimates subjugation. Explaining the Gramscian view of hegemony, he continued: 'To win hegemony is to establish moral, political and intellectual leadership in social life by diffusing one's own world view throughout the fabric of society as a whole, thus equating one's own interests with the interests of society at large'. This Gramscian view of hegemony is a set of ideas by which the dominant group in society, the ANC, secures the consent of the groups below it to ensure its rule.

Passionate attachments, reflexive turns and resignifications

Butler's theories of political subjectivisation, passionate attachments, reflexivity and resignifications (1997: 2-30) are used where the divisive role of the FBJ is explored. I scrutinise the organisation's revival, within a non-racial, democratic South Africa, and then its quick implosion in the light of the majority of black journalists having stated that they saw no place for such a forum in a new South Africa. For them, race was not seen as Master-Signifier around which to unify, showing resignifications to past attachments. The comments of the journalists Justice Malala, Chris Bathemba, Phylicia Oppelt and Ferial Haffajee, who were not in favour of the blacks-only forum, showed a lack of reiteration to norms which oppress, for example singular, linear, race identity. For Butler, neither norms nor identities are fixed, and even within these reiterations there are possibilities that they will be repeated in unpredictable ways; that they will be re-appropriated, so to speak, showing resignifications. The case of those black journalists who did not give validity to the FBJ reflects the operation of Butler's concept of resignifications. On the other side of the coin was Abbey Makoe (who initiated the revival of the FBJ) who embraced the very terms that injured him. He repeated the norms of racial oppression that simply returned him to a position of subjection, which reflects the operation of Butler's passionate attachment. It is the radical dependency on norms and a reiteration of those norms that lead to subjection. Using Butler's concepts of attachments and resignifications I show the circularity and reproduction of race-based subjection, as in the case of the FBJ. The example of journalists in South Africa with free floating, multiple (rather than fixed) identities also make the theories of Butler pertinent. Employing these concepts shows that the media is not one entity which is fixed. Nor is democracy a process that has an end point. It is continuously contested and reinvented – fluid, open-ended and always in a process of becoming.

Other works that I have utilised include Diane Macdonell's elucidation of discourse theory (1986) which states that discourse has a social function. She explains the role of ideology, meaning, understanding and language in discourse, with the starting point that meanings of words and expressions are not intrinsic but, rather, dependent on the particular contexts in which they are articulated. I have also referred to Pecheux (1982) who explained the relationship between ideology and discourse. Pecheux's view was that words, expressions and so on change their meanings according to the positions held by those who use them. Similarly, Torfing explains that there is always something that escapes processes of signification within discourse, partially fixing meaning, and this produces a surplus in meaning which escapes the logic of discourse (1999: 92). The field of irreducible surplus is the field of the discursive, a terrain that is undecidable, unfixed and in flux. This is discourse, in Laclau and Mouffe's theories, which elucidates that no one signifier has a special status above all others: meaning is acquired through a particular signifier's configuration and relationship with others. This is how I use the term discourse theoretically in this book.

Thus my theoretical underpinnings are a blend of radical democratic theory and psychoanalysis theory, interlaced with a postmodern approach. The theories elucidated are those which argue for a radical democracy within pluralism, as do Laclau and Mouffe, Žižek and Butler, theorists who have all grappled with, and continue to grapple with, the new globalised world and how to deal with what is often called a post-ideological world in which liberal democracy seems to be taken for granted as the only system to endorse. This capitalist liberal framework, however, has not brought about equality in the world. Quite the contrary, and for this reason I have sought to explore an alternative radical democratic theoretical framework – but I must say from the outset that the focus is on the contribution the media *does* make (albeit an imperfect one) to the democracy-in-process.

Radical democracy

One way to understand radical democracy is through a theoretically post-Marxist, poststructuralist perspective which challenges liberal democracy's lack of inclusion of all sectors of civil society. It aims for a deeper and more expansive democracy than what is currently on the table in the western world. Radical democracy emerged in response to the crisis that affected western left wing thought in the second half of the twentieth century. These crises included dissatisfaction and disillusionment with the Marxist project and the rise of social movements which, according to Little and Lloyd (2009), included feminist struggles, gay and lesbian issues, and environmental concerns, among other particular micropolitics. Another way to understand radical democracy is through post-Marxism as defined by Iris Marion Young who averred that it was inspired by socialism and was critical of capitalist economic processes (2009). But this achievement of equality or true democracy can never be fully realised, is open-ended and conflictual by nature, always contested, and not open to final realisation or reconciliation. Civil society is important in radical democracy, as the various plural struggles and microstruggles contest unprogressive hegemonies. This book shows how contestations in South Africa between the ruling party's understandings of democracy, developmental journalism and freedom of the press exemplify the conditions described above. It also elucidates the overlap between radical democracy, which is conditional, and a postmodern state of fluidity and lack of decidability. In my argument the media is precisely one such space, part of the public sphere. It is a pluralistic space in which different views can be expressed and where dynamic deliberations and contestations can and do take place. Why a 'radical democracy' framework rather than 'liberal democracy' framework or simply a 'democracy' framework? Because a radical democratic framework demands the acknowledgement of difference.

Postmodernism

By its very nature, the term postmodern appears to be more apt as the description of a process rather than of a fixed period. It describes the condition post the modern era which was characterised by rationalism and consensus politics. Postmodernism developed in the 1950s and 1960s as a breakaway from the universalism of the enlightenment, the rationalism of modernism and the class essentialism and reductionism of Marxism. There are different interpretations of postmodernism in politics. The key word in politics and postmodernism is 'process'. In other words, postmodernism calls for a rejection of modern politics, a radically different politics, a rejection of essentialism and a celebration of difference and contingency. As David West (1996: 199) stated:

> If the mood of post-modernity is defined in terms of incredulity towards meta-narratives, the politics of post-modernity is radically errant of grand projects and ambitious political programmes, which are a prominent feature of modern states and ideologies. Attempts to unify society

artificially according to some grand, 'totalising' theory or ideology are no longer convincing.

These are really more akin to descriptions, rather than full definitions, of post-modernism. They mark what the postmodern condition entails, or is charac-terised by – fluidity, undecidability, multiple identities and dispersed identities, with no fixed signifier and a plurality of struggles within 'the social' – while acknowledging the split nature of society and the split nature of identities too.

Psychoanalysis

The theoretical framework is not a psychoanalytical one *per se*. It is rather the use of Žižek's Lacanian tools that mark it as psychoanalytic. To be more precise, it is the use of terms such as social fantasy, gaze, surplus, excess, and hysteria that are drawn from psychoanalysis. Lacan's psychoanalysis was itself a method of reading texts, oral or written. It is in this sense that I use the psychoanalytic.

The main use of Lacan's psychoanalysis by Žižek is the understanding of transference, the belief in 'the other', as in the false belief that the analyst knows the meaning of his or her patient's symptoms. This is a false belief at the start of the analysis process, but it is through this false belief that the work of analysis can proceed. Political power, I argue, is symbolic in nature and through the roles and the masks, and through interpellations (naming, hailing, labelling, subjecting, calling) ideological subjectivisation (subjugation) can take place. In this book, there are two important Lacanian theoretical concepts: subjects are always divided between what they consciously know and say, and their unconscious beliefs (Žižek 2006a: 2-21). For example, the media is a signi-fier without a signified. And, in the same way that Žižek has argued that no one knows precisely what they mean when they talk about 'the nation' or 'the people', I argue that the ANC does not know what it means when it talks about 'the media'.

It is in Žižek's use of Lacan's conceptual tools of fantasy, gaze, rigid desig-nator and *jouissance* that his radical departure emerges. According to Lacan, *jouissance* might mean enjoyment but its real meaning resides in that which is too much to bear, and so most of the time it is about suffering. It is linked to paranoia and to something outside or some agency external to it, for example television, which becomes 'the other', as Darien Leader and Judy Groves (1995) have explained. The argument developed in this book is that the ANC's gaze on the media since democracy has been characterised by an excess and surplus enjoyment which is the last support of ideology. Kay suggests that in Žižek's usage enjoyment is usually identifiable with what Lacan calls 'surplus enjoy-ment' (*plus de jouissance/plus de jouir*). In other words, 'enjoyment' comes in 'the form of a surplus, or remainder that permeates all of our symbolic institutions as their obscene underside ... ' (2003: 161).

Is the ANC aware of what it is doing? Is the fantasy that the media is threatening democracy conscious or unconscious? If Žižek were writing this he might say, 'yes, please',[8] which means both. In the same way, I argue that for the ANC its fantasy is both conscious and unconscious.

This book attempts to find answers about what is 'really bugging' the ANC. The qualitative data – the interviews with journalists and editors of some South African English language newspapers which are dispersed throughout the book – show that the ANC conflates 'the people' with 'the ANC', the consequence of which is that any criticism of the ruling party translates, conflates and collapses into a construction that the critic is anti-transformation and anti-democracy. This statement is further supported by evidence drawn from 'Letters from the president' in *ANC Today*, as well as other interpellations where the media is constructed as the enemy, for example in the discourse over the proposed media appeals tribunal. I show how the ANC desires consensus, harmony, or unity with the party. Through discourse analysis in the next chapter I show how all three post-apartheid presidents, Mandela, Mbeki and Zuma, have desired this unity and have attached an excess to the media, with an unconscious fantasy in operation. Discussions with various editors and journalists indicated that there is a conflation of the party and 'the people'.

How I conducted the research

The research for this book hailed from my PhD in Political Studies with the topic 'The role of the media in a democracy: Unravelling the politics between the media, the state and the ANC in South Africa'. The main research question was 'What is the intersection between the floating signifier, democracy and an independent press?'.

This work of political philosophy engages concepts and case studies. The concepts outlined above were utilised to shed light on the complex relationship of democracy to the media and how attempts are made to pin down 'democracy', a floating signifier, into a fixed meaning tied to transformation and loyalty to the ANC. The qualitative findings, through interview material, newspaper stories, letters from the public to newspapers, recorded meetings, panel discussions, protest action, and the range of ANC and other documentation, have been examined through the prism of the conceptual analytical tools discussed above. This has enabled the drawing together of reflections, the identification of patterns or attachments, the splits and contradictions, and the ambivalences on the part of both the media and the ANC. Critical discourse analysis has been used primarily to understand the ideological workings in the tensions between the ANC and the media, specifically the press.

This work adopts a multi-pronged integrative methodological strategy in order to provide a richer and fuller (as opposed to a linear) interpretation of the relationship between the media and the ANC. First, events that have occurred since 1994 have been elucidated and a historical context has been provided. While these 'events' can be called case studies, they are not case studies in the classical and traditional sense; nor will they be used for any traditional empirical or quantitative purposes. The methods of discourse analysis will, rather, be used to foreground the ideological underpinnings that help us to understand the positions adopted by different actors.

Besides the theoretical conceptual method, critical discourse analysis has also been deployed throughout the book. It is through language that subjugation takes place and, according to Lacan, 'hysteria' emerges when a subject starts to question, or feel discomfort in, his or her symbolic identity (Žižek 2006: 35). For the ANC, the media's reaction to the proposed media appeals tribunal has been 'hysterical'. Macdonell (1986) also explained, in *Theories of Discourse: an Introduction*, that the field of discourse is not homogeneous. Discourse is social, and the 'statement made, the words used and the meanings of the words used, depend on where and against what the statement is made'. She drew on the works of Pecheux, for whom 'words, expressions and propositions, change their meaning according to the positions held by those who use them'. As a result, 'conflicting discourses' can develop, even when 'there is supposedly common language'. Words do not have universal meanings, but change over time and at any given moment the same word can hold different meanings. Pecheux, according to Macdonell argued that meanings are part of the 'ideological sphere' and discourse is one of ideology's principal forms.

The interview method, which comprises a reflective commentary, was an important component of my research. A sample of journalists from the English-speaking newspaper media was interviewed. They were over the age of thirty-five and were able to look, in perceptive ways, backwards to their days as reporters under apartheid, during the transition to the new dispensation, to the present, and forwards to the future. A selection of media academics, lawyers and non-governmental activists was also interviewed.

Other sources of information came from newspapers; letters from the public as an indication of the views of civil society and citizenry; academic journals; Letters from the President in *ANC Today;* statements from media bodies including the FXI and Misa; and official policy documents, as well as attendance at and recordings of panel discussions and seminars on media freedom such as the Right2Know Campaign launch and colloquium. Media figures from the ANC's communications department, as well as the SACP intellectual Jeremy Cronin were interviewed on the subject of developmental journalism. These interviews and recordings enriched the project with 'real, live' voices from South Africa's unfolding democracy.

The theoretical conceptual research method I adopted aims to deepen our understanding of the significance to a democratic society of a self-regulating and independent media. Is political philosophy and theory pie in the sky? Butler (2000: 265) also questioned the value of theory. She turned to Aristotle, who had reflected: 'As the saying goes, the action that follows deliberation should be quick, but deliberation slow'. The philosophical arguments between Butler, Žižek and Laclau are united by their foundation: they are 'motivated by a desire for a radically more restructured world, one which would have economic equality and political enfranchisement imagined in much more radical ways than they are' (op. cit.: 277). However, the question is how to make the translations between philosophical commentary in the field of politics and the re-imagining of political life. My work is motivated by a commitment: to media freedom, to wanting to see this aspect of life in South Africa flourish, believing that media independence makes a difference to the deepening of the unfolding and unrealised democracy.

As I use terms 'the ANC', 'the media', 'the social' 'independence' and 'free', I acknowledge that these organisations, terms and entities are split, and not unified. I have used the terms 'independence' and 'free' while acknowledging that 'the media', can only be relatively free and independent. It has to be responsible and accountable to the public, qua the citizenry, plus its readers, viewers and listeners' to the Constitution; and to its code of professional ethics. And so I have to agree with Ramphele's opening quotation to this chapter, that gratitude for liberation should not mean unending gratitude to the leading movement in that process. It would be irresponsible and a shirking of one's duty to entrust the future of society solely to a party, or parties, associated with the liberation struggle.

NOTES

1   Dr Mamphela Ramphele, from a speech made at the University of Cape Town at the launch of the Open Society Monitoring Index ('House of Freedom is open to all', *Mail & Guardian*, 13-19 August 2010).

2   'Interpellation' means naming, hailing, labelling, calling and subjecting that person to that name, for example: lesbian, black, white, racist. Ideological interpellations are demands or social injunctions with the aim of subjecting and making the subject toe the line – the subject becomes the subject by heeding the call, acknowledging the hailing – for example, 'enemy of the people'.

3   The *point de capiton*, in Žižek, is a knot, an upholstery button, which pins down or ties up meaning to avoid slippages and slidings.

4   Had the law been in place at the time, the following stories would not have been published legally according to experts polled in August 2010: the Oilgate story about the payment of R11 million in PetroSA money by a private company to the ANC's 2004 election campaign; a story on the link between the wife of minister of state security, Siyabonga Cwele, and an international cocaine ring; a story on the SABC wasting R49 million on dud shows; and the 2007 exposé of baby deaths at the Mount Frere hospital in the Eastern Cape (see *Sunday Times*: 'Read all about the info bill': 15 August 2010).

5   He was in possession of an apparently fraudulent letter of resignation, which the premier of Mpumalanga, David Mabuza, was supposed to have penned to the president. The letter was subsequently traced back to the premier's office and it would seem that the journalist had become a victim of power politics in the province of Mpumalanga. The arrest of Wa Afrika was a sign of sheer intimidation (see *Mail & Guardian*: 'Sin doctor red faced over fake letter and the nine lives of Wa Afrika': 13-19 August 2010).

6   The use of the term 'transitional' raises the question, of course, of transitional from what to what? I use the term in a Derridean way: democracy is never fully realised; it is constantly unfolding. That is what Derrida meant when he wrote 'democracy to come' which means that democracy is a philosophical concept 'an inheritance of a promise'. In *On the Political* Mouffe writes that democracy is something uncertain and improbable and must never be taken for granted. In *The Democratic Paradox* she offers that the moment of realisation of democracy would see its disintegration. I use the terms unfolding democracy and transitional democracy, then, in this Derridean and Mouffian sense.

7   It was Essop Pahad, formerly minister in Mbeki's presidency and subsequently publisher and editor of *The Thinker*, who said in a speech at a colloquium at Wits University, *Media Freedom and Regulation*, on 15 September 2010, that the ANC found the way 'the Info Bill and the Media Tribunal was being linked is hysterical'.

8   In *Contingency, Hegemony and Universality* Žižek explains the famous Marx brothers joke about 'coffee or tea?'. 'Yes, please!' It is a refusal of choice.

2.

The relationship between the media and democracy

Secrecy obstructs democracy by keeping the public ignorant of information that it needs to make wise policy choices.[1]

This chapter argues that the media is a legitimate adversary – rather than an enemy of the people – in a fluid, changing and unrealised imperfect democracy. The 'free' press (and 'free' is used here in the sense of free from political interference, control and state intervention, not from economic, cultural or social interference) poses something of a challenge to the ruling alliance's hegemonic discourse, with its desire to limit the polymorphic voices of a diverse media.

A dissonance has crept in between the Constitution's ascription to independence of the media on the one hand and the government and state's actions on the other, creating tension in the relationship between the media and the ANC. One of the ANC's main problems with the media is what it conceives as inadequate and negative representation of its views as the ruling party. For example, at the launch of the ANC's online publication *ANC Today* in 2001, the 'Letter from the President' noted:

> Historically the national and political constituency represented by the ANC has had very few and limited mass media throughout the ninety

years of its existence. During this period, the commercial newspaper and magazine press representing the views, values and interests of the white minority has dominated the field of the mass media. This situation has changed only marginally in the period since we obtained our liberation in 1994 (*ANC Today*: 26 January-1 February 2001).

One of the issues raised throughout this book is the compulsion of these discursive interventions, which are in many respects inappropriate to a constitutional democracy. While tension between the ruling party and the media is not a recent development, it became increasingly pronounced during the first decade of the new millennium and at the ANC National Policy Conference in Polokwane in December 2007 when a media appeals tribunal to regulate the media was proposed. This occurred against the backdrop of the ANC wanting a media which would act in the 'national interest', one which would reconcile conflicting interests towards national consensus. In July 2010 it was announced that the Gupta Group, which was closely linked to President Zuma, would fund a daily national newspaper, *The New Age*, which was due to launch in mid-September 2010 (*Business Day*: 6 July 2010). By mid September 2010 the paper had not launched, citing technical difficulties with the new technological systems from India, and a new date for the end of October 2010 was set. The paper launched on 6 December 2010 after a few shaky starts.

Although the main player behind the paper, Essop Pahad, denied that the paper would be affiliated to the ANC, it was clear that it would in fact be more than sympathetic. For example, the editor, Vuyo Mvoko, in an interview on Radio 702 on 23 July 2010, said: 'We will show the positive side of government; it cannot be that our nation is just about crime and corruption'.

The struggle for freedom of the press from state control was a continuous one during the apartheid years, which culminated with press freedom becoming firmly entrenched and encapsulated in the 1996 Constitution. In 2005, South Africa received a favourable rating on a renowned international free press scale from Reporters without Borders, and was ranked thirty-first in the worldwide Press Freedom Index. But by October 2007 it was ranked forty-third on the same index, lower than Mauritius (twenty-fifth), Namibia (twenty-sixth) and Ghana (twenty-ninth).

In October 2007, editors gathered through Sanef to hold the third Media and Society Conference at which the independence of the media from political control was discussed. This took place thirty years after Black Wednesday, 19 October 1977, the day the apartheid government banned *The World* and *The Weekend World* newspapers, together with nineteen black organisations, and detained journalists, editors and anti-apartheid activists.

During the apartheid years there were three distinct streams of media. The mainstream media was made up, first, of the national broadcaster, and, second, of the English and Afrikaans language newspaper blocs (Jacobs 1999), a duopoly split between the Afrikaans conglomerates Naspers and Perskor and the English conglomerates South African Associated Newspapers and Argus Holdings. A third stream existed too, an independent or alternative press, consisting of smaller print publications such as the *Weekly Mail, Vrye Weekblad, South* and *New Nation*.[2] The first two streams had very different approaches to reporting on the government of the day. The mainstream media tended either to toe the government line ideologically or to support the then whites-only opposition party (Berger 1999; Tomaselli and Muller 1989; Steenveld 2007; Hadland 2007b). Any criticism of the government was in the context of accepting the *status quo* and voiced from within the confines of that *status quo*. The English language newspapers tended to take a liberal perspective that criticised certain aspects of the apartheid policies, but in a way that did not challenge the *status quo* outright. The role of the South African Broadcasting Corporation (SABC) and Afrikaans language newspapers was much more obvious – to support the National Party government and its policies. During this time the voices of the majority, the oppressed, were seldom heard via the mainstream media, and outright dissent was rare. Although there were newspapers and radio stations aimed at black South Africans, these tended to have little impact on the perceptions of those in power. Except for the 'alternative or independent press', the net effect was that the bulk of the media did little to challenge apartheid. In essence, the South African mainstream media promoted apartheid and the government supported the mainstream commercially driven media.

Nonetheless, the role the media played during apartheid is an uneven one. There were also instances of exposures of corruption of the ruling class and brutality from police and prisons. Over and above the prohibition of information that came from the banning of political opponents and the general milieu of repression, the National Party government also introduced a host of legislative acts at various times during its rule that affected the media either directly or indirectly, creating an environment that controlled the information reaching the public and violated freedom of the press. Between 1950 and 1990 over a hundred laws were introduced to regulate the activities of the South African media. The most prominent was the Publications Act of 1974 (Durrheim *et al* 2005), outlining the rules and regulations imposed by the state on the media. According to Steenveld (2007), three acts ensured the political climate of media repression: the Internal Security Act of 1982 which prohibited the circulation and debate of ideas relating to alternative social and political policies for South Africa; the Protection of Information Act of 1982 which prohibited the obtaining of forbidden information and its disclosure to any foreign state or hostile organisation; and the Registration of Newspapers Act of 1982, which gave the press the option of falling under the Directorate of Publications (the state censorship machinery) or subjecting themselves to self-regulation under the Media Council.

In addition to the constraints imposed on the media by the political climate, economic imperatives and ownership of the media also affected its role and independence. Until 1990 the concentration of print media ownership in the hands of one or two conglomerates also acted as a threat to media independence. William Gumede (2005: 3-4) was one of the academics arguing that it was necessary to include financial independence, not just political independence, in any discussion of democracy and media freedom. For him, although there has been a proliferation of new newspapers and radio stations throughout South Africa since the inception of democracy, often as a result of the interplay between old and new technology, the real danger in the media being free to report as it sees fit is that content is increasingly shaped by economic imperatives. His argument is that the pressure to remain profitable can result increasingly in urban, consumer-focused media with a declining concern for the voiceless who cannot pay and the race for profits.

To understand the ANC and the media, it is necessary to sketch the ANC media policy and note its shifts over the years. The question I pose is why the ANC, given its stated commitment to the democratic objectives of the Constitution, should be so ambivalent, if not downright opposed to, the freedom of the media. The negotiated settlement that led to the compromise of a liberal constitutionalism (albeit with critical social democratic elements) reflected the triumph of one ideological strand, the liberal one. It was a far cry from socialism or what was called 'democratic centralism'.

The shifts in ANC media policy

It could be argued that not all members of the ANC supported a negotiated settlement. There was disagreement and ambivalence between the hawks and doves in the ANC, some arguing for an armed insurrection via Umkhonto we Sizwe (MK), the military wing of the ANC, as a means to end apartheid, while others were in favour of peaceful negotiations. These differences were also reflected in media policy. Ruth Tomaselli (1994) pointed to the distinction between these two positions as reflecting, on the one side, a more militant position and, on the other, the more pragmatic approach of the doves. The ANC first discussed media policy in November 1991. There is a small clause in the Draft Workers Charter, also of 1991, which states: 'Big business and the state must ensure effective workers' access to all sections of the media' (ANC, 1991). Prior to this date, 'media' policy or issues were like a 'second cousin' to the ANC, Tomaselli observed, noting that there were more pressing concerns for the ANC at the time, concerns such as housing, social welfare and education – but also the South African Broadcasting Corporation. The discussions on media in November 1991 were then drafted and adopted in January 1992. The Media Charter stipulated basic rights and freedom, democratisation of the media, public media, media workers and society, education and training, and promotional mechanisms. Tomaselli noted that the focus was on the broadcast media and the SABC, but she also observed that the charter was framed in 'idealistic terms' and should be seen as a philosophical statement of intent. The document did not specify how a future ANC-led government would fulfill such terms. However, what was happening politically at the time also had a bearing on how media policy was viewed by the ANC. Tomaselli wrote: 'In media policy, as in other policy debates, ANC pragmatists came to realise, by late 1992, that the traditional hardline assumption that the liberation movement would ascend to government in the form of a "people's assembly" following a seizure of power though "mass insurrection"[3] was an unlikely scenario'.

The reality, Tomaselli pointed out, was a standoff situation in which the National Party and the ANC had to negotiate at every level of policy planning. Having researched ANC media policy, Jane Duncan (2009) also pointed to the shifts from the broad guidelines of the Media Charter, adopted in 1992, to the changes in the 2000s. Upon a careful reading, one senses that the shifts are not for more liberalisation, nor for more democracy. Some of what has taken place between the media and the ANC signals a definite shift for tighter state control over the media. Duncan noted that the evolution of the ANC's media policy was closely linked to the transformation of South Africa's apartheid media and in the run-up to the 1994 elections the ANC 'focused on the need to establish independent media institutions rather than to exert its own control over the media'. This culminated in the Media Charter. She pointed out that the ANC's 49th and 50th conferences in 1994 and 1997 did not focus on media policy, suggesting that it was not a serious issue at the time.

A decade and a half after the ANC first discussed media policy, Duncan noted that there seemed in fact to be a swing back, from a focus on diversification to the desire for more state control.

Ambivalence

In its renewed call for a statutory media appeals tribunal in 2010, Point 58 of the ANC's discussion document 'Media transformation, ownership and diversity', drafted in preparation for its National General Council (NGC) on 20-24 September 2010, stated that a 'cursory scan of the print media reveals an astonishing degree of dishonesty, lack of professional integrity and lack of independence'. Yet research by Media Monitoring Africa (MMA), in a paper 'The state of South Africa's media', presented to Sanef's Media Summit on 30 August 2010, showed that it would require a significant study involving a variety of quantitative and qualitative methods carried out across a substantial sample of media to prove the statement made by the ANC. William Bird, director of MMA, observed: 'To then be able to make an informed claim to the extreme of, an "astonishing degree" would require a comprehensive study and not a "cursory glance". To our knowledge a comprehensive study of this nature has not been carried out in South Africa. No evidence for these claims is presented in the document' (MMA 2010). The MMA's research found in its survey of election coverage, for instance, that eighty-four per cent of stories were fair, without any bias towards any political party, while the media's role during the 2010 World Cup was to encourage social cohesiveness and was overwhelmingly positive. The ANC's arguments that the media needed control because of its 'false reporting', 'irresponsible reporting' and 'consistent anti-ANC bias' was belied by the small number of complaints to the ombudsman by the ANC and government officials in the previous year (ending August 2010) about stories published – twenty-four out of tens of thousands.

On the other hand, according to the ombudsman, four stories about the ANC or ANC Youth League were found to be unfair or inaccurate in the past three years, from eight complaints lodged (*Sunday Times*: 29 August 2010). That is a fifty per cent success rate for articles taken to the ombudsman by the ANCYL.

The ANC and the SACP's calls for a media appeals tribunal did not remain static before the September 2010 NGC. Blade Nzimande, the SACP general secretary and minister of higher education, and one of the main proponents within the alliance calling for curbs on the print media's excesses, did an about-turn after the party's Central Committee meeting in Johannesburg on 30 August 2010. He announced that a media appeals tribunal should not be used for pre-publication censorship, and should not be appointed by parliament, but from a range of representative structures from society, to guard against political manipulation (Nzimande 2010b). Cosatu's general secretary, Zwelinzima Vavi, announced the week before the SACP's about-turn that the media appeals tribunal would be a refuge for the corrupt and the federation would not support it (*Mail & Guardian*: 27 August-2 September 2010). While Cosatu's view on an independent media could be seen to be consistent, as there was no history or evidence of the workers federation hailing the media as 'enemies of the people', the SACP's about-turn showed ambivalence. For example, just three weeks earlier, Nzimande had stated that the media was a threat to democracy: 'If there is one serious threat to our democracy, it is a media that is accountable to itself ... we have no opposition other than the bourgeois media' (*The Times*: 2 August 2010). In another, more glaring, example Pallo Jordan wrote that 'the value we place on a free media, independent and outspoken press in democratic South Africa cannot be overstated ... I cannot imagine an ANC government that is fearful of criticism' (*The Times*: 20 August 2010) yet announced in a press conference on 24 September that the ANC had adopted a resolution to forge ahead with the media appeals tribunal and said it was an example of the ANC's 'commitment to press freedom' (see Appendix 2 for the resolution adopted). And in October he told the Pan African Parliament that the media was not reflecting the transition to democracy (*Sunday Independent*: 24 October 2010). There most certainly is ambivalence, but is there a fetishistic split too? Kay explained the fetishistic split in Žižek's theorising, using his example of Tony Blair: 'We voted for Tony Blair in Britain because he is deceitful and a master of spin, even though we also believe he is sincere' (2003). The fetishistic split that ensured his success ran something like this: 'We believe he is upright and moral, but all the same, we know he is scheming and underhand and thus can be relied upon not to change things much, though he may make the status quo work a bit better'. How can we apply this to the media and the ANC in South Africa? We can do so simply by suggesting that the ANC believes in media freedom and supports it, as it states frequently, but that it wants a media appeals tribunal anyway, because it is insecure and afraid of press freedom. While this split might not be so obvious at this stage in the book, what is clear is that there was ambivalence.

The ANC's gaze on the media displays an ambivalence which also characterises the swings in Žižek's theories. For example, in *The Sublime Object of Ideology* Žižek argues, from a fairly liberal perspective, for freedom, while in his later work, *Did Somebody say Totalitarianism?* (2002a), he argues for more state intervention and control which limit democracy. His theoretical ambivalence reflects the lived experience of confusion and ambivalence reflected in the ANC's approach to freedom of expression and democratic culture. A possible explanation for the ambivalence is the history of democratic centralism embedded both in Žižek's theoretical background as an intellectual and in the ANC's past as an underground organisation marked by Soviet Marxist influences. This is the undecided nature of the ANC today, as it is the undecided nature of Žižek's theoretical framework – both with one foot in a Stalinist past and the other in liberal democracy. Before delving too deeply into psychoanalysis and exploring the relationship between the idea of democracy as a floating signifier (without fixed meaning to 'democracy') and an independent press in South Africa, we need first to turn to the origins of democracy and democratic theory in order to understand its varied manifestations historically.

History of democracy

David Held, tracing models of democracy, cited the political ideals of Athens as 'equality among citizens, liberty, respect for the law and justice' (1994: 16). The Athenian city state was ruled by citizen-governors, while citizens were at the same time subjects and creators of public rules and regulations. Citizens are intrinsic to democracy, but not all people are citizens and this was true for Athens as much as for modern forms of democracy. So Aristotle was not a citizen as he was from elsewhere. Women were not citizens either, nor were certain categories of 'commoner'. Direct democracy, Held commented, encompassed the idea that citizens could fulfill themselves through involvement in the polis, a commitment to civic virtue towards the common good, in an intertwining of the public and the private, as he argued in a later work (2006).

Still, not all were included in the original 'democratic' project. Women and slaves, for example, were excluded from citizenship. While some theorists still insist on dating democracy to the Athenians, and maintain that democracy is as old as the hills – over 2 500 years old – it was clearly not real democracy because of its exclusion of aspects of society, or its elitist and sexist nature. Women and slaves combined would have made up more than half the population during Athenian 'democracy'. Democracy has travelled a significant journey towards greater inclusiveness since then, according to Dahl (1998: 43) but the journey is not over. For many post-structuralist theorists: Derrida, Mouffe, Laclau, Butler and Žižek, the journey can never end, hence this framework, which supports radical democracy.

Mouffe elucidated in *The Democratic Paradox* that the commonest trend, and the most talked about model of democracy was the deliberative democratic model but, in her view, this was merely the revival of the fifth century Athenian model or a process of deliberation between free and equal citizens. She argued that the so-called 'new' paradigm was a model of deliberative democracy that had come full circle, 'the revival of an old theme, not the emergence of a new one'.

Antagonism, therefore, was ineradicable and pluralist democratic politics would never find a final solution. This was the democratic paradox. 'What the deliberative democracy theory denied was the division of undecidability and ineradicability of antagonism which is constitutive of the political. A well-functioning democracy called for a vibrant clash of political positions' Mouffe said in 2000. She argued that deliberative theorists negated the inherently conflictual nature of modern pluralism. She explained the meaning of 'agonistic' in her work: an agonistic approach acknowledges the real nature of democracy's frontiers and the forms of exclusion entailed, instead of trying to disguise them under a veil of rationality or morality. Because there is the ever-present temptation in the deliberative model of democratic societies to essentialise identities, the radical democratic model is more receptive to the multiplicity of voices in contemporary pluralist societies. This argument is important in understanding the role of the media in South Africa's democracy.

Antagonism takes place between enemies, or persons who have no common symbolic space. Agonism, on the other hand, involves a relationship not between enemies but between adversaries or friendly enemies. They share a common symbolic space but they are also enemies because they want to organise this space in a different way. Thus, according to Mouffe, the radical pluralist democracy model advocates a positive status to differences and questions homogeneity. So, then, applying this argument, the media and the ANC have a common symbolic space, democracy, and this must be accepted. Within this space there is no room for labelling such as 'enemies of the people'. Mouffe's argument with deliberative theorists such as the liberal democratic theorists Rawls and Habermas is that their approach, far from being conducive to their aim of a more reconciled society, ends up in jeopardy because the struggle between adversaries becomes, rather, a struggle between enemies.

The above distinction is pertinent to my analysis of the role of the media in democracy in South Africa, to show how the ANC seeks consensus with the media, how it attempts foreclosures, and how it exemplifies an unprogressive and narrow hegemony. There can be no rational consensus for a true democracy. However, for society to function there has to be some minimal consensus although, to avoid unnatural foreclosures, we should relinquish the very idea of rational consensus.

In this argument, then, homogeneity and political unity as a condition of possibility for democracy constitute an unprogressive hegemony which applies to the unravelling of the relationship between the media, the ANC and democracy in South Africa. This point will be highlighted when I discuss what various journalists and editors in South Africa argued in relation to whether the independence of the media was contingent on a particular historical context – in this case, early stages of democracy in South Africa, or a transitional democracy.

The argument for a radical democracy is helpful when I discuss the ANC's use of 'us and them', as well as the ideological interpellations or labelling of the media as 'enemies of the people'. Mouffe's concept of an agonistic pluralist democratic project typifies this tension in South Africa where there is an inability to distinguish between adversaries and real enemies. Agonistic pluralism advocates viewing the 'us and them' in a different way, not as an enemy to be destroyed but as a legitimate opponent. Both Mouffe and Žižek would lean towards a Lacanian definition of democracy with a socio-political order in which 'the people' do not exist – certainly not as a unity. In this argument, which I incline towards and use in the forthcoming analyses, the radical differences in a democratic society are intrinsic. The opposite would be totalitarianism or the complete closing off of spaces. In this mode of thinking, totalitarianism, then, is an attempt to re-establish the unity of democracy. The argument for radical democracy, adapted from Mouffe and Žižek, is that because of the open character of society there will naturally be conflict and there cannot be a 'unity of the people'.

As Mouffe notes, 'democracy is something uncertain and improbable and must never be taken for granted. It is an always fragile conquest that needs to be defended as well as deepened' (2006: 6). The empirical in the research leading to this book will show the fragile, contradictory and ambivalent nature of South Africa's democracy – and, in fact, the fragile and ambivalent nature of the independence of the media. For example, even though a resolution was taken by the ANC to investigate a media appeals tribunal in December 2007, by 2010 there was still no certainty about it: whether it would indeed be implemented; and if it were to be, who would oversee it and what form would it take. But the threat remained, hanging over us like a black cloud of foreboding uncertainty. This remained the case in 2012.

Transformation of the media in post-apartheid South Africa

To the ANC and its alliance partners, transformation of the media after apartheid meant deracialisation and diversification of ownership of the media companies, of the newsroom (the journalist), and of content (who and what is written about).

The changes in the media landscape of 2000, compared to 1994, were exponential. In a 2000 paper 'Deracialisation, democracy and development: Transformation of the South African media 1994-2000', Guy Berger plotted the changes in ownership and staffing by race, class and gender. He argued that the transformation contained new challenges, which were part of global changes and showed the growing global cross-ownership of media and telecoms, entertainment or computer software companies; the outsourcing and multiskilling of media workers; the internationalisation of supply and market-chains; technological convergence and the Internet; satellites and broadband networks; and the decline of classical journalism in the face of rising entertainment. He noted that the 'media has emerged from apartheid significantly transformed from what it was before. Racism exists in South Africa, but it no longer rules in either politics or media. Democracy and development are part of the daily diet of a transforming society'.

Berger did however point out that the end point of transformation was the doing-away with racial distinctions altogether. His paper examined transformation in the media, deploying the categories of race, democracy and development, and scrutinising ownership, staffing, conceptions of political role, content and audiences. The apposite point Berger made was that the final destination of the transformation was not meant to be re-racialisation. However, if you look at newsrooms today, you will see that the racial composition changed anyway, as the majority of reporters and editors are black.

According to an ANC discussion document, Media in a Democratic South Africa (ANC National Conference, Stellenbosch, December 2002):

> Considerable progress has been made and some significant milestones achieved with regard to ownership patterns, licensing of new media, increasing of black and women journalists, repositioning of the SABC, a measure of diversity in ownership with black empowerment groups and union funds controlling some of the assets ... These are putative first steps towards the transformation of the media industry.

In an unpublished paper on the tabloid newspapers, presented to a politics and media discussion group in Johannesburg, May 2009, Anton Harber observed of the ANC's comment above: 'It is apparent that the ANC's definition of transformation was based on three elements: diversity of ownership, particularly the need for black owners; more representative staffing and management; and content less hostile to the ANC-led transformation project'. (The argument that race in the media should be a Master-Signifier is deconstructed in Chapter Four in a discussion on the Forum for Black Journalists and its ultimate failure to re-launch.)

In Berger's 1999 critique of the changes and concentration in media ownership, 'Towards an analysis of South African media. Transformation 1994-1999', he suggests that there is some ambiguity in the effects on competition and democratic outcomes. On the one hand, plural democracy itself might be compromised by concentration, yet the competition prompted the launch of more diverse newspapers that added to the deliberative quality of the media. There were other changes that came in with the new democratic era: in 1994, the Irish businessman Tony O'Reilly bought thirty-five per cent of the Argus Company).

The company name changed from Argus to Independent Newspapers, under whose umbrella reside *The Star, Cape Times, Natal Mercury, Pretoria News* and *Sunday Independent*. By 1999, O'Reilly had bought out the whole company. As Berger commented:

> Considered in terms of concentration, this foreign investment was not a positive development from the vantage point of pluralistic democracy, in that in Cape Town and Durban the same company now owns both morning and evening papers. However, at the same time, the entry of international capital saw a noticeable increase in competition in the newspaper industry – even if this was only at the higher end of the market. It took the form of more vigorous competition by Independent titles with those of other groups ...

There were other changes regarding the trend in foreign ownership, he noted. The English company, Pearson PLC, bought half of *Business Day* and the *Financial Mail* from Times Media Limited (Times Media then became Avusa at the end of 2007). Partnerships with foreign investment also occurred in 1998, when *The Guardian* in London bought sixty-two per cent of the *Mail & Guardian*, which prevented the closure of the paper. Subsequently, in 2001, it sold most of these shares to the Zimbabwean newspaper mogul Trevor Ncube, still the majority owner and publisher. Another foreign ownership-cum-partnership occurred when Swedish group Dagens Industry bought twenty-four per cent of black-owned Mafube Publishing. Berger noted the irony that liberation in South Africa saw the death of the liberation movement's media as funding dried up because donors felt the country was now 'normal'. The small newspapers *South, Vrye Weekblad* and *New Nation,* met their demise in the early 1990s.

In addition to the above foreign partnerships and ownership trends, there were significant racial changes in ownership, according to Berger. He noted five main developments. Dr Nthatho Motlana formed New Africa Publishing (owned thereafter by New African Investments Ltd or NAIL) and in 1993 he bought the *Sowetan*. This was then bought by NAIL, a black economic empowerment (BEE) company. Second, thirty-four per cent of the holding company of Times Media Ltd, Johnnic, was sold to a BEE group, with the ANC politician and subsequent businessman Cyril Ramaphosa spearheading the deal. This group, the National Empowerment Consortium, consisted of: NAIL, the National Union of Mineworkers (Num), and the SA Railway and Harbour Workers Union (Sarhwu), precursor to the Transport and General Workers Union (T&G) which became the South African Transport and Allied Workers

Union (Satawu). Third, Berger noted a partnership between Kagiso Media and Perskor in 1998 but this split in 1999. Subsequently, Caxton bought Perskor and took ownership of the *Citizen*. Then the Union Alliance Media (UAM), a subsidiary of Union Alliance Holdings representing the two major union federations, Cosatu and Nactu, each with over two million members at the time, acquired shares in media companies.

These were major changes in media ownership. Owners included blacks and workers, and were a shift from the old patterns under apartheid, of white, male, capitalist owners. According to Jane Duncan, in an e-mail interview on 17 March 2008 for an article I wrote in *Enterprise* magazine, 'The media's political and economic landscape', this period could be described as 'the golden season of diversification'. She outlined the three main shifts. The first was between 1994 and 1996 when transformation of the media ensued with attempts to unbundle the three major newspaper groups which were owned mainly by the mining and finance houses. Attempts were made to introduce some level of black ownership. The second, Duncan said, was the financial crisis of 1996 which led to the introduction of Gear (Growth Employment and Redistribution – the growth strategy of the ANC under Mbeki) when 'credit became more costly' and 'black empowerment deals unwound'. This then led to the third, the 'reconsolidation of media into three big groups once again, Johncom (now Avusa), Independent Newspapers and Media 24/Naspers'.

The shifts that Duncan highlighted showed that as quickly as diversification took place the deals just as quickly unravelled. The government used the opportunity to call for measures to curb concentration while at the same time trying to muscle into the free space of the media. In the same interview, Duncan pointed to the 'growing executive control' of the media:

> Government advertising is also used as a means of exerting political pressure on media; recently the government threatened to withdraw advertising from the *Sunday Times* newspaper after it carried reports critical of the health minister ... The ANC is also investigating the setting up of a media tribunal to address the 'deficits' in the self-regulatory system, which may well lead to greater statutory control of the print media, considered to be a thorn in the side of many in positions of power.

As the story of the fight for democracy between the ANC and the media unfolds it becomes clearer how the ANC has used the concentration of media ownership as an excuse for its political subjections.

Media and democracy in South Africa

Using the conceptual tools of radical democracy and psychoanalysis my argument is that the trend of the interpellations against the media was based in ideology which is meant to mask antagonism within the ruling party itself: it deflects attention away from its own shortcomings by focusing on the media's shortcomings. Evidence will be provided in the case studies to follow. These interpellations began with Nelson Mandela and became quite intense during Thabo Mbeki's time as president. During Jacob Zuma's presidency we see legal interpellations in the form of law suits against media groups and individuals, for example the cartoonist Zapiro, and we see the Protection of State Information Bill (which would impede the work of investigative journalists) and the proposed media appeals tribunal.

The interpellations began with Mandela and it is noteworthy that, while the first democratic president was not paranoid about the media, he too showed misunderstanding of the media's role in democracy and assumed that because you were a black journalist you would necessarily be soft on the ANC and its flaws. To a group of Sanef editors, he said, in 1997: 'While there are a few exceptional journalists, many like to please their white editors' (cited in *Rhodes Journalism Review* 1997). It could be said that Mandela desired unity with the press, and expected it of black journalists. I argue that this kind of unity suggests foreclosures which are not ideal in a radical democracy characterised by heterogeneity, open spaces, and fluidity. Mandela's statement appears to be an attempt to create hegemonic unity out of irreducible heterogeneity, and an attempt to hermetically seal off the multiplicity of space, but using race.

Mbeki's first interpellations against the media were recorded by the journalist Mark Gevisser in his 2007 book, *The Dream Deferred*. He recalled how the 'first volley' by Mbeki against the press took place in 1994 just after his appointment as deputy president. In an address to the Cape Town Press Club he mounted a critical assessment of the media, accusing it of 'harbouring a tendency to look for crises and to look for faults and mistakes', an allegation that became his pattern, and then that of the ANC. Gevisser wrote that by September 1995 Mbeki was branding any media criticism of the ANC as racist.

The interpellation took place on two levels, one against black journalists and another against Anton Harber, former editor of the *Weekly Mail*. Looking at Harber, Mbeki said: 'Now criticism and complaining is what I expect from him. This forum, on the other hand, has to see itself as change agent, and not just criticise. The message to black journalists, I wrote at the time, was clear: Roll up your sleeves and stop whingeing like a whitey. Get with the programme' (Gevisser 2007: 644). In Mbeki's understanding, or misunderstanding, of the media's role in a democracy, he fails completely to recognise that the media is a relatively independent agent, independent from the ruling party and his rationale is that if you are black you will automatically heed the ideological interpellations of the ruling party. In other words, you will recognise that you are indeed an enemy of the people if you do not and you will begin to toe the line ideologically rather than report critically.

I would also argue, drawing on Mouffe, that Mbeki did not make a distinction between a legitimate adversary such as Harber and an antagonist; he viewed the editor as an antagonist, in the sense of not being supportive of the ANC's programme of transformation as the ANC saw it. Mouffe disagrees with Carl Schmitt whose argument did not permit a differential treatment of conflict but could only manifest as antagonism, 'where two sides are in complete opposition and no common ground exists between them. According to Schmitt, there is no possibility for pluralism – that is, legitimate dissent among friends' (Mouffe 1999: 5). In this sense, Mbeki's interpellation of Harber was Schmittean.

A further misunderstanding, or even deliberate misrecognition, of the role of the media in a democracy can be witnessed from the discourse of the president of the ANC, Jacob Zuma, when he said on the ANC website:

> We are faced with the virtually unique situation that, among the democracies, the overwhelmingly dominant tendency in South African politics, represented by the ANC, has no representation whatsoever in the mass media. We therefore have to contend with the situation that what masquerades, as 'public opinion', as reflected in the bulk of our media, is in fact minority opinion informed by the historic social and political position occupied by this minority. There are many examples we can cite to illustrate this point. Every day brings fresh instances of a media that, in general terms, is politically and ideologically out of sync with the society in which it exists (*ANC Today*: 18-24 January 2008).

In Zuma's gaze the media should be 'ideologically in sync' with society. How does he know this? How does he know what the whole of society thinks? It seems to be a conflation: society equals ANC. It is within this discourse that we can see what Torfing meant, in *New Theories of Discourse: Laclau, Mouffe and Žižek*, when he described the difference between discourse and the discursive (1999: 92). There is always something that escapes processes of signification within discourse, and the partial fixing of meaning produces a surplus. In other words, a surplus of meaning (what is not said, but is implied or read into meaning) is illogical and leads to an indefinable surplus, a meandering discussion which is off the point. There is surplus attached to the media in all three discursive interventions by Mandela, Mbeki and Zuma. Their expectations are in excess of the role of the media. Both the former presidents of the ANC and the current president appear to be obsessed by the media.

Their words show an attempt to create a hegemonic unity out of irreducible heterogeneity. But a radical democracy is exemplified by the acceptance of the multiplicity of spaces (and the media would be one such space): all open and not hermetically sealed, with fierce contestations and engagements all in flux. The call for too much unity, and consensus about everything, limits the free speech and criticism that are good for democracy. From the ANC presidents' words and their interpellations on the media, it can be seen that they would prefer a media that is at unity with the ANC, but this is not the role of the media in a democracy. This brings us back to the topic at hand: what is the role of the media in a democracy? It is not to be in sync ideologically, or to curry favour with politicians, and it is not – contrary to what the ANC desires – a media which should be involved in 'nation-building'.

On the one hand, there is support in the ANC for an independent media (in theory) while on the other it appears as though the ANC find the media goes too far in its criticisms. Take, for instance, Zuma's lawsuits against Zapiro, totalling R7 million for defamation (this amount was reduced to R5 million in 2011). Zuma says that he supports the free press, and yet he persists with the lawsuits, saying this is his right as a citizen (*The Weekender*: 15-16 August 2009).

The media's responsibility is to report news truthfully, accurately and fairly, according to the South African Press Code (see Appendix 1), and to keep public spaces open for debate and dissension, according to the democratic theory visited in this chapter. 'Truth' here, is to be understood in journalistic terms rather than in any transcendental philosophical way: that is, reporting the facts, and giving the citizenry as many different voices as possible. By playing the role of watchdog and holding power to account and by exposing corruption, the media plays a critical role in civil society. But is it that easy and is it that simple? It is worth pausing here to turn to three journal articles in *Social Dynamics* on public spheres, by Cowling and Hamilton (2010), Cowling (2010) and Serino (2010). The article by Serino discusses how topics for debate enter the South African public sphere, using the *Sunday Times* as an example. This takes place, research showed, through professional journalistic norms (for example what is newsworthy) but also through the *Sunday Times'* notion of what is in the public interest, in the context of its role in transformation and democracy. Through the selection or non-selection of stories and use of expert opinion, the *Sunday Times* sees itself as an agenda-setter; and therefore there is some orchestration of debate (Serino 2010). Serino also noted that there was a level of 'self impor-tance' attached to the way in which this was done and conveyed. Cowling and

Hamilton (2010) agreed with Serino on the 'orchestration' question, arguing that while it is an accepted practice in journalism there is not enough responsibility attached to it. 'The idea of public interest is thus a fuzzy but critical concept at the heart of journalistic practice' vis-à-vis choices of topics for debate governed by public interest, but it is undefined and learnt by journalists from their engagement with the news production process, and through negotiation and discussion. However, it could also be argued that perhaps even more should be left undefined and fuzzy in order to make the process of news selection more authentic. Cowling and Hamilton's research showed that on AM Live presenters played a key role in constituting the show's form; the mode was carefully orchestrated; and finding the 'right' guest was important. Therefore, their argument goes, why was there such a fuss about the SABC banning certain commentators? A point that Cowling and Hamilton raised was that, given that the paymasters were the SABC, who shared the ideas of the ANC on the developmental state and nation-building or, as the two authors put it, 'the national project of development', journalists nonetheless acted according to their own professional standards. A further point that they raised was that in the selection and production process there is a lot taken for granted and journalists are often not critically engaged. Then there is the question of 'orchestration', which implies deliberate, almost cynical and sinister, undertakings whereas in my experience of newsrooms in the last two decades, as an employee and freelancer, I found selection to be much more random than this, having much more to do with the public interest, production process, deadlines and what 'fits a page', rather than any coherent and conscious ideological positioning.

There is also the question of 'self-importance' that Serino (2010: 110) raised, quoting Mondli Makhanya starting off a 2007 news conferences by asking (referring to his paper): 'What will the highest court in the land say this week?', and 'the *Sunday Times* will select topics that it believes can advance the discussion of issues of relevance to South Africa'. This is interesting and thought provoking. Let's now turn to a piece by Peter Bruce, editor of *Business Day*, which might show this 'self-importance' (but I think he was merely observing certain facts). This is an extract from Bruce's column, *Thick End of the Wedge*:

> I think there's a case to be made for newspapers not being owned by
> public companies at all. When you consider the contribution they make
> to democracy it may be worth ruling that only newspapers owned by
> trusts or something similar can register as newspapers with the Post
> Office. Having said that, it was a newspaper (*City Press*) owned by the
> mother of all local listed media companies (Naspers) which for the second or third week in a row yesterday gave us some insight into how

Julius Malema has made his millions, and, in turn, added to the insight into why he feels he can't be contained. Why? Because with R54m in your bank account no one can tell you what to do. Only, thanks to *City Press*, we know now that Malema hasn't paid any tax on his ill-gotten millions and that could mean he goes to jail. Fantastic! But will it happen? [...] By cheating the government, by 'winning' tenders to be paid for with public money even though you have no chance of meeting the conditions of the tender, you are robbing the public purse and, therefore, you are robbing the poor. Looked at that way, Malema is a thief, but he is treated like a hero by the poor (*Business Day*: 8 March 2010).

Bruce was celebrating the uncovering by the media in February 2010 of the ANC Youth League leader Julius Malema having been caught with several companies registered in his name through alleged fraudulent tenders and having R54 million in his bank account while his salary was R20 000 a month. The stories showed details of fraudulent tenders, and the media called him a 'tenderpreneur' and remorselessly subjected him to scrutiny. This exposure is the role of the media in a democracy. The public was given the chance to question where taxpayers' money was going – into the pockets of corrupt leaders or towards solving the country's crime, unemployment and flailing infrastructural problems. If South Africa had a media that was ideologically in sync with the ANC, there would be no exposure of fraud and corruption. As Bruce said in the above column, it's the exposure of cheating the government by winning tenders, and the 'thieving' (*Business Day*: 8 March 2010) that made him proud of being in the profession.

Malema talked back. He refused identification with, or declined to appropriate, what Judith Butler had called 'the injurious term' (Schippers 2009: 78). He said he was just a 'poor child' and the media was jealous of him; he was not guilty of corruption and had nothing to hide from the South African Receiver of Revenue (SARS) (*Sunday Independent*: 28 February 2010). He also accused journalists of being opportunistic and having a conspiracy against him (*The Times*: 3 March 2010). The details of Malema's corruption are not the focus for this discussion, but the fact that he was exposed and that there was the space for this to occur signalled something encouraging for the media's role in this democracy. Malema also received a chance to talk back, via the media, when he claimed to be a poor child. What all this showed was the media playing the professional role according to the South African Press Code: 'The primary purpose of gathering and distributing news and opinion is to serve society by informing citizens and enabling them to make informed judgments on the issues of the time, and, the freedom of the press allows for an independent scrutiny to bear on the forces that shape society'. There are shortcomings in the way the media operates, as noted by Cowling and Hamilton, and by Serino. For example, a lot is taken for granted and often not critically engaged with. There may be some self-importance. Nonetheless in playing this role, even in a less than perfect way, the media does hold power to account. (In my experience journalists can sometimes be lazy with a penchant for desiring 'freebies' more than they should. They can also be unethical but this is not commonplace. In June 2010, Ashley Smith, a *Cape Argus* journalist, admitted to having taken payment from Ebrahim Rasool, the former ANC provincial leader in the Western Cape, to write stories favourable to the ANC. The press body condemned this, made it a big story in the newspapers and broadcast media, and also condemned the fact that the government appeared to be going ahead with its plans to appoint Rasool to the US as ambassador.)

Through the Malema example we can witness how secrecy can obstruct democracy by keeping the public ignorant of important information. It can be argued that there is little secrecy in South Africa because the media appears to be loyal to its professional – although we don't know how much is hidden, of course. Reconciliation of society (à *la* the theories of Žižek and Mouffe) that is, unity between the media and the ANC, seems impossible, and this is good news for the unrealised democracy. Moreover, as Johannsen, quoted at the beginning of this chapter, observed, 'Secrecy obstructs democracy by keeping the public ignorant of information'.

NOTES

1   Johannsen RC (1994) Military policies and the state system. In Held D (ed.) *Prospects for Democracy: North South, East, West.* Cambridge: Polity Press.

2   Newspapers such as the *Weekly Mail* called themselves independent, not so much for being independent from political parties but for being commercially independent. In other words, they were not part of the big newspaper conglomerates (Perskor, Naspers, or the Argus Group), and were not profit driven.

3   Tomaselli was quoting Mzala, a writer and radical within the ANC, who penned some of the ANC's analysis, strategy and tactics.

3.

The media's challenges:
legislation and commercial imperatives

The Protection of Information Bill currently before Parliament is meant to replace an apartheid-era law dating from
1982 ... it would virtually shield the government from the
scrutiny of the independent press and criminalise activities
essential to investigative journalism, a vital public service.[1]

This chapter first examines specifically how the legislative apparatus left over
from the apartheid period hindered the work of journalists but remained
because it suited the democratically elected leaders of the post-apartheid era.
Then, it examines how the growing uses of technology, coupled with commercial imperatives, affect the media's role in a democracy. The argument here is
that these forms of subjection and interference have had a negative impact
on the 'free' and 'independent' media. Then there is the raft of legislation that
has an impact on journalism, and, specifically, the ANC's efforts to promote
and explain its insidious creation, the Protection of State Information Bill
(Secrecy Bill) through which, as the US media body, the Committee to Protect
Journalists, said in the opening quotation, the activities of the independent
press would be criminalised while the government of the day would be shielded
from scrutiny if this had to be enacted.

The chapter proceeds to an overview of the South African media, to provide
details of how it has grown from a small and narrow set of players three decades
ago to the more diverse, amorphous and fluid media landscape in the new
dispensation – although it also shows the shifts from concentration of media

ownership to fragmentation and then back again. The chapter then describes the legal conditions under which journalists have to operate and how, in some instances, the laws have changed to accommodate the free flow of information while, in others, the legislation is deliberately obstreperous: The Promotion of Access to Information Act of 2000, for example, stands in stark contrast to the Protection of State Information Bill, which went before Parliament in July 2010 and again in September 2010, then again in November 2010, and was then passed by the National Assembly in 2011 before amendments were made in May 2012, which included a public interest defence. But then these were withdrawn in June 2012.

The chapter then looks at commercial imperatives and new media and the impact this has had, and continues to have, on the world of traditional journalism. It also shows how the meaning of the term 'media' has changed – from the traditional sphere of television, radio and newspapers providing the public with information and a public sphere for debate and analysis, to a broader view that encompasses citizen journalism, blogging, online publishing, and social networking sites, as well as cellphone technology used to pass on news to fellow citizens and to the traditional media.

Nick Davies is a journalist at *The Guardian* newspaper in London. His 2009 book, *Flat Earth News*, which subjects the profession to critical scrutiny, argues that journalism has been short-changed throughout the world. Owing to subjection by commercial imperatives, newsrooms have been slashed to half their original size in some cases, and desk journalism (where reporters sit at their desks 'dialing a quote' rather than venturing out to the site of the scene or to interview someone personally) is all-pervasive. Journalists write more stories in less time, with no time to check the facts, and they often regurgitate press releases from public relations companies. It amounts to what Davies calls 'churnalism' (2009: 70), stories churned out mindlessly from press releases, with the deadline rather than the accuracy of the facts in mind. While Davies's research is based primarily in the United Kingdom there are interesting overlaps with (and differences from) the situation in South Africa, as this chapter will show. Indeed, Anton Harber observes in the introduction to the book *Troublemakers: The Best of South Africa's Investigative Journalism* (2010), edited jointly with Margaret Renn, that there has indeed been a juniorisation of newsrooms, with age and experience levels having dropped in the post-apartheid era. He argues, however, that this romanticises journalism under apartheid, suggesting that some unspecified universal high standard of journalism was set, while it is debatable that coverage was then more accurate or substantial. The chapter then turns to the South African media landscape, with a particular emphasis on newspapers, and examines concentration of ownership, state interventions, and commercial imperatives, arguing that these are all different kinds of pressures which, it can be argued, are subjections.

The South African media landscape: an unprogressive concentration of media therefore a lack of diversity?

The claim that there is too much concentration of media ownership necessarily means a lack of diversity and, in turn, a need for state intervention to curb media excesses is a spurious one. My argument expresses the contrary: that the media is amorphous and fluid, lacking in unity and cohesion, with as many opinions as there are journalists in a newsroom. There is no one ideological agenda in 'the media', and journalists, by and large, exercise agency and act within the codes and ethics of their profession.

The media grew significantly in the last quarter of the twentieth century, and again from 2000 to 2007. What the figures below highlight is the growth from a small, narrow field of operators to a broader more diverse terrain. The media in 2007 consisted of seventy-one television stations, whereas in 2000 there were fifty-six, and in 1975 there were none. Similar growth trends can be seen in the number of radio stations. In 2007, there were 124 radio stations, in 2000 there were 105, and in 1975 there were seven. In March 2010, the Media Club South Africa website estimated that about 14.5 million South Africans buy the urban dailies, while community newspapers have a circulation of 5.5 million. There were twenty-two daily and twenty-five weekly urban newspapers in South Africa in 2010. In 2011, the state of newspapers showed these trends, according to *The Media* magazine of March 2012: newspaper distribution was double what it was in 1997, but there was a decline in the rate of growth over the last few years. Free community newspapers, however, have shown enormous growth: in 1997 there were 83 titles and in 2011 there were 195. While dailies' numbers are up since 1997, they show a downward trend over the last four years, as Tony Banahan wrote in an article, 'The figures don't lie' (*The Media*: March 2012). The following is a list of newspapers with sales and circulation figures from 2011.

- *Beeld* is an Afrikaans language daily, owned by Media 24, with copy sales of 36 754 and a total circulation of 76 321.
- *Die Burger* is an Afrikaans language daily paper, owned by Media 24, with copy sales of 35 680 with a total circulation of 78 901.
- *Business Day* is an English language daily owned by *Business Day/Financial Mail* in association with Avusa and the London-based Pearson, with copy sales of 8 532 and a total circulation of 36 103.

- *Cape Argus* is an English daily circulated in the Western Cape and is owned by the Independent Newspaper Group, with copy sales of 22 363 and a total circulation of 45 128.
- *Cape Times* is an English language daily, owned by the Independent Newspaper Group, with copy sales of 21 636 and a total circulation of 43 274.
- *The Citizen* is an English newspaper published six days a week, distributed in Gauteng and owned by Avusa/Caxton, with copy sales of 51 487 and a total circulation of 69 649.
- *Daily Dispatch* is an English newspaper in the Eastern Cape and is owned by Avusa, with copy sales of 22 634 and a total circulation of 22 394.
- *Daily News* is an English language daily based in KwaZulu-Natal and is owned by Independent Newspaper Group, with copy sales of 12 246 and a total circulation of 33 214.
- *Daily Sun,* the most-read newspaper in South Africa, distributed nationwide, is a tabloid owned by Media 24, with copy sales of 374 341 and total circulation of 374 400.
- *Diamond Fields Advertiser* is based in Kimberley in the Northern Cape and is owned by Independent Newspaper Group, with copy sales of 6 768 and a total circulation of 9 495.
- *The Herald* based in the Eastern Cape is one of the country's oldest newspapers, launched in 1845, and is owned by Avusa, with copy sales of 15 178 and a total circulation of 22 139.
- *Isolezwe* is an isiZulu newspaper published Monday to Friday, based in KwaZulu-Natal, owned by Independent Newspaper Group, with copy sales of 105 713 and a total circulation of 106 734.
- *Ilanga*, owned by Independent Newspapers and distributed in KwaZulu-Natal, has copy sales of 135 359 and a total circulation of 135 706.
- *Sondag* is an Afrikaans newspaper owned by Media 24, with copy sales of 46 304 and a total circulation of 47 286.
- *The Mercury* is an English language Durban morning paper, owned by Independent Newspaper Group, with copy sales of 14 462 and a total circulation of 31 474.
- *Pretoria News*, an English daily based in Pretoria but also distributed in the provinces of Mpumalanga and North West, is owned by Independent Newspaper Group, with copy sales of 12 630 and a total circulation of 23 148.
- *Sowetan* is a daily English language newspaper aimed at a literate black readership, owned by Avusa, with copy sales of 86 892 and a total circulation of 116 347.

- *The Star* an English daily published in Johannesburg but circulated throughout the country is owned by Independent Newspaper Group, with copy sales of 58 321 and a total circulation of 136 552.
- *The Times*, one of South Africa's newest papers, is an English language tabloid, the sister paper to the *Sunday Times*, owned by Avusa, with copy sales of 38 579 and a total circulation of 142 024.
- *Volksblad* is an Afrikaans language daily based in the Free State and is owned by Media 24, with copy sales of 13 169 and a total circulation of 21 353 for the daily edition.
- *The Witness*, an English language daily newspaper based in Pieter-maritzburg, owned by Media 24, has copy sales of 8 971 and a total circulation of 21 908.
- *The New Age* is an English daily with sales and circulation figures unavailable.

The weekly newspapers:
- *City Press* is an English Sunday paper, owned by Media 24, with copy sales of 155 247 and a total circulation of 157 306.
- *Saturday Star* is a weekly, based in Johannesburg, owned by Independent Newspapers, with copy sales of 57 121 and a total circulation of 97 257.
- *Independent on Saturday*, owned by Independent Newspapers, has copy sales of 22 473 and a total circulation of 46 008.
- *Isolezwe nge Sonto*, owned by Independent Newspapers, has copy sales of 81 041 with a total circulation of 81 553.
- *Ilanga Langesonto*, owned by Independent Newspapers, is distributed in KwaZulu-Natal and has copy sales of 85 726 and a total circulation of 85 726.
- *Mail & Guardian*, owned by Mail & Guardian Media, has copy sales of 35 324 and a total circulation of 45 692.
- *Post*, owned by Independent Newspapers, has copy sales of 25 831 and a total circulation of 43 413.
- *Soccer Laduma* owned by Media 24, distributed nationwide but also in Botswana and Swaziland, has copy sales of 345 088 and a total circulation of 345 088.
- *Rapport*, owned by Media 24, has copy sales of 215 479 and a total circulation of 231 911.
- *Sun*, owned by Media 24, is an Afrikaans language Western Cape tabloid, with copy sales of 103 056 and a total circulation of 103 056.
- *Sunday Independent*, owned by Independent Newspaper Group, in Gauteng, Western Cape, KwaZulu-Natal, Mpumalanga, Northern Province, has copy sales if 14 621 and a total circulation of 39 569.

- *Son op Sondag* is owned by Media 24; distribution is in the Eastern and Western Cape, with copy sales of 60 174 and a total circulation of 60 174.
- *Sondag* is owned by Media 24 and distributed in Gauteng, Free State, Northwest, Mpumalanga, Limpopo, KwaZulu-Natal and Northern Cape, with copy sales of 46 304 and a total circulation of 47 286.
- *Sunday Times*, owned by Avusa, is distributed nationwide with copy sales of 253 721 and a total circulation of 451 361.
- *Sunday Tribune* is owned by Independent Newspaper Group, distributed in Gauteng and KwaZulu-Natal, with copy sales 41 344 and a total circulation of 82 477.
- *Sunday World*, owned by Avusa, distributed in North West, Northern Cape, Free State, Eastern Cape, KwaZulu-Natal, Mpumalanga, Limpopo, and Gauteng, has copy sales of 127 490 and a total circulation of 147 614.
- *Weekend Post* is owned by Avusa and distributed in Western Cape and Eastern Cape with copy sales of 19 899 and a total circulation of 23 656.
- *Weekend Argus* is owned by Independent Newspapers and distributed in the Western Cape with copy sales of 49 217 and a total circulation of 70 212.
- *Weekend Witness*, owned by Independent Newspapers and distributed in the greater Pietermaritzburg area, has copy sales of 12 549 and a total circulation of 21 908.

Some trends

In an analysis of the above list a number of different trends emerge, but I cannot focus here on all of them. While there is a variety of newspapers, the majority in English, they are geared towards different readerships. Some tabloids target niche markets, for example those interested in sex and scandal, as reflected, for instance, in the *Sun*. But although there are many newspapers there are very few owners. A point worth noting is that, according to Harber (2009) the growth of the *Daily Sun* suggests that the reading public is widening. The *Daily Sun* is the country's biggest newspaper, aimed at black, working class people, offering local news and gossip, and focusing on the everyday lives and struggles of people rather than on intellectual debate. While the *Daily Sun* is the most widely read daily newspaper in the country, Harber said, daily papers aimed at an intellectual market, on the other hand, do not survive, and he provided the example of the attempt by the *Weekly Mail* in 1990 to launch a daily, the *Daily Mail*. This paper could not sustain itself and lack of funding meant that it met its demise less than two months after launching. *ThisDay*, a national intellectual daily to compete with *The Star* lasted a year, from October 2003 to October 2004, running up debts of up to R14 million (www.bizcommunity. com/article/196/90/4987). The problem was that neither was able to capture a sufficiently large advertising market or to reach a broad enough audience. The *Weekender* followed the same pattern as the *Daily Mail* and *ThisDay* when it shut down in November 2009. *Business Day/Financial Mail* (BDFM) launched the *Weekender* in March 2007. It serviced an intellectual readership, and at its second birthday in March 2009, according to the All Media and Products survey (AMPs) of 2009, the paper showed a significant following of 71 000 readers per issue. However, by November 2009 the management of BDFM closed the paper because of financial constraints. Again, it was a case of not enough advertising and not enough sales. In the meantime, at the lower end of the market the tabloid *Daily Sun* – launched by Media 24 in 2003 – sold 508 000 copies daily in March 2004, when it was not yet one year old (Harber 2009), and the AMPs survey showed growth from 1.4 million readers in 2003 to 3.4 million by 2005 (AMPs 2009).

A further trend, evidenced by the last point, is that newspaper readership's decline has been arrested, according to the South African Advertising Research Foundation (*Business Day*: 1 April 2010). Newspaper sales stabilised, according to the research, and the number of South Africans reading newspapers had increased to 15.324 million, compared with the figure of 14.5 produced by Media Club South Africa in March 2010 cited earlier in this chapter. A fifth trend to be gleaned from the above listing of newspapers is that there is a concentration of ownership by four main players: Avusa, Independent Newspaper Group, Caxton and Media 24. This concentration cannot be a good thing. We need more media, we need a diverse media, and we need media where all voices, from all classes, races and genders are heard – but does this concentration translate into an unprogressive hegemony by big capital? There are far too many issues that are conflated in a discussion of media freedom in South Africa. According to the ANC, in a discussion document for its September 2010 NGC, 'Free, independent and pluralistic media can only be achieved through not only many media products but by the diversity of ownership and control of media' (ANC 2010). This is a curious statement, given that the ANC wishes to exercise political control of the media via a media appeals tribunal. It could be claimed that the ruling party's argument for diversity and transformation is a spurious one, that it is self-serving and a disguise for its more insidious intentions of controlling the free flow of information and criticism. Readers of newspapers in fact have pointed to arguments for diversity as a 'guise' to mask the ANC's efforts to control and limit the role of the media. The extract below from a letter to *The Times* shows how one reader responded.

It is an open secret that the ANC realises that its inevitable decline in power and control of the country has arrived, now the only option it has is to close access to information. It is not by coincidence that the Protection of Information Bill and the media appeals tribunal are being proposed simultaneously (*The Times:* 16 August 2010).

Is this concentration of ownership an unprogressive hegemony?

Four big companies own the lion's share of the commercial print media. This concentration of ownership does not translate into four views in the media, as is sometimes implied by the ANC. I will argue that this assumption reflects reductionist logic and is a simplistic and inaccurate answer to the question of the concentration of ownership. The ruling party uses the concentration of media ownership to try to limit the free space of the media. The stranglehold of big media companies has provided a platform for the government to initiate laws and policies under the guise of development, transformation, protection of privacy and state security, which threaten to close the discursive spaces for open criticism germane to developing a democratic culture and society.

There are different ways of looking at what 'diversity' means in relation to concentration of ownership. In response to the long-held belief that ownership and control of commercial media translate into determination of content, Thabo Leshilo, the veteran journalist, then columnist at *The Times* and public editor at Avusa Media, argued: 'The idea that such concentration of ownership is a threat to democracy is far-fetched and can only succeed in inflaming passions' (*Sunday Times:* 8 November 2009). He pointed out that the big four did not form a news cartel. 'They all compete fiercely for market share, even to the point of wanting to kill one another's titles' he argued. Leshilo was responding to the Media Development and Diversity Agency (MDDA), a section 21 company set up by the government in the new democracy to investigate media ownership and lack of diversity. The stated aims of the MDDA were to give adequate space to women, children and people with disabilities, and for the self-regulatory mechanism for newspapers to be aligned with legislation. Leshilo explained that in South Africa there was little correlation between shareholders and the stories that appeared in papers, radio or television. Nic Dawes, editor of the *Mail & Guardian*, made the same point: 'Editors I know and respect would resign if given instructions by management, advertising and shareholders on what news content should be. In all major SA newsrooms, at least those that I know of, they keep a strict Chinese wall between advertising and editorial' (cited in *Daily Maverick*: 2 October 2010).

Leshilo wrote: 'What shareholders care about is the return on their investment. They do not scrutinise papers to check if they do a good job on covering women or people with disabilities, for example' (*Sunday Times*: 8 November 2009). In South Africa, he further expounded, shareholders appoint a board, which appoints management, which then appoints editors. While Leshilo conceded that papers could do a better job of covering marginalised communities, women and children, it was not for a government agency to be policing newspapers or the news. He added that some methods proposed at the MDDA meeting were hugely problematic:

> They betrayed a veiled desire by representatives of government, state organs and the ruling alliance to impose their own set of values on society and determine what is acceptable to publish. Their suggestion to resuscitate debate on the ANC's ill-conceived idea of subjecting independent media, privately funded media to a state media tribunal or some other government agency is a dead-giveaway of their intentions (*Sunday Times*: 8 November 2009).

In theoretical terms, what Leshilo was describing was the unprogressive hegemony of the ANC and the attempted closure of media spaces. A government agency, wanting more diversity to sympathetically reflect the concerns of neglected rural people, blacks, women, children and people with disabilities, is deployed as a disguise for more political control of the media. This constitutes an unprogressive hegemony in disguise as openness, which would ironically limit and hinder free speech and freedom of expression – hallmarks of what is required to sustain democracy – even more than the so-called concentration of ownership. Attesting to this view would be the following point made by Mondli Makhanya *en passant* in an interview conducted in 2008: 'Cyril Ramaphosa has greeted me a few times as we've passed each other by on the escalator, not once has he called me in for a chat, nor has he visited me in my office ... '. Yet Ramaphosa is one of the owners of his newspaper. While the area of ownership and media concentration is not the focus of my argument, I have raised it here to show that there are different ways of looking at diversity. In particular, the argument for a direct relationship, or even a correlation, between ownership and journalistic freedom of expression, is too reductionist and conflates ownership with control of information and opinion dissemination. Moreover, it does not add up to the real experience of journalists within a particular newspaper. This is not to deny that the world of journalism is affected by profit motives of owners, as the closure of newspapers suggests, nor is it to deny that rural areas are inadequately covered and that the majority of newspapers have a middle class bias. In addition, the new world of technology has made the old world of newspapers struggle for its space. The traditional media world has been subjected to significant competition, an onslaught, if you like, over the last decade, with the wave of new technology that has rolled in to compete for its space. However, as media analyst Paula Fray pointed out in an interview in March 2008, if you remove cell phones from the equation of new media only a small percentage of South Africans have access to the Internet: 'Fewer than ten per cent of adult South Africans surf the Internet but its impact is still significant,' she said, but technology has certainly changed the way our children consume information:

> Increasingly news needs to be more interactive, shorter, targeted and media now face the challenge of building relationships with their online users. The flood of information on the Internet actually promotes targeted media because people are looking for products that serve their needs. In the last year particularly, I've seen the online websites of print products become more interactive and multi-media.

Fray observed that the traditional world of the media was changing from one in which media meant radio, television and newspapers, to an expanded view which embraced a range of technology, including the Internet. In this new technological age the consumption of information has spread and expanded. Despite rapid technological changes, the question of who has access to these developments remains. The former *Weekly Mail* editor and the first journalist in South Africa to begin publishing online, Irwin Manoim, commented on the results of Internet usage in South Africa in the wealth trends survey in Gauteng (*Sunday Times*: 22 June 2008). His research showed that 493 000 people had accessed the Internet over the four-week monitoring period; twenty-one per cent of them had read the news online, and eleven per cent had read a daily paper online. Manoim commented that the wealthy were probably reading business news online, which the Internet provided as it unfolded, but which print can only provide the next day. 'Internet news can be read on your office computer while you are working. It even prompts you when news that is of interest to you comes up,' he said.

While this was the trend in the upper end of the wealth scale, or living standards measure, the Gauteng Wealth Survey also showed that printed news was doing better than ever at the lower popular tabloid end of the market (*Sunday Times*: 22 June 2008), reflecting the same trend in other developing countries in Africa and the East, for example China and India. Nevertheless, South Africa's newspapers were affected by the global economic recession of 2008 and the move away from advertising in print to advertising on the Internet, which is cheaper according to Manoim. Many newspapers and magazines have closed down. For example, *Maverick* magazine folded in October 2008, *Ymag* in November 2008, *Enterprise* magazine in December 2008, *The Weekender* in November 2009, and *Femina*, South Africa's oldest women's magazine, in February 2010. Before a more detailed discussion of the complex question of commercial imperatives and the intersection between media and democracy, this chapter now turns to an overview of the legislation, a severe form of subjection which hinders the work of journalists and the free flow of information, thus signifying significant closures for democracy.

State subjection via the law and civil society reaction

A free media is guaranteed in Section 16 of the Constitution under the principle of freedom of expression. The section reads:

16. Freedom of expression
Everyone has the right to freedom of expression, which includes
a) freedom of the press and other media;
b) freedom to receive or impart information or ideas;
c freedom of artistic creativity; and academic freedom and freedom of scientific research.

It is inherent in the Constitution that no right is absolute. It would be within this context that the media's fight for independence from political control, as in the Protection of State Information Bill and the proposed media appeals tribunal, would take place should the issue reach the Constitutional Court. The scrutiny of the independence of the media did not begin only in 2010, as we saw in Chapter Two. The civil society watchdog body, the FXI, in a booklet entitled *The Media and the Law*, pointed out that while media freedom is constitutionally protected and the country has one of the freest media in Africa, as the 'honeymoon phase of our new democracy fades, so it becomes clear that attacks on media freedom are increasing'.

Over the past few years, the FXI has charted a trend of increasing censorship of the media and individual journalists. This censorship is not only directly applied through laws and lawsuits, but also indirectly, through a withdrawal of advertising and self-censorship. A favoured method to silence the media is the defamation lawsuit. Media freedom is also under threat from the courts in the form of interdicts brought by aggrieved parties against the media. This amounts to pre-publication censorship and, although the interdicts are temporary, by the time the interim period lapses, the news story is out of date and the banned copies must be pulped, with severe financial implications. Another increasing threat to media freedom has been the pressure brought to bear on journalists and media to reveal the confidential sources of their information (Freedom of Expression Institute 2008).

In the above extract there were three main issues of concern to the FXI: increasing censorship through laws and lawsuits, particularly the defamation lawsuit;[2] interdicts to prevent publication and the pressure to reveal confidential sources. The legislation that impacts on media and non-media freedom of expression is discussed below. This includes the two Bills that have not yet been passed in parliament. If the two Bills are enacted they will profoundly affect the work of journalists.

- **Promotion of Equality and Prevention of Unfair Discrimination Act** (No. 4 of 2000). The aim of this Act was to prohibit hate speech but it also raised freedom of expression issues. According to the Act, no person may publish, propagate, advocate or communicate words that could reasonably be construed to demonstrate a clear intention to be hurtful, harmful or to incite harm; or promote or propagate hatred. This raises the question of how journalists would report on issues that might offend. The most likely effect on editors and journalists would be self-censorship.

- **Films and Publications Act** (No. 3 of 2009). The aim of this Act was to protect against child pornography. However, it could also be used as a form of pre-publication censorship, which would counter the media freedoms guaranteed in the Constitution. Three media organisations, the FXI, Sanef and Misa, felt that there was no record of newspapers or news broadcasters having contravened the common law crime of displaying child pornography or of exposing children to pornography. In the end, the Bill was enacted without the government having consulted adequately with the media and subsequent to complaints from media NGOs, a clause was included to protect bona fide newspapers, but, according to Raymond Louw, deputy chairperson of Sanef's media freedom committee and publisher and editor of *Southern Africa Report*, about 700 publications and magazines were not included in the clause and therefore have to comply with the Act (*Business Day*: 12 November 2009). Dene Smuts, a Democratic Alliance MP and the former editor of a woman's journal, said: 'No one at all should be conducting pre-publication inspection. That is censorship of the most primitive kind, whether imposed on broadcasters or print media, and it is plainly unconstitutional' (*Sunday Times*: 6 May 2007). In a public survey conducted by TNS Research, citizens were asked whether new laws were needed to clamp down on the media to curb child pornography, and seventy three per cent of South Africans said that it was 'important to have independent TV stations, radio, and newspapers so that we get unbiased news' (*Sunday Independent*: 6 May 2007). Out of a total of 2 000 respondents in Johannesburg and Pretoria, eighty seven per cent agreed on the need for independent uncensored news; seventy seven per cent from Soweto agreed; seventy two per cent from Cape Town and Durban. Bloemfontein came in lowest with sixty per cent.

- **National Key Points Act** (No. 102 of 1980). This Act prevents publication about security arrangements at key strategic installation points called national key points. The law prevents reporters and photographers from reporting and taking pictures of, for example, the security wall built around the president's and cabinet ministers' homes in Pretoria. Any state department or public entity could be declared a national key point by the minister of safety and security in the interests of national safety and security. In an interview which took place in January 2008, Hopewell Radebe observed that, 'Sanef is struggling to get laws repealed and, as Justice Pius Langa warned, if editors don't let the laws be promulgated, it's hard to have them repealed. In effect the National Key Points Act means you could get into trouble for taking a picture of a Post Office!'

- **Protection from Harassment Act** 17 of 2011. The aim of the Act was to protect victims from stalkers. However, investigative journalism would be impeded, because it sometimes requires what could be conceived of as 'stalking'. In effect, for doing their work, journalists could have faced criminal charges or damage claims. Sanef made submissions opposing the Bill on the basis that this would have the unintended consequence of impeding investigations by journalists. By 2011, when it was enacted, an exemption clause had been added in for journalists.

- **Protection of State Information Bill** (B6 – 2010). This Bill was before Parliament in 2009 and for most of the second half of 2010. If enacted, it would prevent certain stories from being published as it allowed a broad range of information to be classified as secret. Owing to the wide outcry over this Bill, that its classification is too broad and that too much power is vested in the minister of security to decide what classified information is, it was withdrawn temporarily in 2008, to return in 2009, and again in 2010. In June 2010, the Bill came before Parliament with twenty-three submissions from civil society groups and editors concerned about the implications for journalists gaining access to state information. The editors were concerned that a journalist could be jailed for up to twenty-five years for publishing classified information. In May 2012, the Bill before the National Council of Provinces was amended to include a public interest defence.

The Bill seems to suit the ruling party's hegemonic purposes and one can argue that it reflects an agenda for what could be defined as an unprogressive hegemony, a closing of the open and free spaces for civil society action in order to create a society where there is secrecy rather than transparency. The curtailing of media freedoms – if the Protection of State Information Bill were to be enacted without a public interest defence – would criminalise investigative journalism and jail sentences of between three to twenty-five years would be imposed for those in contravention. If enacted, it would mean that newspapers would not be able to question whether a president is fit for office, nor expose misconduct and corruption by public figures. In fact, the media's function, as discussed in earlier chapters, of holding power to account and exposing abuse of power, would have been curbed. In June 2012, parliamentary discussions on the Bill were postponed to September 2012.

The Secrecy Bill

The main focus of this section is to present evidence of the public discourse around the Bill through letters to some newspapers, rather than to unpack clause by clause the legislation itself. First, if the Protection of State Information Bill (or 'Secrecy Bill') were to become law without amendments, it would create a secret society, as it would stop the free flow of information as stipulated in the Promotion of Access to Information Act of 2000. According to a 'Civil Society Statement' (2 August 2010)[3] the Secrecy Bill, if enacted, would mean that: a document containing state information may be classified as confidential, secret, or top secret. You, as a member of the public, a whistle-blower or a journalist, would be liable for a criminal offence if caught with such a document, as you ought to have reasonably known that it was dangerous. Besides the absence of a public interest defence, there are other problems with the Bill. These include:

- It gave the state security minister huge power, including extending to the right to classify information in any organ of state. The criteria for classification are not spelled out.
- The sentences are harsh: twenty-five years in jail for the disclosure of 'top secret' information, fifteen years for 'secret' information, and five years if the information was classified 'confidential' or if the offender 'should have known' that this would 'directly or indirectly' have benefitted another state or non-state actor or prejudice national security. Even possession or disclosure, regardless of whether there is prejudice, could translate into jail terms of up to five years. And if that possession or disclosure was in respect of information classified by the State Security Agency the penalty rose to ten years.
- The state argues that the public's right to information is met by the Promotion of Access to Information Act (Paia) and the whistle-blower provisions of the Protected Disclosures Act and Companies Act. The Secrecy Bill undermines this by overriding Paia as whenever there is a clash, the Secrecy Bill should take precedence.
- The Bill's scope was ostensibly narrowed to national security matters only. This is eroded by the introduction of broad concepts such as 'economic, scientific or technological secrets vital to the Republic' and 'state security matters', defined as anything and everything the State Security Agency considers its business.
- The idea of a classification review panel that was introduced after much protest appears to lack true independence, as it would be chosen by and would report to Parliament's joint standing committee on intelligence, which works behind a veil of secrecy.

Civil society groupings launched the Right2Know campaign to oppose the Secrecy Bill, in Cape Town on 31 August 2010 and in Johannesburg on 16 September 2010. In the launching statement, the Right2Know said that, if enacted, this Bill would create a 'society of secrets', criminalise whistle blowers and impinge on press freedom in South Africa. It would become close to impossible to investigate those in positions of power for corruption or abuse of office, and it would lead to self-censorship by journalists afraid of imprisonment. There were many articles written by the media itself, as well as by political analysts in the media, about the Bill, and letters from the public show how some citizens felt their lives would be affected negatively by a media clampdown. The majority of these letters indicated that many members of the public could see that the controls were political. The letters variously described the purpose of the Bill as ideological obfuscation and constituting a desire to cover up the ruling party's own inadequacies and its tarnished image owing to the many exposures of corruption, and they serve to show that many did not believe in the ideological social fantasy that the 'bourgeois commercial media' was merely serving the interests of their 'capitalist bosses', or that the 'neoliberal media' was a threat to democracy. Many disagreed with the comment made by Blade Nzimande, the minister of higher education that: 'We have a huge offensive against our democracy ... the print media is the biggest perpetrator' (*The Star*: 11 October 2010).

Letters from *The Times*:

ANC wants grip of iron

President Jacob Zuma's contention that the media are suspect because they were 'not democratically elected' (August 12) once again shows how misguided the ANC's conception of democracy is. Democracy means to be able to exercise choices. No newspaper forces me to buy and read it. It is the proposed media tribunal that is undemocratic because it removes choice ... (Louis van Rooyen, Klerksdorp, 16 August 2010).

We've no one to blame but ourselves

All this chaos about the media tribunal and the Protection of Information Bill started the day President Zuma and his supporters were voted into power ... Now, despite Zuma's promises to preserve the freedom of the media and freedom of expression, his attention-seeking police chief, Bheki Cele, is arresting and harassing reporters and newspapers. How could the media pose any threat to the revolution? (Sabelo Mkhaliphi, Johannesburg, 12 August 2010).

We must protect public's right to know

Our government's proposed controversial Protection of Information Bill and the ANC's plans for the establishment of a media tribunal that would regulate the media are against the Constitution ... Freedom and access to information are some of the main features of a democracy. Democracy centres on investigative and fearless reporting, and independent media that are truly free from any interference. Critical and probing questions are essentials of good journalism. A free media also helps prevent abuse of power, and promotes accountability and transparency. Media independence from the government is crucial to encourage public discussion and participation. Democracy requires an informed populace. Freedom of the press is something we should not forego (Abdullah Saeed, 10 August 2010).

We should be opening up our democracy

The proposed media tribunal and the new classification [of information] laws set a dangerous precedent. It is the fine detail and the letter of the law that count. Control of the media is a disaster. We do not need an army of officials classifying documents. We should be opening up and relying on a mature and democratic public to see its way through. The ANC should withdraw the bills and look for other ways to open debate, discussion and action in a democracy (Graeme Bloch, by email, 10 August 2010).

Elites want to seize control of media

In view of the bid by the ANC to establish a media tribunal, and the mafia style arrest of Sunday Times journalist Mzilikazi wa Afrika, I am reminded of Marxist sociologist Ralph Miliband … 'They share power with others only when it is in their interest, and they never voluntarily surrender power. To rule their society, elites employ techniques such as dominating the economy, using the police and military forces, and manipulating the educational system and the mass media.' He said elites often believe that leadership by an elite is the natural state for people to live in and that people are easily led. For me, this view accurately explains the government's attitude to the media (Tshilidzi Tuwani, by email, 10 August 2010).

Tribunal a bid to keep a lid on top-level rot

I am quite disturbed by the ANC's proposed media appeals tribunal and the Protection of Information Bill. Though the party might claim that the media tribunal would adjudicate complaints from citizens about the press, it has become quite apparent that it is the ANC's strategy to stop the media from exposing the corruption of top officials. It seems the ANC wishes to build a state in which people are not allowed to know the evil deeds and mischief of the leaders they have elected (Thalukanyo Nangammbi, Pretoria, 11 August 2010).

One of the most important points to note is that citizens made the link between the Protection of State Information Bill and the media appeals tribunal and seemed to find that these were not isolated or randomly proposed regulations and laws but laws that would work together to close the spaces for democracy. What was apparent from these readers' comments was that a connection was being made by many of the public that there was, on the part of the ANC, ideological obfuscation at play, and the media were used as a scapegoat for the ruling party's problems. There are resonances with Žižek's explanation of the 'symbolic over-determination': the basic trick of displacement was to displace social antagonism into antagonism between the sound social texture, social body, and – in his example – the Jew as the force corroding it. Thus the force of corruption was located within a particular entity. (1989: 125). In an explanation of how surplus supports ideology, Žižek wrote that the displacement is supported by a condensation of features: Jew as profiteer, Jew as schemer, Jew as seducer of innocent girls, Jew as corrupt and anti-Christian, and so forth, so that a series of heterogeneous features and floating signifiers became condensed, and it is this very surplus which becomes the last support of ideology. In South Africa, we have a similar ideological interpellation or hailing of the media as unsupportive of transformation or as capitalist bastards or as enemies of the people and as a threat to democracy and a law unto themselves, of whom Jackson Mthembu wrote in the article 'Big stick to beat errant journalists', if 'they need to be jailed then they need to be jailed' (*Mail & Guardian*: 23-29 July 2010).

The function of ideological fantasy, deployed from Žižek's theory, is to mask inconsistency. It is precisely the way antagonistic fissure is masked. This explains the ANC's gaze on the media. The ANC needs to close the media spaces in order to create a mirage of unity, so that it seems as though society is united and harmonious. In a 2008 interview, Hopewell Radebe described the phenomenon journalistically:

> The ruling party just wants happy stories, finish and *klaar*. We try and put all sides of the story together, and so they call us enemies of the people. We once reported on a housing story in Mpumalanga's Bushbuckridge area. The people were happy they received houses, yes, but they were not happy with the type of houses they got. It had changed their culture of living and builders had just looked at cost effectiveness. The housing department took exception to the story.

From the fantasy gaze of the ANC, the media is the cause of social antagonism, which prevents society from achieving its full identity as a closed, homogenous totality. As some of the letters from the public showed, citizens were not blinded by the ANC's ideological stratagems. They tell of a paranoid construction of 'the media' with a symbolic over-determination invested in it. As Ferial Haffajee, editor of *City Press*, commented in a Special Assignment programme on SABC 3 on 17 August 2010: 'I really wonder why the ANC is not as obsessed about poverty, the delivery of housing, and unemployment as it is about the media'.

Žižek (1989) described how in the Soviet Union those who disagreed with 'the Party' as representatives of the people were positioned ideologically as traitors or enemies of the people: 'Fantasy is a means for an ideology to take its own failure into account in advance' (1989: 126). It constitutes the frame through which we experience the world as consistent and meaningful. The letters from the public showed that the writers understood that the ANC was indulging in an ideological social fantasy and was attempting to structure the media as outside democracy to suit its own purposes, masking its own inadequacies and inconsistencies. So then, we give houses to the poor, but do not let anyone know that the poor were not happy with those houses for that would make you an enemy of the people. Not all the letter-writers accepted the ANC's ideological interpellations of the media as 'enemy'. I would call them cases of rejection of the ideologically interpellating voice of the ANC.

The letters below, from the *Daily Sun*, show a similar trend, except the second letter which points to a terrible mistake the media made when it published a wholly inaccurate story about Kgalema Motlanthe's private life.

Tribunal a warning
The ANC's media tribunal is uncalled for and must not be allowed to happen. The tribunal's main objective is to hide the corruption of under-performing politicians. Why can't the ANC first establish a tribunal into corruption by political office-bearers? ... (Julius Sadiki, Jo'burg, 4 August 2010).

We DO need a media tribunal
I would like to add my voice to the call for a government regulated media tribunal. We have seen in the past how the media has failed to use self-regulation mechanisms like the press ombudsman. A lot of people's rights have been infringed in the name of freedom of speech and freedom of the press. Let me remind my fellow South Africans of Kgalema Motlanthe's love-child saga, and of Zapiro's cartoons depicting our president pulling his pants down and getting ready to rape Lady Justice. These are just two examples of how the media targets and demonises people they don't like. If a false story makes headlines, it's read by millions. A retraction is normally a small column that goes unnoticed. The media is being used by certain individuals to distort the image of their rivals to further their own agendas. We need a media tribunal – finished and *klaar*! (Sipho Nsibande, Pretoria, 2 August 2010).

Media bill a bad idea
The proposed media tribunal is a very bad idea for a country like ours, where corruption is common ... Those who have a lot to hide will support this tribunal. But those who have nothing to hide will understand that

journalists are the ears and mouths of ordinary people. If you know that a newspaper story about you is true, you will want to form a media tribunal that will consist of your political allies, who will cover up for you (Patrick Sekgala, Kanana, 11 August 2010).

Media bill a cover-up for corruption

I am strenuously opposed to the proposed law calling for a media tribunal and the Protection of Information Bill by the ANC and its alliance partners. To me this smacks of a total abuse of power. Those who argue that media self-regulation is not enough either have skeletons in their closet and fear the media will expose them or do not want the masses to know how their tax money is being spent. Why is it only the media that is being targeted with this tribunal? ... the ruling party does not want them to know about their public shenanigans. Service delivery is horrible but the ruling party conveniently isn't calling for a tribunal to deal with their failure to provide basic services! (Puleng Mmila, Seokodibeng, 11 August 2010).

ANC wants to keep us all in the dark

Why does the ANC insist on this media tribunal? Why do they hate a free press? Why do they want to turn SA into Zimbabwe? What are they trying so hard to hide from the public eye? Do they prefer the dark? The media is there to inform the public on matters that concern them as South African citizens. According to the ANC, the media is their biggest enemy at the moment. Is this because it is spilling the beans on the corruption of party leaders? This attempt to gag the press has nothing to do with protecting the dignity of South Africa or the needs for journalistic accuracy, as the ANC claims. Free speech and access to information are the lifeblood of our democracy. Why is government trying to take that away from us? (Zama Mhlambi, Pretoria, 3 August 2010).

Media face major threat

The media in our country face a massive threat if the proposed media tribunal law is passed. This is a poor decision by untrustworthy politicians who want to manipulate the media in order to praise their achievements, conceal their crimes and promote their questionable agendas in the full knowledge that they will not be found out ... The media are a mirror of society and should continue to cast light in the dark corners, exposing all wrongdoings regardless of the powers involved (Jerry Pingurai, Port Elizabeth, 3 August 2010).

The media must not knock ANC

Although the proposed media tribunal might not be the perfect solution to the shoddy and biased journalism in this country, few would deny that we need an effective regulation mechanism to curb the excesses of some of our media. The SA media has positioned itself against the ANC. There seems to be desperation to link every Tom, Dick and Harry to the ANC. For a ruling party that has enjoyed a two-thirds majority, it is inevitable that most people will be linked to them. Print media hire males to slander the ruling party. Personal opinions and conservative columns rubbishing the ANC cause major irritation – hence the calls for a fairer system to regulate these excesses. Rubbishing and denigrating the ruling party is the work of the political opposition, not the media! (Patrick Rampai, Klerksdorp, 16 August 2010).

ANC doesn't have monopoly on truth

In 1994, Nelson Mandela proclaimed that no person or group could claim to have a monopoly on the truth. He further warned that any prejudice that hampers freedom of expression is a disservice to society. Indeed, Madiba was spot on! At the root of media freedom lies a mirror through which the concepts of accountability, transparency and openness – are to be realised. Constitution – Why fear media criticism if your affairs are above board? (Puleng Mmila, Seokodibeng, 17 August 2010).

Media Bill to protect corrupt ANC cadres

The ANC has two major problems. One: keeping their promise of bettering the lives of the people. Two: corruption is rocking the mighty Titanic in all sorts of undesired directions! The ANC of Oliver Tambo has in recent years been infiltrated by greedy, unpatriotic and insensitive men and women … The liberal media of our country, a product of the democracy fought for by the ruling party, have gone to great lengths to hold government accountable, with high professional standards. That has meant reporting on stories of corruption within the ANC, which has led to the downfall of a few cadres. Is the media getting too close to even bigger wrongdoers? It seems so. Why else would we need a Protection of Cadres Bill – sorry, I mean the Protection of Information Bill? For the ANC to continue with its proposal for a media appeals tribunal would be to concede that corruption has won the day and we must shut up and watch soapies! (Christopher Mazibuko, Soshanguve, 26 August 2010).

SA a democratic state no more

Censoring the SA media is a big mistake by President Zuma and his political cronies. It not only undermines freedom of speech but the integrity of journalists to be transparent in their work … Ironically, the people who are pleading for a tribunal have made headlines for mismanaging taxpayers' funds. If the Information Bill is passed, corrupt officials will have no boundaries … The media only tells people about information, not what to do with it … South Africa is slowly sliding off the democratic radar! (Thabo Mthombeni, no place provided, 19 August 2010).

Evil lurks in ANC

… Untrustworthy politicians are proposing a bill that will protect them from being exposed by media when they steal from government coffers. Tender irregularities will then go unpunished, as we will never know about it. The proposed media tribunal could be good as long as independent people are appointed to run it and they aren't accountable to Parliament. The real evil now is the proposed Information Bill, which I suspect is meant to cover up corruption … (Patrick Sekgala, Ndhambi Village, 26 August 2010).

One of the letters in support of the ANC's proposed legislation to curb the 'excesses' of the media points to a good example of irresponsible journalism when the Independent Group ran a story of Kgalema Motlanthe's love child. This story proved to be false. It was indeed irresponsible reporting. The retraction, as the reader correctly pointed out, was very small in comparison to the hurt and damage the big front-page story must surely have caused. This was a reason for more control of the media, according to the writer, 'finished and *klaar*'.

Another member of the public felt, in the same way that the ANC feels, that the media was positioning itself as an opposition party. The statement that the print media hire 'males to slander the ruling party' is quite inexplicable. However, the other letters showed that many readers were not so easily hoodwinked. The views against the Secrecy Bill and the media appeals tribunal showed an awareness that the ruling party wanted to cover up corruption (for example tender irregularities); that those who wanted it 'had a lot to hide' while the Secrecy Bill was a Protection of Cadres Bill; that the media was the 'voice, ears and eyes' of the people; that this would instil fear in journalists; free speech and access to information was the lifeblood of democracy; democracy was under threat from the ANC and not the media and it smacked of abuse of power; that 'South Africa was sliding off the democracy radar';

that the ANC does not have a 'monopoly on the truth'; wanting to hide the incompetence regarding the provision of service delivery was the real issue; the public had the right to know what was happening in their country; and the agenda is self-enrichment.

Understanding these letters

Some members of the public saw through the ideological obfuscation of the ANC, showing that the social reality is conflictual by nature and that the ANC had deliberately created an 'us' (the ANC and 'the people') and a 'them' (the media). It does this because it does not recognise sufficiently the role of a critical and independent media in a democracy. Conflict is necessary in a plural society, but of course there has to be some kind of consensus (Mouffe 2005: 131-32) which could be based on the ethico-political values informing the political association, although there will always be different meanings attached to the way they will be implemented. This is what we find playing itself out in South Africa today regarding the fight for democracy between the media and the ANC. And so we have something called 'lawfare' where, at the drop of a hat, all parties run off to the courts to have disputes resolved.

The media is caught in a deep slumber

Prior to 2010 there appeared to have been considerable complacency within the journalist profession about media freedom and attempted subjugations, for instance in their response to the Secrecy Bill. By 2010, however, the media profession had begun to realise that a different challenge existed, and exercised considerable resistance following the three events alluded to in the first chapter: the further push for the media appeals tribunal by the ANC, the Protection of State Information Bill before Parliament, and the arrest of a *Sunday Times* journalist, Mzilikazi wa Afrika, outside the newspaper offices on 4 August 2010.

Ferial Haffajee referred to this earlier 'complacency' when she observed that the media does not 'scream' loudly enough, when it feels its independence is at stake. Haffajee was a speaker at the Second International Media Forum South Africa, held on 21-22 May 2008, in a panel discussion entitled 'Is the media free in South Africa to report what it wants?' She argued: 'Our media should get constructive criticism awards. The National Police Commissioner has been suspended after a series of articles exposing him. The media should be marketed as a key component of freedom.' The chair of the panel session, John Perlman, asked whether 'the media scream too loudly' when they think that press freedom is under threat. Haffajee answered, 'No, we don't scream too loudly. Look what happened in Zimbabwe, in tiny fractions democracy disappeared and it all started with media freedoms being whittled away. Now it's all gone. We must not apologise for screaming loudly'. Concurring with Haffajee, Franz Kruger, head of the Radio Academy at Wits Journalism, and also *Mail & Guardian* ombudsman, suggested in an interview that there seemed to be little resistance to attempted subjections, reflecting that, for example, with regard to the possible media appeals tribunal, the ANC could 'couch it in terms of development, transformation and democracy. In many ways the ANC feels it owns these terms because it was democratically elected, having won the struggle'. Kruger also said '[The ANC] hasn't taken on what it means to have an independent media. Yes, there would be a constitutional challenge, there will be reaction, but will it be enough?'

However, there were also cross-cutting moments of optimism, if one considers a new non-racial organisation, Projourn, formed at the end of 2009, which aimed to tackle precisely such closing interventions by the state, as well as to address other concerns related to journalism. Projourn, according to Michael Schmidt, at the time a member of the steering committee,[4] is an organisation 'for journalists by journalists' because most in the industry were tired of decisions being made for them by either Sanef, or NGOs not directly involved in the day to day working lives of journalists. By the end of 2009, Projourn had already attracted 300 members. For Schmidt, the reason for the existence of this organisation was to protect media freedoms and he concurred with Kruger's concern when he observed that:

> Things can change with the Constitution and we need to be organised. We held a dialogue on the issue of Media Appeals Tribunals and we said this would be the first issue we would take up as state interference would be intolerable. We do need to find a way on how to acquire teeth.

Projourn is open to all working journalists, freelance journalists, community journalists, broadcast journalists, print, radio, magazine, traditional and new media. 'We don't want to look after just our own interests but the interests of democracy in general,' said Schmidt. This perspective shows the intersection of professional codes with the ideal of democracy. But while there was some hope reflected in the formation of Projourn there were others who sensed inertia and a lack of awareness about the state's hindering of a free media. Leshilo made an apposite observation: that not too many journalists wrote about the implications of the Protection of State Information Bill. The Bill, if enacted, would have direct bearing on the work of the media. Yet, Leshilo wrote, there were no protests inside or outside Parliament by journalists, nor many stories written about it (*Sunday Times*: 25 October 2009). He observed a most curious and inexplicable fact that on the occasion of Media Freedom Day, 19 October 2009, none of the newspapers sent their reporters to cover the event held at the University of the Witwatersrand. For him it was an important historic event, but it went largely unnoticed by its own industry. He wrote:

> I am dejected because of the scant regard our newspapers gave to the celebration of Media Freedom Day on Monday. Am I missing something here or do such occasions no longer matter? Is it not important to take stock and ponder how well we use and protect our freedom of speech? Does our nation not deserve to know why the South African National Editors Forum (Sanef) continues to urge vigilance against threats to press freedom, given that we have the freest media on the continent?

Leshilo also pointed out that, besides the reporters, newspaper editors did not bother to attend an event that Sanef, their own lobby group, was party to organising. There were a paltry four paragraphs on the wire service, the South African Press Agency (Sapa), on the event and, even more ironically, the *Sowetan*, which co-hosted it, completely ignored it too. It can then be said that very possibly a state of inertia existed within the journalist profession with regard to their freedoms. They took freedom for granted. Here was an opportunity for the media to talk to its citizenry about media freedom, freedom of expression, constitutional guarantees, and new laws which threaten freedom. The Secrecy Bill provided the ideal news angle, and was put before Parliament in the very same month as Media Freedom Day. It was a missed opportunity and signalled complacency and lack of resistance within the media industry in 2009. Managing partner at the M&G Centre for Investigative Journalism (nicknamed amaBhungane),[5] Stefaans Brümmer captured the essence of the situation when he reflected, in an interview, that the media was 'caught in a deep slumber':

> I am very, very concerned about the impact a number of legislative developments may have on journalists' ability to do their work. Last year it was the Protection of Information Bill, which would have handed the power easily to classify documents to a very wide array of functionaries and would have imposed very stiff penalties, which journalists or their sources could have suffered just for possessing such documents. The Bill

was withdrawn, but may be back soon. This year we have the Protection of Personal Information Bill and the Protection from Harassment Bill, each with features which are likely to impede the flow of information to journalists or prevent them doing things they habitually do in democratic societies. So this is about the defence of hard-won democratic space and yes, I am concerned that the media has been caught in a deep slumber. I am not suggesting that journalists should toyi-toyi yet … But unless we engage and make ourselves heard, these consequences may well become part of the legal arsenal available to public figures who do not like the media›s probing attention.

Brümmer was concerned, in 2009, that there were very few voices from within the journalist profession protesting about the Bill and no sense of urgency or outcry save for legal submissions. His other noteworthy observation was that had we been living in the apartheid days there would have been action. 'I'm sure had the perpetrator been the apartheid state there would have been more of an outcry. But the outcry would have come from the alternative press.' What he was alluding to was that a serious complacency, inertia, or burying of heads in the sand existed in 2009. It could be that there was still trust in the ANC-led government that freedom of the media would continue, even though this was by no means certain given the legislation that was being considered by the government.

In order to fulfil their watchdog role in society, journalists, NGOs and civic-minded members of the public need access to public records. But Brümmer explained that these individuals' access would now be limited because of the Bill's definition of 'personal information', for instance civil and criminal records as maintained by the courts, or titles and other deeds, bonds, and antenuptial contracts as recorded by the Deeds Office:

> The type of public records described are needed by journalists (and others fulfilling a watchdog role) to warn when public figures (whether in the public or private sector) may abuse the trust of the public, such as by hiding a conflict of interest between their public duties and their private interests. While the person of interest would be a public figure, it is often necessary to examine the public records of persons who are not public figures to 'follow the money' to public figures.

Brümmer added that 'The type of public records described are also needed, regardless of whether the information subject is a public figure, to warn of physical or moral danger to the public, such as when toxic waste is leaking from premises or when an unsafe or contraband-laden aircraft is seen taking to the sky'. These records, he said, tended to be freely available in developed democracies. Sam Sole, Brümmer's co-managing partner at amaBhungane, commented about the issue of personal information:

> The definition of what is public is very vague leading to the default position being that it is private, given the general intentions of the Bill. The journalistic exemption is based on having a code, which contains the same principles – which is not on – given that the principles in this Bill are very restrictive – such as the need to inform the subject, the need to collect only information that is directly relevant to a specific purpose etc. The Bill also basically invites the regulation of journalistic conduct via the issuing of a code for journalists by the regulator. I can't believe the law commission came up with such an Orwellian approach. We know the state has the capacity to gather and process ever more personal information – and no doubt does so. This essentially grants the state monopoly control over that process and de-democratises information.

For the work of these two investigative journalists, the passing into law of the above Bill would mean an obstruction to the flow of information necessary for their investigations. They would not gain access to information easily, nor would their stories be able to be published in the detail they would otherwise have been. In short, it would impede democracy because holding power to account, one of the tenets of independent journalism, would be curtailed. However, in 2011 an exemption for journalists was included on personal information.

While the state, from above, hinders the flow of democracy and the free flow of information through its foreclosing impending legislation, commercial imperatives and new journalism and social media have also had an impact on the world of journalism. While Brümmer and Sole both accept that citizen journalism, blogging and the Internet have increased the flow of information, there have been others who argue that this has had a detrimental effect on traditional journalism. This will be shown in the next section. The argument is that traditional journalism, for instance the world of newspapers, for all its flaws is more reliable than bloggers' views and citizens' opinions. The next section puts the world of South African print journalism within the international context of newspapers' struggle for survival. It shows that while politics and ideology is the focus of this book, the changing world of technology also affects the media, the traditional media, in this case, the world of newspapers. It is a tangent to the main argument here but it is a huge change in the world of journalism.

Commercial imperatives and the impact of new media

'It's the consumer, stupid!' wrote Arianna Huffington, founder of *The Huffington Post*, when she also stated that the ' ... key question is whether those of us working in the media (old and new) embrace and adapt to the radical changes brought about by the Internet or pretend that we can somehow hop into a journalistic Way Back Machine and return to a past that no longer exists and can't be resurrected. As my compatriot Heraclites put it nearly 2500 years ago, "You cannot step into the same river twice"'(Huffington 2009).

Touché, Huffington. The pattern in the developed world is that the newspaper industry is in decline. In fact, the industry is shrinking at a rapid rate. The question posed by media analysts has been whether South Africa will follow this trend or the trend of developing countries (for example, India and China, where newspaper circulation is rising) or whether the Internet will replace newspapers. It seems that South Africa is part of the developing world trend if one considers the increase in the number of South Africans buying newspapers, from 14.5 million in 2008 to 15.234 million in 2009, as shown in the first section of this chapter. However, if it is true that the traditional world of journalism in South Africa is in decline, albeit not at the same rate as that in the developed world, this will have implications for the kind of journalism that will replace it. Nobody seems to know what the future holds for newspapers, or what precisely will replace them. As Clay Shirky commented:

> So who covers all that news if some significant faction of the currently employed newspaper people loses their jobs? I don't know. Nobody knows. We're collectively living through 1500, when it's easier to see what's broken than what will replace it. The Internet turns forty this year. Access by the general public is half that age. Web use, as a normal part of life for a majority of the developed world, is less than half that age. We just got here. Even the revolutionaries can't predict what will happen (Shirky 2009).

The World Association of Newspapers Newsroom Barometer showed in a 2009 survey of 700 editors and senior news executives in 120 countries, the following: eighty-six per cent believed that integrated print and online newsrooms will become the norm; eighty-three per cent believed that journalists will be expected to be able to produce content for all media within five years; two-thirds believed some editorial functions will be outsourced despite frequent newsroom opposition to the practice; forty-four per cent believed that online will be the most common platform for reading news in the future, compared with forty-one per cent in 2008; a majority of editors, fifty-six per cent, believed that news in the future will be free (this was up from forty-eight per cent in the 2008 survey; and only one-third of the editors believed the news will remain to be paid for while eleven per cent were unsure (Harber 2009). The World Association of Newspapers showed, at the end of 2009, that the circulation of quality dailies and tabloids in the United Kingdom had dropped: circulation for dailies was down 4.2 per cent, Sunday papers were down 7 per cent, and the circulation of *The Guardian* was down 14.8 per cent, *The Independent* was down 7.2 per cent and *The Times* had fallen 9.4 per cent while the *Financial Times* dropped 9.2 per cent (Redman 2009).

The global economic recession of 2009, wreaked havoc with the traditional media world, especially print. In fact, in a matter of two years from 2007, when the newspaper industry worldwide showed growth, to 2009 when the industry was imploding, there were massive changes, according to Manoim (2009: 51). The first 'culprit', he observed, was the global recession: currencies slipped, newspaper prices rose, and advertising revenues collapsed. The recession, however, merely hastened the real culprit, media experts pointed out (Harber 2009; Kruger 2009; Manoim 2009), which has been the increased use of the Internet to access news over the past decade. This has created a culture in which consumers are becoming accustomed to receiving news for free. There has, additionally, been the growth of cellphone technology to pass on news between citizens and to traditional media (citizen journalism). Worldwide, the Internet has scored two damaging blows against print media. The first is that it took away readers, especially young readers. As Manoim noted:

> Back in 1993, some thirty-five per cent of the USA population read a newspaper every day. By 2008 that figure had dropped to thirty-four per cent. Less than two per cent of Americans used the Internet for news in 1995, but by 2008, the figure was thirty-seven per cent, slightly higher than the number reading newspapers. While older people are still reading newspapers, the bad news is that younger people are hardly bothering to start (2009: 55).

The second impact of the Internet is that it managed to take away advertising from print media. It is cheaper to advertise online, and in some cases it is free. While one argument is that the above scenario, the decline of print, is a developed world phenomenon, and that print sales in India and China are increasing. In Zimbabwe, where Internet penetration is even narrower than in South Africa, citizens used cellphones to pass news on via small message service (SMS) technology, according to Dumisani Moyo (2009). This occurred in Zimbabwe during the last election of March 2008, when there was a virtual blackout of news owing to harsh clampdowns by the ruling party, Zanu–PF.

The School of Journalism and Media Studies at Rhodes University in Grahamstown launched a cellphone-based technology project, *Lindaba Ziyafrika* ('the news is coming' in isiZulu), with the idea that such technology can be used to increase social capital and social bonding, and help civil society to better engage with the government, according to Dugmore (2009: 30), who said that the basis of the project was to facilitate citizen reporting and opinion-sharing through cellphones, which are now ubiquitous in South Africa. The idea was that if 'ordinary people can better receive information', and also have a say, it would be a great boon for local democracy.

Media commentators have noted that online penetration in South Africa is indeed small compared to the global trend – five per cent compared to the global average of twenty five per cent, according to Wertheim-Aymes (2009). However, with the use of cell phone SMS technology and with increased band-width, more people will gain access to the Internet on their cellphones. Another important fact related to the decline of print media, not just in the developed world but also in South Africa, is that advertisers, on which newspapers depend for revenue, are increasingly putting their money online. Wertheim-Aymes said that 'Advertisers in SA are still pumping billions of rand into television, print and radio. Only three per cent of ad spend goes to the web. But this will change as cellphone rates come down and once there is more equitable and affordable access to broadband. It's not a question of if. It's a matter of when'.

The closure of *The Weekender* newspaper

The Weekender, a publication of *Business Day/Financial Mail*, owned by Avusa locally and Pearson in the UK, seemed to have been founded with the ratio-nale that if you produce a quality high end product, with 'interesting, lengthy, discursive stories full of good writing and respectable intelligence, eventu-ally people will come. Well, scratch that idea,' Tim Cohen wrote in the *Daily Maverick* (10 November 2009). It was closed down on 7 November 2009. I had a contract with *The Weekender* at the time of its closure, to write a series on media in a time of political change. The contract was one week short of the last article. I was devastated at the closure. I felt the same loss and bewilderment when the *Daily Mail*, a daily started up by the then *Weekly Mail*, where I was a junior reporter, was closed down in 1990.

There are two reasons for this sub-section on *The Weekender's* closure. First, it shows how commercial imperatives impact on the world of journalism and, second, through the letters on the closure, it shows the need the public had for this paper's function as a public sphere for debate, albeit an intellectual, middle and upper class sphere. There are two ways to view the closure on *The Weekender*. It seems to be a pattern in South Africa that newspapers targeting high-income earners do not survive because the intellectual readership is insufficient to carry the paper in sales. But a second gaze could show that this is also the trend overseas, where newspapers are fast becoming anachronisms as people read the news on their laptops and iPads. This is not so in working class markets, as the tabloid expansion shows. *The Weekender* was also South Africa's first newspaper casualty of the global recession of 2008-2009. The closure was suddenly announced on the 7 November 2009. According to a report by Jocelyn Newmarch in the last edition of the paper (*The Weekender*: 7-8 November 2009), the BDFM board made a decision to shut down the paper because of 'the ongoing economic crisis and difficult trading conditions' (advertising was down by twenty per cent). The columnist Jacob Dlamini told readers in his last column for the paper about his rationale for writing: 'If I do not remember the stories and the books of my childhood in Katlehong, who will?' (*The Weekender*: 7-8 November 2009). It was not just journalists who felt the loss of one of the democratic spaces in society. The following letter to *Business Day* showed the space that *The Weekender* provided:

> … *The Weekender* was much much more than a newspaper to its readers. It raised the intellect of all South African society. It gave me the same opportunity to be in the same auditorium as the greatest thinkers and politicians in the country. I shall miss the debates and public lectures as much as I shall miss the excellent articles throughout the paper … Please reconsider your decision [to close]. While the board of any company should always consider its bottom line, the board of a newspaper should consider its responsibility to building a free society of committed citizens – and *The Weekender* did exactly that (Sizwe Majola, Midrand, in *Business Day*: 11 November 2009).

The essence of the letter was that the reader would miss the space for stimulating intellectual debate, independent analysis, breaking news, and thought-provoking stories which he felt the paper provided. In the end, commercial imperatives held sway with the board of BDFM, as *The Weekender* had cost and lost the company R20 million since its launch in March 2006, according to editor of *Business Day* and editor in chief of *The Weekender,* Peter Bruce (2009). Bruce stated in his blog that while this was a large sum of money, it was not nearly enough. It would be easy to assess *The Weekender*'s closure as a one-off event in the landscape of South African media but this would be a narrow focus and would be ignoring the conditions that have affected the world of traditional media. Some of these conditions included: the global recession of 2008-2009; the increased use of the Internet to access free news, where advertisers could advertise cheaply or for free; the high costs of printing; and an increased awareness of the environment and therefore the need to save paper and trees. On the other hand, it could be argued that intellectual quality newspapers just don't survive in this country, given the performances of *The Daily Mail* and *ThisDay*. Besides the bottom lines of profits from media companies, there are citizenry's bottom lines too. Thabo Leshilo cited the commercial imperatives of the citizenry in the decline of print media:

> Newspapers cannot compete with bread and milk when families struggle to fill empty bellies on shrinking budgets. I would love to say that all that shall pass when the economy starts picking up. But I'm afraid to say the halcyon days of high circulations are over for newspapers (*The Times*: 27 November 2009).

The trick, according to Leshilo, was to stop conflating journalism with the printed word. Most newspapers have grasped the future by going multimedia, for example, and the debate is far from local. These issues were being grappled with in the developing world in the new millennium, where the demise of print has led to many debates about the future of journalism.

My case for the continued role of traditional journalism is the investigative side of the profession, as well as the context that journalism can provide to the news. Can the average citizen make sense of the Wikileaks cables? Does the citizen have the resources to investigate a story and write it up without being paid for it? It remains to be seen whether the South African media will work out the challenges posed by the commercial imperatives it is faced with but these facts remain: new and social media are growing, and use of the Internet to access news is growing.

The figures below indicate where South Africa stood in 2009 in relation to new media and traditional media and show the numbers of people who read print and who read online.

Newspapers readers:
- *Sowetan* – 1.5 million
- *The Times* – 375 000
- *The Daily Dispatch* – 298 000
- *The Herald* – 232 000

Online readers:

- *Sowetan Online* – 6 million unique page impressions a month and 288 000 unique users
- *Times Live* (the *Times* and the *Sunday Times*) – 4 million
- *Daily Dispatch* (including Saturday) – 1.4 million
- *The Herald* (including *Weekend Post*) – 1.7 million
- *Sunday World* – 1.1 million page impressions and 80 000 unique users
- (*The Times*: 27 November 2009)

There is indeed a space for citizen journalism and new media, which includes blogging and social networking, but if it replaces traditional journalism this would be a loss of professional and investigative journalism. This intersection between the role of the media in a democracy and the fight for independence from political interference is my main argument but it should be made clear that the fight for democracy takes place within a highly competitive commercial climate and the increasing use of technology.

'It's the consumer, stupid', and 'you cannot step into the same river twice' (meaning you can't go back) was Huffington's (2009) unoriginal but instructive point but I have argued that if newspapers disappear completely it will be a loss to democracy.

After numerous postponements the Bill was passed by the National Assembly on 22 November 2011, with 229 yes votes, 107 no votes, and two abstentions. It was then referred to the National Council of Provinces (NCOP), the second tier of Parliament, for further consultations, public hearings and submissions. The NCOP conducted hearings around the country in the first few months of 2012. The Bill has to be passed by the council before it proceeds to the president for gazetting. The public participation process threw up some surprises for the ANC. Citizens from the Cape Flats, for instance, questioned the ANC about service delivery and asked pointed questions about what the party wanted to hide. Forewarned by this attack, the ANC in the Eastern Cape bussed in supporters but the NCOP tried a new tactic. Every time anyone said 'Secrecy Bill' he or she was shot down, and told to address the issue and, further, not to mention service delivery. Reports from attendees at the Eastern Cape hearings, as well as many of the other provinces thereafter, questioned why the government was prioritising the Bill. Given this mixed bag, it was rather perplexing when Parliament issued a statement: '2 February 2012: Bill gets resounding approval'. A careful reading of the statement does not explain why the hearings were to be considered a 'resounding' success. The Right2Know campaign made other findings. Many people do not know the implications of the Bill, but when they do they state unequivocally that they want less secrecy in society, not more.

They want a free flow of information so that they can make informed decisions about their lives. In March 2012, a further postponement was announced, (to 17 May 2012), and only seventeen of the 263 written submissions were approved for presentation to the parliamentary committee. It seemed to be a case of Parliament not wanting to acknowledge all the protests against the Bill. But then, on 10 May 2012, in a surprise and welcome move, a twist, if you like, the ANC made significant amendments to the Bill which would not criminalise journalists and whistle-blowers. It also removed the clause 'ought to have reasonably known' (that something was classifiable), and removed minimum sentences so that if you reveal criminal activity through the use of a document (that could be or was classified) you cannot be criminalised. However, the State Security Agency seems exempt from this. It still falls short on espionage. As a journalist or whistleblower you could fall short of the law if the information you reveal benefits a group hostile to the state and you are endangering the country.

While in the end many of the problematic contentions in the Bill were amended to bring it in line with the Constitution, it did not happen overnight – it was a battle that lasted two years. Moreover, it did not happen without serious interventions and protest action by civil society groupings, legal representations and submissions. The inclusion of a public interest defence, however clumsy or imperfect, was a huge victory for activism, and for democracy. But before you could say 'victory' the amendments were rejected in June 2012 and deliberations on the Bill postponed until September 2012.

NOTES

1   Extract from a letter to President Jacob Zuma by the Committee to Protect Journalists: *Business Day*: 17 August 2010.
2   For example, the lawsuit by President Zuma against cartoonist Zapiro (discussed in Chapter Five), for R7 million, is the largest in the world against any cartoonist or journalist.
3   Some of the organisations which opposed the bill consisted of: AmaBhungane of the *Mail & Guardian*, Cosatu, the FXI, Sanef, the Institute of Security Studies, Media Monitoring Africa, the Committee to Protect Journalists (international), the Alternative Information and Development Centre (AIDC), Anti-Privatisation Forum, Equal Education, the Lesbian and Gay Equality Project (LGEP), Social Justice Coalition, the Open Society Foundation, Misa, Print Media SA, Idasa, and the SAHRC.
4   Schmidt later became executive director of the Institute for the Advancement of Journalism. The remark was made in an interview.
5   *amaBhungane* means dung beetles in isiZulu. The aim of the investigative unit is to get to the bottom (dung) of things to expose corruption and the abuse of power.

4.

Race and the media

There are two meanings of the word 'subject': subject to someone else by control and dependence, and tied to his own identity by a conscience or self-knowledge. Both meanings suggest a form of power that subjugates and makes subject to.[1]

This chapter comprises two sections which examine race, identity and subjection. One is the failure of the FBJ to relaunch. The other considers the firing of a *Sunday Times* columnist, David Bullard, for writing a racist column. Each event shows subjection to past norms of racial identity which oppressed. In the case of the FBJ, however, the majority of black journalists ignored the interpellating (or hailing) to be loyal to blackness, and so the revival of the forum failed. The theoretical point is one that Butler developed from Foucault's theory on power to explain the paradoxical nature of subjection: one is familiar with the idea of power being external to the self, but it is pressed upon one from the outside, and one is also dependent on that power for one's very existence (1997: 2-20). Power forms the subject and also forms reflexivity: the figure of the psyche turns against itself ('turns' is used in this sense in this chapter). In other words, when one faces subjection through interpellation, does one heed the call and turn towards the voice of authority, or does one exercise some agency and turn against the attempted subjection?

The media is not monolithic. Just as Lacan argued that we are hundreds of people in one, so the media is also diverse and fluid in composition in terms of race and in characterisation of different political vents. This chapter shows that race is not simplistically embraced as a Master-Signifier for all black journalists or for the public. But for some it is. The theoretical starting point for 'race' here is its unessential nature, and that it is a social and cultural construct. I argue, as many others have,[2] that it is a marker of identity, where identity is fluid, multiple and contingent. As Norval noted, if apartheid is not only a precise and historically determinate mode of social division, but also an

> identitary logic which attempts to resist the never-ending quest for
> identification by fixing boundaries between identities for all time, then
> the central question with regard to non-racialism concerns the extent to
> which it will be able to foster and sustain difference in such a manner
> as to keep spaces open for identification with a democratic order
> (1996: 293).[3]

Using the two specific events from 2008 as examples, this chapter uncovers an aspect of the deliberative role that journalism plays in the public sphere, bringing to the fore the diversity of 'attachments' that surround different events, and underlining the significance for democracy of the debates engaged in by journalists. It further seeks to show how impossible it is to completely unify society, to totalise and essentialise identity.

In examining the two events, I use the postmodern concepts of 'Master-Signifier', 'subjectivisation', 'passionate attachments', 'resignification' and 'reflexive turn'. A Master-Signifier is a signifier that puts an end to the chain of meaning. It is a transcendental signifier that anchors all meaning or ties it to one thing. A Lacanian understanding of 'Master-Signifier' hails from a subject identifying with certain signifiers. For example, if someone identifies himself or herself as a 'communist' the meanings of a whole array of other signifiers are ordered in quite different ways from someone who thinks of himself or herself as a 'liberal', 'democrat', or 'social democrat'. 'Freedom' for a communist is tied to one thing: freedom from the exploitative practices in capitalism and 'democracy' comes to mean 'the dictatorship of the proletariat'. Žižek opined that 'the struggle for democracy (today's Master-Signifier) is in what it will mean, which kind of democracy will hegemonise the universal notion' (2006c: 37).

In other words, all other meanings are stabilised at a nodal point through the Master-Signifier. For this discussion, it is the signifier 'race' that will be shown to be the Master-Signifier in the world of some journalists, while it is the floating signifier – a signifier that doesn't have full meaning, whose meaning is not closed off and has not been attached or linked to another signifier – to many other journalists and readers of newspapers.

Turning 'race' into the Master-Signifier means rendering it the most important rallying point or call, and when it is said that, for some subjects, 'race' is a Master-Signifier, what this involves, what its content is, and how this subject itself relates 'race' to its other identities should be spelled out. What sort of evidence counts here in determining whether some signifier is a Master-Signifier?

Subjection consists of more than the standard model of power that imposes itself upon us from the outside. Often, weakened by this imposition, we come to accept subjection, according to the Butlerian theoretical formulation of power deployed here. What this account fails to note is that 'we' who accept such terms are fundamentally dependent on those subjugating norms and terms for 'our' existence (1997: 2). She found that, as a form of power, subjection is paradoxical: it signifies the process of becoming subordinated by power as well as the process of becoming a subject, whether by interpellation in the Althusserian sense or by discursive productivity, and no subject emerges without a passionate attachment to those on whom he or she is fundamentally dependent (even if that passion is negative in the psychoanalytic sense). (An example used by Butler includes the dependency of the child, and while this is not political subordination in the conventional sense, the formation of primary passion in dependency renders the child vulnerable to subordination and exploitation.)

According to the argument, a reflexive turn takes place through passionate attachments to one's own subordination through the workings of power. However, agency is possible through unsettling passionate attachments and through resignifications, meaning not reiterating (or repeating) norms. In this way freedom can emerge. This chapter will deconstruct and analyse the failure of the FBJ and the firing of Bullard from the *Sunday Times*. We turn first to the attempt to re-launch the FBJ, the reaction of journalists, and the 'turns' they made towards the interpellations of the voice of 'authority' ('Turn' here means the reflexive turn which is at one and the same time an external turn towards the law or voice of authority in the Althusserian sense, and a turn against oneself, the turn of conscience as in the Nietzchean sense: 'conscience doth make subjects of us all' (Butler 1997: 115).)

Two events marked the moment when we begin to see how attempts were made to conceive of race as the Master-Signifier in the journalism profession. The first was when Jacob Zuma accepted an invitation by some journalists in February 2008 to a relaunch luncheon of a blacks-only journalists' forum, the FBJ. This organisation was first endorsed in 1996-1997 with the blessing of the then deputy president, Thabo Mbeki, and was officially inaugurated in 1997.

The 2008 event sparked concern among many journalists, political analysts and media academics who believed it was unconstitutional to have a blacks-only journalist event. There was also an outcry that white journalists who attempted to attend the event in Sandton were turned away. Subsequently, Radio 702 lodged a complaint with the SAHRC, which held a hearing on the matter. Radio 702 won its appeal against the FBJ. It was found to be unconstitutional and unfair that some journalists, because of their colour, should be excluded.

The second event was when David Bullard, a columnist at the *Sunday Times* for nearly a decade, was fired in April 2008 after publishing a column deemed to be racist. He stereotyped black people and made unfounded racial assertions and implications that, for example, blacks do not care enough for their babies and if one died they would simply have another. The column is printed in full in the analysis of this event, followed by the very diverse reactions, showing multiple and split identities and subjectivities. The event brought to the fore the ambivalence with which freedom of speech is viewed within the context of the Constitution, as it balances other rights, such as human dignity, as well as hate speech, which is unconstitutional.

Both events enable an examination of race identity, its fluid contingent nature in a democracy in transition, and its radical indeterminacy which shows also how division and conflict are unavoidable with competing and ambivalent interpretations of freedom, equality, freedom of expression, and association. Finally the events show the role of journalism in relation to the floating signifier, democracy.

The failure of the revival of the Forum for Black Journalists

In February 2008, the president of the ANC, Jacob Zuma, was invited to attend a relaunch luncheon of the FBJ. He accepted the invitation. On 22 February, Yusuf Abramjee, group head of news and talk programming at Primemedia Broadcasting, attended the blacks-only forum, together with Kieno Kammies, a talk show host. They raised the objection that white journalists were excluded from a meeting with Zuma and they then walked out in solidarity with their white colleagues, who were ordered out. Abramjee said that as they walked out they were called 'coconuts' (black on the outside but white inside) (*Mail & Guardian*: 29 February-6 March 2008). Katy Katopodis, the editor of Talk Radio 702 and 94.7 Highveld Stereo, laid a formal complaint with the SAHRC following the refusal to allow white journalists into the meeting.

Commenting in *Business Day*, a political reporter, Hajra Omarjee, wrote that some viewed Zuma's acceptance of the invitation as a 'move to woo certain sections of the media, that is, black journalists' after he had begun to wrangle with the media, and she pointed to the political context: the ANC's declaration of its intention to institute new mechanisms of control in a media appeals tribunal (*Business Day*: 22 February 2008). This tribunal had been mooted at the ANC Polokwane Conference in December 2007. It would apparently supplement (not replace) self-regulatory mechanisms already in place. The proposal for more media regulation and control must be understood in the context of Zuma's suing several media houses for defamation (before Zuma became ANC president in December 2007 he had served legal papers on *Sunday Times* columnist, David Bullard, and on cartoonist Jonathan Shapiro, for defamation) including reprimanding journalists for reporting on the corruption charges against him (Zuma had charges of alleged rape, fraud and corruption against him, in all of which he was found not guilty by April 2009 when he was elected president).

Commenting on a racially exclusive gathering with Zuma, Anton Harber, head of Wits Journalism and media commentator in *Business Day*, felt 'hard pressed' to find different and distinctive challenges facing black and white journalists in South Africa (*Business Day*: 5 March 2008). Zuma's inane response to being criticised for accepting such an invitation was: 'There isn't a forum of white journalists that has invited me' (*The Weekender*: 23-24 February 2008). The FBJ's argument to exclude whites was that an exclusively black gathering was needed so that black journalists could discuss issues that affected them, for instance 'development', or absence thereof, in their respective newsrooms. The head of the FBJ, Abbey Makoe, who initiated the revival of the forum and was also political editor of the SABC at the time, wrote:

> Our aim, then and now, was to ensure that all journalists from previously disadvantaged backgrounds were organised into a meaningful group that would frequently get together and discuss matters of mutual interest. For example, in a transition, what is the role of the black journalist interpreting change – good or bad? There is no denying that the replacement of apartheid by democracy is good change. But what change in the glaringly unequal newsrooms? (*Saturday Star*: 1 March 2008).

Ostensibly, the 'glaringly unequal newsrooms' was the reason for the relaunch. Yet, when the SAHRC ruled against the relaunch, Makoe's response was that the SAHRC's 'understanding of racism is dubious. SAHRC has found us guilty of being black. We are pronounced guilty of being black. No banning order will stop us' ('HRC rules against forum': www.journalism.co.za, 12 April 2008). Here is shown the slide into the unhappy consciousness, the passionate attachment

to norms of the past, bonded to apartheid, and its limits on freedom and liberation, as, clearly, no one had found Makoe 'guilty of being black'.

Taking issue with Makoe's fixation on race, journalist Wilson Johwa wrote
in *The Weekender* that journalism was 'a liberal profession where colleagues
judged each other on the strength of their writing and sharpness of their
thinking' (*The Weekender*: 23-24 February 2008). 'Colour,' he said, 'had largely
taken a back seat in South African journalism'. He then proceeded to note that,
of the thirty-two newspapers in the country, nineteen had black editors. Johwa
quoted journalist, Fiona Forde, who was turned away from the blacks-only
journalist meeting. She observed that 'although black journalists had a genuine
case to ensure their self-development, they needed to raise it with management
and media owners but not your peers; we need each other' (*The Weekender*:
23-24 February 2008). The rallying call on the basis of race was not univer-
sally accepted, nor was it a success, given the response from several other black
journalists. Race was a floating signifier, ambiguous, with no full or fully-fixed
meaning. For example, in a column in the *Citizen* newspaper, Chris Bathembu,
who attended the forum, stated:

> Yes, the profession has a very gruesome past and yes, there may still be
> some challenges facing black journalists in newsrooms, but is the FBJ the
> solution? What about white journalists who stood by their black col-
> leagues in the apartheid era? Surely what happened on Friday is an insult
> to them and all white journalists who do not subscribe to racism. This
> racism is unacceptable, no matter how hard the FBJ tries to justify it. No
> way in hell am I joining such an organisation (*Citizen*: 25 February 2008).

Bathembu had turned away from race as the Master-Signifier. Another columnist, Justice Malala, wrote that the blacks-only forum betrayed the ANC's
founding principles, that the initiative was 'hypocritical', and intellectually
bankrupt. Indeed, he felt that actually being black was not enough; 'you needed
to have the right political bias too' (*The Times*: 25 February 2008). In the same
article Malala also pointed out that many big newspapers and radio and television news departments were already run by blacks, and he observed that
Makoe, the spokesman of the forum, worked at the SABC, where news management was almost entirely black.

> He [Makoe] is therefore in a position to solve many of the problems that
> pertain to blacks …The ANC fought a long and exhausting struggle to
> get rid of a system that institutionalised the oppression of blacks by
> whites. It did not win it by excluding whites. It won it by including

whites; not because they were white, but because they too believed in a non-racial, united democratic South Africa. The conclusion is that the blacks-only FBJ has nothing to do with journalism. The forum is an organisation that clearly wants to influence black journalists to toe a particular party or leader's line.

Malala's reasoning and conclusion underscored the way in which race was being manipulated for political purposes. His argument resonates with the theoretical underpinnings of this chapter, which assert that subjects can easily turn towards the voice of power, but also that attempted subjection can be ignored, as can ideological interpellations or hailings. The attempt to revive the forum had less to do with the racial 'disadvantage' of black journalists than with a racialised ideology that interpellated black journalists in order to summon them to toe a particular party or ideological line.

The ANC might not have done this directly, but the opportunity was given to them by the invitation of the FBJ. The FBJ was itself falling into the ANC's attempts at subjectivisation to create a 'sweetheart press'. What the revival, and subsequent failure, of the FBJ also showed was the lack of homogeneity among journalists. Race issues aside, in newsrooms themselves there was no one voice that spoke, but rather a myriad of views, as seen in the following example of how the *Mail & Guardian* reacted to the news of the FBJ. The newspaper published a lengthy spread on the issue under the title 'Race and the media'. The editor at the time, Ferial Haffajee, wrote that 'we live in a liberated zone' adding that she would not go to the forum's gatherings 'because journalists are not so easily boxed and as editor it would feel wrong to go where some of my colleagues cannot tread' (*Mail & Guardian*: 29 February-6 March 2008). Her newsroom held an open meeting to discuss the FBJ. Some of her black colleagues challenged her views. For example, Fikile-Ntsikelelo Moya asked, 'Can we as a newsroom honestly say that the black staff does not have issues they feel particularly unhappy about? Can we assuredly say that we have created a newsroom that makes black journalists not need an FBJ?' Another black journalist, Matuma Letsoalo, asked whether the story was chosen by the byline. Haffajee surmised that he must be referring to the investigative team whose writings dominated the lead stories. Stefaans Brümmer responded by asking, 'Who says I'm white?', constituting a challenge and indicating how race is a social construct and, more pertinently, how identities can 'float' rather than be fixed.

Nevertheless, as Haffajee commented in the same article, for Letsoalo the reality was that we should confront the issue of who was trusted to deliver the front page goods. She pointed out that a significant number of journalists at the *Mail & Guardian* felt 'deep unhappiness with the FBJ for what it practises and what it might portend: an era of racial access to news and newsmakers and a return to a past many have spent their adult years fighting'. Tim du Plessis, editor of *Rapport,* said: 'I see no objective for such an organisation. What special issues can black journalists still have after fifteen years of newsroom transformation? The most influential editors today are black. The leadership of Sanef is predominately black and has been for more than a decade' (*Mail & Guardian*: 29 February - 6 March 2008).

Expressing significant difference with Haffajee's view was the then editor of *City Press,* Mathatha Tsedu, who felt that whites intruding on the luncheon with Zuma to relaunch the FBJ, and creating a 'stink' was 'sheer arrogance to me. Black journalists have a right to decide for themselves that they want to talk among themselves, while being addressed by whoever they choose to invite'. In direct contrast to Tsedu's view was that of the then editor of the *Daily Dispatch,* Phylicia Oppelt. When asked about the need for such a forum, she remarked:

> I don't think there is a need. What are the pressing issues for black journalists in this country when most news organisations are being led by black editors or managers? By giving attention to the forum, it gives it some life, credence and justification for existing. I think it is unnecessarily divisive and reactionary. Makoe's comment that 'they' would respect the right of white journalists to gather along the same lines is trite and mischievous because he knows there would be outrage if they did so. I would like to see an organisation of South African journalists where issues of professionalism, skills and common problems are explored and debated (*Mail & Guardian Online*: 5 March 2008).

Oppelt hit the nail on the head when she asked what the pressing issues were for black journalists when most news organisations were being led by blacks. Her view, that she would like to see common problems experienced by all journalists tackled, resonated with the comment by the researcher at the FXI, Tendayi Sithole, who also refused to join the forum. As he said in an interview in March 2008, he felt that journalists should be uniting to oppose the media appeals tribunal proposed by the ANC to regulate freedom of the press, an issue that could unite all journalists in an inclusive and non-racial 'unified forum'.

When Abramjee accompanied his colleague Katopodis to the SAHRC hearing, he told the panel that he objected to being labelled a 'coconut' when he walked out of the FBJ meeting because his white colleagues were excluded (*Mail & Guardian*: 29 February-6 March 2008). 'We are of the view that the term coconut is not only insulting, it is discriminatory.' He said: 'I said at the start of the FBJ meeting that whites should not be excluded on the grounds of freedom of association. The Constitution should not be used selectively. The Constitution also doesn't allow for any form of racial discrimination'.

These varied perspectives showed that there was no homogeneity, either on transformation and democracy or on identification on the basis of race. It was also clear that many black journalists did not support the FBJ because they found it inappropriate in the new democracy. There is a strong argument then to conclude that 'the media does not exist in itself as a closed entity, nor is there a unitary black bloc', or indeed a white bloc (*The Weekender*: 3-4 October 2008).

The above comments, deliberately chosen mainly from black journalists, showed that even within one newsroom there were significant differences of opinion. This heterogeneity of views and multiple identities signals plurality. The attempted hegemonisation, subjectivisation and interpellation by one group of journalists in relaunching the FBJ, failed. The existence of heterogeneity among black journalists, and of resistance to ideological conformity, portends well for democracy.

How might we interpret Makoe's attempt to revive the FBJ in post-apartheid South Africa? I turn to Butler's theories of power and subjection. In a re-reading of Hegel's *Unhappy Consciousness*[4] she stated: '…we are given to understand an attachment to subjection is formative of the reflexive structure of subjection itself' (1997: 58). She continued that 'wretchedness, agony and pain are sites or modes of stubbornness, ways of attaching to oneself, negatively articulated modes of reflexivity … because they are given regulatory regimes as the sites available for attachment, and a subject will attach to pain rather than not attach at all' (1997: 61).

The point of drawing on Butler's thoughts is to suggest that the reiteration of racial subjection remains a dominant theme in post-apartheid South Africa, but not in all quarters of society. The continued reference by some to racial subjugation means that former subjects remain trapped within an 'unhappy consciousness' of 'agony and pain' which must limit the development of their own capabilities to free themselves. Instead of embracing the removal of the regulatory regime of apartheid and exploring the freedom to create new imaginaries of non-racialism, Makoe's efforts to recreate a safe zone for racial exclusivity revived the very regimes of negative exclusion that characterised apartheid. But this attempt to reposition race as the Master-Signifier was highly contested, as we saw from the very diverse responses of some black editors and black journalists in different newsrooms: Oppelt, Malala, Bathembu, and others. Oppelt's comment that she would like to see professionalism, skills and such common problems explored and debated (*Mail & Guardian Online*: 5 March 2008), showed resignifications from past attachments, rather than the reiteration of norms of the past. Her turn, unlike Makoe's, could not be called a reflexive turn, or a turn against oneself. Bathembu's question about the exclusion of white journalists who had stood by their black colleagues during apartheid showed an unsettling of past attachments – in other words, he was not attached to his race suffering from apartheid days.

Voices such as these turned away from the interpellating voices. But of course there were also some views in-between which show some splitting or ambivalence. Take for instance, the *Mail & Guardian* journalist Fikile-Ntsikelelo Moya, who asked: 'Can we as a newsroom honestly say that the black staff does not have issues they feel particularly unhappy about? Can we assuredly say that we have created a newsroom that makes black journalists not need an FBJ?' (*Mail & Guardian*: 29 February-6 March 2008).

How then are we to understand the failure of the revival of the FBJ (by 2009 there was not even one mention of the FBJ in the news)? There were some black journalists, such as Makoe, who attached to norms which oppress, and turned towards the interpellating voice of the ANC but there were others who did not slide into unhappy consciousness and who would, in Butlerian terms, be showing 'resignification'. The failure of the FBJ to relaunch showed that race was not ultimately the Master-Signifier, and that the media was not a homogeneous entity, either by race or within one newspaper. It showed the indeterminate nature of race as a signifier in post-apartheid South Africa. It showed that race was primarily a floating signifier, not a Master-Signifier, and attempts to render it as one failed, signalling an optimistic moment for democracy. It also showed the half turns towards the voice of power, as in the case of Fikile-Ntsikelelo Moya when he expressed ambivalence about whether there was a need for the FBJ.

Subjectivities, however, change, are fluid and do not remain static. For instance, in 2010 Makoe wrote a highly progressive piece entitled 'Orwellian trend is emerging', in which he said that freedom of speech is much bigger than the ANC, or even the media, but is about people's rights to express their thoughts (*The Star*: 2 September 2010). In a turn away from allowing subjection, Makoe wrote:

> When the ANC goes overboard in tackling a critical building block in a democracy such as the media, historians and social commentators might pause and observe an Orwellian trend where the persecuted have now turned into the persecutors ... In any meaningful democracy, the media and all other exponents of free speech need to be treated like what Stone calls 'civic treasures – guides to a better way of life – instead of a menace'.

This is a powerful statement. Through his 2010 turning, Makoe showed that he was siding with the ethical codes of the profession and loyalty to the ideal of democracy, rather than with the ANC's closed vision, hegemonic purposes and ideological hysteria against the media. While he has not refuted his stance about race, nor his insistence on the place for the FBJ in post-apartheid South Africa, the above piece was written in the same manner as all others in the profession who denounced the Secrecy Bill and the media appeals tribunal in the interests of a society not hermetically sealed. While this chapter deals specifically with the issue of the FBJ and race, the above turning against the repressive ANC and state proposals by Makoe in 2010 positioned him, along with other journalists, as a legitimate adversary in a democracy.

Legitimate adversaries, passionate attachments and resignifications

Drawing on conceptual analytical tools from Mouffe (legitimate adversaries), Butler (passionate attachments, subjectivisation and resignifications) and Žižek (enemies of the people), I argue that the South African Constitution allows us to think of 'fights' internal to democracy as fights between legitimate adversaries rather than enemies. It then also allows for resignifications so that new pathways or new floating attachments can be made, unsettling old passions and attachments, which can happen if one does not reiterate norms from the past. However, a trend established by the ANC from the time of Mbeki's deputy presidency, through Mbeki's two terms as president, and then carried through to 2008 by Zuma, was the attempt to create a subordinate, compliant, uncritical and even unified press. The danger of labelling critics as illegitimate opponents, and the suppressing of any form of dissent, would push this society towards totalitarianism. Mouffe had criticised Carl Schmitt's argument about, or fear of, the 'loss of common premises and consequent destruction of the political unity', calling for a distinction between legitimate adversaries and antagonists, the key task facing democratic politics today being to make room for conflictual pluralism, given the increasing fragmentation of identities and the multiplication of new forms of conflict. Mouffe disapproved of Schmitt's argument because it would not permit a differential treatment of conflict, which could only be manifest in the mode of antagonism, 'where two sides are in complete opposition and no common ground exists between them. According to Schmitt, there is no possibility for pluralism – that is, legitimate dissent among friends' (Mouffe 1999: 5). But during the saga of the FBJ we saw in operation the maxim that you need a plurality of competing forces for a radical democracy.

In their argument for a democratic revolution, Laclau and Mouffe assert that politics should be founded 'on affirmation of the contingency and ambiguity of every essence, and on the constitutive character of social division and antagonism' rather than on the dogmatic postulation of an 'essence of the social' (1985: 193). The trend in the discourse of the ANC is to place political unity above all else. In the case of the media, this political unity means that the ANC and journalists should be of the same frame of mind and political persuasion. This is what Mouffe argues against in her analysis of Schmitt. In placing political unity above all else, she comments, the space for pluralism, and therefore more tolerance in a democracy, is closed off (1999: 5). By promoting a blacks-only forum for journalists, which reiterated the logic of race and aligned itself with the hegemonic political party and leadership of Jacob Zuma, the 'space for pluralism' in South Africa would be under threat. However, the attempt appeared to have failed.

Althusser's central thesis was that ideology interpellated individuals as subjects. And Butler, using the often quoted example of the passer-by subject turning towards the authoritative voice of a policeman who said 'hey, you', explained further that the man in the street did not know that the policeman was hailing him in particular, but turned towards the voice of authority anyway, as though he was indeed the one being hailed (Butler 1997: 107). Why? Butler ventured that subordination took place through language and through interpellation.The turning around, she explained, is an act conditioned both by the 'voice' of the law and by the responsiveness of the one hailed by the law. Butler further explained that there would be no turning around without first having been hailed, neither would there be a turning around without some readiness to turn.

Justice Malala was against the same sort of subjectivisation of journalists through the FBJ. The issue of race, for Malala, was really an excuse; race was actually political ideology at work and the FBJ was an attempt to hegemonise black journalists. But of course, as Malala commented, the real motive for forming the FBJ was to reel them in politically, to block them from being free and independent thinkers and agents; to render them supportive of the party line. He also wrote that because racism was known and experienced, one should not reduce oneself to the pain of that exclusion again: 'That is why so many of us are outraged that those who claim to know the pain of exclusion on racial grounds can suddenly be sanguine about the Forum for Black Journalists kicking whites out of a meeting. It is not right when it is done to us. It is not right when it is done by us to others, either' (*The Times*: 3 March 2008). What the response of those black journalists who were not in favour of the blacks-only forum showed was a refusal to reiterate the norms which oppressed, in this case the norms of race identity. For Butler, norms and identities were not fixed and even within these reiterations there were possibilities that they would be repeated in unpredictable ways; that they would be re-appropriated, so to speak, showing resignification.

In the case of the black journalists who did not accept the FBJ a process of Butlerian 'resignification' was at play. On the other hand, Makoe's actions signify embracing the very terms that injured him through a repetition of the norm (race oppression) to which he was 'passionately attached'. For Butler, it was the radical dependency on norms and their reiteration that led to subjection. But if Makoe was radically dependent on race in 2008, in 2010 there seemed to be some 'unsettling' and 'unpredictability' when he wrote against the ANC's attempts at subjugating the independent media, going as far as to call it an Orwellian trend (*The Star*: 2 September 2010). Orwellian implies ideological obfuscation, manipulation and a denial of truth and when Makoe says this trend is creeping into the ANC he makes a powerful statement.

A free subject would think for himself or herself, and not be passionately attached to subjugation. This must apply particularly to the profession of journalism, where the principles of fairness, truth and balance should apply. In the same vein, Pecheux would say that the journalists I have referred to aimed to do what they were supposed to do – that is, to think for themselves. He considered a 'bad subject' to be, in short, a 'trouble maker'(1982: 22) who counter-identified against the discursive formation imposed on him. His argument for democracy was that one must 'dare to rebel ... nobody could think in anyone else's place and one must dare to think for oneself'.

It was not the first time that attempts at racial divisions were created between journalists, as discussed in Chapter Two, when in 1995 Mbeki was branding any criticism of the ANC as racist (Gevisser 2007). Mbeki also made a separation between what he expected of white and black journalists at an address to the FBJ: 'Now criticism and complaining is what I expect from him', when he pointed at Anton Harber. 'This forum, on the other hand, has to see itself as a change agent'. He urged black journalists: 'roll up your sleeves and stop whinging like a whitey. Get with the programme'.

In the Butlerian-Althusserian sense then, this hailing or interpellation, ironically enough, was to bring the black journalists into line. Mbeki had given up on Harber himself – after all he was white, and a lost cause – so he turned to black journalists, making race the rallying call. Mbeki singled out the *Mail & Guardian* and did not treat 'the media' as a homogeneous bloc, which later became the case. Bad subjects, for him then, would be all black journalists – and there were many – who refused to subvert loyalty to their profession to loyalty to the party.

This was one of Mbeki's first steps in subjecting the media to the hege-monic discourse of the ANC, where 'the rigid designator' was in operation. Žižek contends that '… in the Stalinist universe, the real member of "the People" is only he who supports the rule of the Party: those who work against it are automatically excluded from "the People"; they become enemies of "the People"' (1989: 147). Supporting the rule of the party is rigidly designated by 'the People'. While Mbeki's direct call was against a white journalist, he was, at the same time, hailing black journalists as part of a unitary universe, that of the ANC, but also one that rendered race as the Master-Signifier. At the start of his ascent to power and to the presidency, Mbeki was holding out hope for black journalists. Some would turn, over the next decade of democracy, towards this hailing, this authoritative voice, and more would turn against it. Mbeki had hoped black journalists would heed his call to be loyal to the ANC, conflating this voice and the ANC's voice with the voice of democracy itself.

In subsequent chapters, I intend to show what turn most journalists made, irrespective of race, in an attempt to answer the question of whether 'the media' is, or is not, a hegemonic bloc. What I have demonstrated, so far, through the case of the FBJ, is that journalists are not a homogeneous entity in South Africa, and that black journalists are not a single, totalised, essentialised entity. To talk, then, of 'the media' as the ANC does is inaccurate.

The second example of how passionate attachments act to reproduce racism, was the firing of *Sunday Times* columnist David Bullard over a racist column. Interestingly, not all black readers and writers to newspapers thought he was racist, and not all whites thought he should not have been fired. This showed fluid and free-floating identities, detaching from the signifier, race. The then editor of the *Sunday Times*, Mondli Makhanya, found Bullard's views incom-patible with the ethos of the new South Africa, democracy and the Constitution. So then, the question must be asked: was the firing an anti-freedom of expres-sion act? Was Bullard exercising his right to free speech within the constitu-tional framework, or was he out of bounds in terms of a constitution which espouses the principles of non-racialism and values dignity and respect for all people? I have three intentions. The first is to explore whether these two ideo-logical discourses are two sides of the same coin – in other words, is 'race' a Master-Signifier in Bullard's discourse, as it was in Makoe's? My second aim is to analyse Bullard's column in terms of Butler's theory of passionate attach-ments and resignification. My third aim is to examine what freedom of speech means within the context of democracy.

The firing of David Bullard and the right to free speech

In order to scrutinise and explore the contention that free speech is not a legal and moral absolute, I now turn to the example of the firing of David Bullard, and then further my argument about how race can be a Master-Signifier in unprogressive discourses, discussing Butler's concepts of passionate attachments and resignification.

If there are moral and legal limits to free speech, what are they? The following are some extracts from the column 'Out to Lunch' in the *Sunday Times* of 6 April 2008 that led to the termination of Bullard's employment (which he contested as an 'unfair dismissal' and lost).

Uncolonised Africa wouldn't know what it was missing

Imagine for a moment what life would be like in South Africa if the evil white man hadn't come to disturb the rustic idyll of the early black settlers ... the various tribes of South Africa live healthy and peaceful lives, only occasionally indulging in a bit of ethnic cleansing. Their children don't watch television because there is no television to watch ... They live in single-storey huts arranged to catch most of the day's sunshine and their animals are kept nearby. Nobody has any more animals than his family needs and nobody grows more crops than he requires to feed his family and swap for other crops ... Every so often a child goes missing from the village, eaten either by a hungry lion or a crocodile. The family mourn for a week or so and then have another child ... Praying to the ancestors is no help because they are just as clueless ...

Bullard was fired three days later by Makhanya, who justified his decision by saying that while the right to free speech is something that everyone on his newspaper held dear, 'we are NOT in the business of promoting prejudice'. The relationship of an editor to a columnist is a special one, he said. 'You hand over a piece of real estate to the column, the site for a villa, a mansion or castle. The onus is then on the columnist to treat the space with responsibility and not abuse that freedom from interference.' Over the years, Makhanya said, Bullard 'had fun with the space' but then 'last Sunday he crossed the line ... In a subsequent conversation I had with Bullard, it was clear that he holds the views he expressed in the article – which were essentially that black people are indolent savages' (*Sunday Times*: 13 April 2008).

In a further explanation to the public, Makhanya wrote: 'The *Sunday Times* subscribes to non-racialism and is committed to building a South Africa based on the values enshrined in the Constitution. We will not be a platform for views which undermine the values of our publication'. Prior to the announcement of the firing, the political commentator Xolela Mangcu made this observation on the tension between democracy and free speech: 'Criticism of authorities is at the foundation of democracy' (*Business Day*: 10 April 2008) (a statement, indeed, at the foundation of this book). He continued: 'But democracy is not an invitation to offensive speech'. Mangcu then quoted the political scientist Robert Weissberg on the fine line between legitimate criticism and offensive speech:

> The questioning of sacred doctrine or the challenging of honoured traditions is protected by the principle of protected liberty. Indeed such challenging is not only permitted, it may well be essential to society's intellectual life, invigorating both our capacities and the doctrines themselves. Nevertheless, because mere words can shade into actions and actions may have preventable injurious consequences, the right to one's views is not unbounded.

In Mangcu's view, this right was bound by both social civility and legal proscription in the case of hate speech. It was guesswork to say what Africa would have been like had it not been for colonialism. 'The age Bullard is celebrating was one of uninterrupted European violence against indigenous people all over the world. But it was also an age of barbaric acts of cruelty among Europeans themselves'. The upshot of Mangcu's judgment was that Bullard engaged in hate speech when he described African people as savages capable only of undertaking ethnic cleansing and that 'every so often a child goes missing from the village, eaten either by a hungry lion or crocodile. The family mourns for a week or so then has another child' as this was 'the same stuff that Hendrik Verwoerd used to say about the mental capacity of black people. If this is not racist speech, then what was the point of the fight against apartheid?'

I am persuaded by Mangcu's argument that Bullard's views had rings of Verwoerdianism to them. Those views hail from a racist and colonial past based on stereotypes. The content of the column and the firing of Bullard raised debate and showed a varied and dispersed set of opinions on the subject from editors and readers alike. What is interesting, and feeds directly into my argument about multiple and fluid identities and disparate subjectivities, is that not all white readers agreed with Bullard on the greatness of colonialism, and not all black readers believed that it was correct to fire him. The following are some views from the profession. In his column about the firing of Bullard, the editor of *Business Day*, Peter Bruce, wrote:

I don't think he is a racist and he makes me laugh. Still, I would have canned 'Out to Lunch' as well after his last effort in the *Sunday Times*. For Editor Abuse (EA) is a virus common among columnists. It makes you stop caring what the editor thinks about your work or what the political or commercial effects of it may be on him or her *(Business Day*: 14 April 2008).

From another perspective, the then *Sunday Independent* columnist Jeremy Gordin (also known as Karen Bliksem), took a light view of Bullard's column:

> The Bullfinch column of Sunday April 6 that caused all the trouble is one of the weakest, blandest and most tedious bits of nothing that any-one has written lately – and, therefore, to hold it up as the acme of rac-ism is to devalue, so to speak, serious racism. To take umbrage at some-thing Bullfinch says is to get angry at the bleating of a dead sheep (*The Sunday Independent*: 13 April 2008).

By contrast, an editorial in *The Weekender* was more serious:

> David Bullard overstepped his mark and his axing was justified, but it should not be cause for other writers to censor themselves ... A sense of humour is a handy tool in a country like SA, where the only available options often seem to be either to laugh or to break down in despair. But this is not a licence for columnists to spew invective or encourage racial intolerance and hope to escape responsibility by accusing critics of being spoilsports (*The Weekender* 12-13 April 2008).

The editorial's conclusion was that 'it would be a pity if the result [of the firing] is that other writers censor themselves for fear of inadvertently crossing a line that is all too often invisible'. Then, Anton Harber wrote in a *Business Day* column:

> There is no freedom of speech issue here ... Columns are an essential part of a newspaper, bringing opinion and debate to break through the tedium of news ... A sensible editor carries a healthy range of challeng-ing opinions, but makes it clear that there are certain views which go beyond the bounds that will not appear in the paper (*Business Day*: 16 April 2008).

None of the above editors or columnists was able to say what exactly the line was, or what the 'bounds' were. Harber didn't explain why this was not a freedom of speech issue or what these 'certain views' were, which go beyond the bounds. Gordin's comment that Bullard's column was just weak, bland and tedious bits of nothing, also made one think. Could Gordin be correct? However, more importantly for the argument here, another commentator, Bryan Rostron, pointed to the similar 'inanity' of Bullard and Makoe:

> Then, with democracy, we got David Bullard on the one side and the departing SABC political editor on the other. Bullard has been fired for supposed 'racism', while Makoe, as chairman of the FBJ, fulminated when the Human Rights Commission judged that the FBJ's exclusivity was unconstitutional, that we have effectively been found guilty of being black. Both Bullard and Makoe are well known, and each has a following, so it is the sheer inanity of their views that is depressing …The irony is that Makoe was defending the need for an all-black forum, while Bullard pretty much writes for an all-white forum (*Business Day*: 15 April 2008).

By likening Bullard to Makoe, Rostron showed that race was indeed a Master-Signifier to both subjects. I disagree, however, with Rostron in that Bullard wrote for 'pretty much … an all-white forum'. The letters from the public to newspapers showed otherwise. They showed that for these readers race was a floating signifier: it did not have full and definitive meaning attached to it. These views showed that there were resignifications happening, while the debates showed the deepening of democracy taking place in and through journalism. *En passant*, David Bullard apologised in an article in *Business Day* on 18 April 2008, for the content of his column. His intention, he wrote, was to:

> … make the point that some black South Africans blame white colonialism for all the country's problems … The article was never intended to offend, but it has, and that offence has caused the column's disappearance from the *Sunday Times*. For that I offer sincere and heartfelt apologies to those who were offended, including Mondli Makhanya, my friend and former editor, whom I respect enormously. Particularly offensive to so many was the suggestion that a family who had lost a child would mourn for a week or so and then have another. Despite my claim that this is fantasy SA, I realise that this was an insensitive remark to make and I humbly apologise (*Business Day*: 18 April 2008).

However, one day later, Bullard announced that he would sue the publisher Avusa for unfair dismissal, and for two years of lost income. His complaint was not on the basis of free speech but unfair procedure in terms of the Employment Act (*Saturday Star*: 19 April 2008). He argued that he was given no warning about the content of his writings over the years of his employment at the *Sunday Times*, and his services were terminated over the telephone, after the publication of the offending column.

Trevor Ncube, publisher of the *Mail & Guardian*, said in an interview on 12 August 2001 that he believed Bullard should not have been fired but that 'the issues he raised should have been engaged with and debated'. Philosophically, he would be on the same side as Voltaire, he said, and he quoted: 'I might not agree with what you are saying but I defend your right to say it'. Ncube cautioned against flying 'too close to censorship', which happens, 'the moment we begin to say we cannot do this and we cannot say that – who among us has a set of values to judge what is proper?'

This is a salient point. However, as Mouffe has also stated (and I agree) that while a radical democracy has to have robust fights, tension and contestations, there has to be some minimal consensus in society for it to function. In South Africa, it is widely accepted that this consensus is inherent in the Constitution, which does contain restrictions on free speech, for example that it should not incite hatred or violence. But this is not set in stone either – it is debated, contested, negotiated and constantly interpreted and re-interpreted.

What the readers said about Bullard's column and his subsequent firing: the emergence of resignification

The following letters from the public illustrate two important things. They show the important public space that newspapers provide for the airing of views and debate. They also illustrate an absence of homogeneity. Several other issues are highlighted. First, it seemed that the space for debate was quite vibrant in the country. Second, not all whites believed that Bullard's column was acceptable in the new discourse of post-apartheid South Africa. Third, not all blacks thought he should have been fired. Fourth, the Constitution and its reference points were debated. Finally, it showed how journalism could be a gate-opener for democracy; how it was one of the spaces in public discourse for airing views and debating controversies. I have selected a few letters from the public to demonstrate some of these reflections.

> The article so lacks balance in that it fails to even mention the brutish-ness of the colonising thugs who, armed with guns and Bibles, trashed the indigenous people's cultures, feeding their greed under the veil of a

fraudulent piety. Bullard's article suffers another defect. He apparently considers himself an ironist, but so heavy handed are his attempts at irony that any redemptive aspect of the article is lost in an adolescent display of failed satire. And this is surely the essence of the matter. Instead of censoring Bullard, why is there no effort to meet him on his own ground and critically deconstruct his flaccid attempt at provocation? (Laurence Berman, *Sunday Independent*: 20 April 2008).

What took the editor so long to fire Mr Bullard? (Mandlesilo Mavimbela, *Sunday Times*: 13 April 2008).

Please accept my heartfelt congratulations for getting rid of that obnoxious David Bullard. Let the little tit run to the DA and squeal. I might even buy the *Sunday Times* again – Bullard has kept me from it for years (Dave Pepler, *Sunday Times*: 13 April 2008).

It is obvious David Bullard went too far for many people with his column, but he is a satirist and his writings should not be taken literally. Satirists use humour to ridicule something that seems to them ridiculous. An apology might have been called for, but dismissal will lessen the country's ability to laugh at itself (Mark Henning, *Sunday Times*: 13 April 2008).

The firing of Mr Bullard is a mistake and will be a great loss to the *Sunday Times*. He may be vulgar and offensive at times but he is always a good read and provokes thought and a different view of the situation that's often pushed out by our politicians and the SABC (Tony Zebert, *Sunday Times*: 13 April 2008).

On Friday I read a most beautiful and poignant letter written by David Bullard: Bullard: an apology to my readers and friends (April 18). After having grown accustomed to his columns, which are sometimes hilarious yet at times out of order and insulting, I think his behaviour was exemplary. It occurred to me as I was reading his piece that this man who has come from Britain has truly metamorphosed into a South African and an African. His apology was so sincere and so moving. I have no doubt that those who embody that unique concept only found in Africa called *ubuntu* would agree with me that that apology was worthy of your acceptance. For that, Bullard, you have my forgiveness and my understanding. SA needs brash and sometimes abrasive not-so-young men like you. Your ownership of your shortcomings should serve as an inspiration to change for some of our patriots who fervently believe what you wrote. Well done bro (Sipho Nkosi, *Business Day*: 21 April 2008).

Let's be perfectly clear on one thing. I do not like David Bullard. I don't particularly like him because he has never written anything that made me think: 'Wow, I wish I had thought of that'. *Au contraire*, his views about the world in general and South Africa in particular tend to be niggardly pernickety hair-splitting diatribes. But they are bloody well written niggardly hair-splitting diatribes (Kanthan Pillay, *Mail & Guardian*: 18-24 April 2008).

The above letters show no unity on race in society. The letters are, in Mouffian terms, examples of how journalism can be a gate-opener for democracy. Interviewer Nick Carpentier put it to Mouffe: 'Gate-openers are interested in providing the options, arguments and perspectives. Instead of closing the gate, it is actually a matter of opening the gate.' Mouffe's reply was: 'Yes, yes, yes, that would be it, if one were to define what ideally the role of the journalist should be' (Carpentier & Cammaerts 2006). The letters also showed passionate attachment to race or to norms that oppressed, as well as exemplifying the concept of resignification, a transcendence, so to speak, of norms that have oppressed in the past. Tying this into the firing of Bullard, but also referring back to the attempt to relaunch the FBJ, the following two letters from readers support the argument that South African society has a diversity of views on race, that identities are not fixed and are often split, and that ultimately race is a floating signifier.

Black journalists' groups belong to the past. If black journalists were barred from attending a white journalists' forum there would have been an outcry, and it would have been worse if such a discriminatory act had been endorsed by an influential white leader … If we are to build a better South Africa for all, we need to learn to live with the past if we cannot leave it behind. There was a time where it was justifiable to have a body such as the one in question, but that was in the past. How do we in this era justify the divide based on race? While people are free to associate with whomever they want to, our Constitution rules against all forms of discrimination. To say to one person, 'I cannot allow you here because you do not have the right skin colour' is as yesterday as the mid-80s (Phumla Khanyile, *The Times*: 3 March 2008).

For Khanyile it was time to stop reiterating norms of the past, in other words, race identification and race suffering, as this was not progressive in moving forward towards real liberation. She cautioned that one needed to learn from the past, rather than imitate it. In the next letter we find a similar aversion to passionate attachments to race.

> Is this the season of hypocrisy, or double speak, or double standards, or is it plain arrogance on the part of the victors? The Forum of Black Journalists (FBJ) that is currently raging is a sign of the victorious black majority's 'entitlement' veiled as empowerment. It is accompanied by hypocrisy as well. The notion that whites enjoyed all the freedom in their time (albeit under a cruel regime) and that now it's 'blacks' time' is sick. That Jacob Zuma (the future president) would be enticed to make a speech to a blacks-only audience does not augur well for this country … Suppose, for arguments sake, that white journalists start their own organisation parallel to the FBJ. And suppose whites break away from all 'common organisations' and form their own. Is that not widening the gap in terms of uniting and bringing the population together? (K Maphosa, *Mail & Guardian*: 18-24 April 2008).

This section has shown how race 'floats' among many identities held by different subjects. It has shown, for example, how some white readers had some sympathy for the FBJ, while some black readers were repelled by the implicit racism in an exclusive race club for journalists. The FBJ and Bullard examples show ambivalence in the journalist profession about the firing of Bullard, with only Ncube stating outright that he should not have been fired, while Gordin felt that Bullard should not have been taken that seriously. The letters from the public showed that Bullard also had a black following, interestingly enough, even though his columns were often racist. 'Uncolonised Africa wouldn't know what it was missing', the column he was fired for, certainly was obnoxious and stereotyped black people in the most vicious ways. Yet, could it also be that South Africans were robust enough to debate with Bullard and show him up for his prejudices? In other words, should this racist space have been kept, like Ncube's libertarian freedom of expression views? Or was it just too obviously hate speech to be tolerated?

Bullard and Makoe

Both Bullard and Makoe were passionately attached to the oppressive norm of race. They both made turns to their past, Makoe to apartheid oppression and Bullard to colonial norms. These were turns against themselves. However, the seeming debacle of the FBJ and the firing of Bullard were exactly that – seemingly disastrous episodes. The episodes raised debate and they enabled contestations to take place. The questions of how to create democracy, what constitutes freedom in a democracy, as well as freedom of speech and freedom of association, were new in a democratic South Africa. Through both of the episodes, nevertheless, the issues of limits and absolute rights and freedoms were tested, creating heated debate. It is only through debate in public spaces, one of which would be newspapers, about issues which clearly lurk beneath the surface, that a radical democracy can emanate. These spaces that are constantly being fought over and negotiated, the heterogeneity in the divided society, are precisely what makes for a democracy in action, a democracy to come, or an unrealised democracy. These spaces must be kept open, for the deepening of democracy.

While the discourses of Makoe and Bullard were highly ideological, both harked back to the past and both were out of sync with the values of democracy or of moving forward. How did the discourses of Makoe and Bullard advance democracy, if they did at all? In themselves and in their content they did not. But the fact remains that they led to robust debate about freedom of speech and its boundaries, and about race. This took place within the newspapers, and between the citizenry, and constituted democratic combative thinking. In so doing, what we saw were the possibilities provided by the media as a public sphere, and through journalism, for what Mouffe called radical democracy, pluralism and agonism. This also echoes Ncube when he said that he agreed with Voltaire's famous statement: 'I might not agree with what you are saying but I defend your right to say it'.

Mouffe, in her interview with Carpentier and Cammaerts, pointed out that journalism was as ideological as society but that there was also a contradictory nature to it (2006: 996-997). This was evident in the Makoe and Bullard cases. Mouffe's point was that argument and debate promote democracy. This can be seen in the arguments and debates that occurred and in the hundreds of column inches devoted to the legitimacy of the FBJ and the firing of Bullard. How different people interpreted the two events, and what they meant – or did not mean – for democracy and freedom of speech, showed a fractured, open-ended society.

Makhanya's decision to fire Bullard was probably correct, and his comments are a useful conclusion to this chapter. They are on the role of journalism in a democracy. Makhanya quoted the French writer Marguerite Duras: 'Journalism without a moral purpose is impossible. Every journalist is a moralist. It is absolutely unavoidable' (*Sunday Times*: 7 September 2008). Makhanya argued that:

Cynics would say that we are a tribe that rummages through closets and hangs out at smoke-filled bars in search of the next sensational headline. They would say 'morality' and 'media' cannot be used in the same sentence. We would argue otherwise. One of the things that attracts journalists to this profession is a sense of idealism – a belief that the world can be better and that each human can do their little bit to make it more livable. And our bit is to tell stories: we inform our readers about their world and their societies; we entertain them; we anger them; sometimes we make them sad and despondent … Most importantly, we hold power to account – be it state, corporate or social power. Sometimes we do this well and sometimes we do not do so as thoroughly as we should. We are not angels and – as idealistic as we are we have never purported to be on a higher plane than the rest of human society. Just as others make mistakes, so will we.[5]

Makhanya conceded that journalists made mistakes too. There was a sense of 'idealism' in the profession, for him, as in the desire to hold power to account. One of the key focuses of this book is to find the intersection between the floating signifier democracy and the role of the media. Makhanya, as well as other journalists I interviewed, show how differently they saw their role from the way the ANC saw it. This chapter showed the fluidity of 'the media' and different identities and subjectivities among journalists. It showed, also, how 'the media' did not exist as a homogeneous entity; how race was not the Master-Signifier for many black journalists; and how the public did not rigidly identify with race. The examples were optimistic moments for democracy in the sense that debate was stirred and the vehicle used was the media. In the end, it became clear how important it is that these debates take place at all and how journalism is often a vehicle for them.

Race was the Master-Signifier for Makoe and Bullard, who both made reflexive turns, showing passionate attachment to their own oppression. However, the ultimate failure of the FBJ to relaunch showed that race was a floating signifier for other journalists, in that race was merely one of many signifiers, as not all their subjectivities collapsed into race identity or being black. By contrast, Makoe attached to apartheid norms and Bullard, through obnoxious scorn, disdain and contempt for black people, also attached to past racist and colonial norms, showing how severely oppressed he was. Ultimately, it became apparent that a racialised discourse would reproduce the 'subjugated' mentality of the past, and prevent and undermine the emergence of a democratic culture. The effect of this in the context of the changes in political power and ideological hegemony of the ANC, might be one that reproduces, too, the oppression of the past, stifles debate and poses a threat to freedom of expression – and ultimately to democratic deliberation.

NOTES

1   The extract is from *The Subject and Power in Ethics: Subjectivity and Truth* (1994), edited by Paul Rabinow.

2   For this argument Derrida's deconstruction theory has been used by a wide range of theorists from Butler on identity and subjection (1997), Mouffe on pluralism (2000), Norval on apartheid (1996), to Biko when he wrote on black consciousness in South Africa (1978).

3   See also Adam and Moodley (2000) who captured the tension of race politics in the new democratic South Africa, saying 'Paradoxically, with the death of legal racism, racial assertiveness abounds'.

4   In the story of the slave and lord, the freed slave was not happy – there was a stubborn attachment of conditions to his past, which gave him reason for being. He fell into 'unhappy consciousness' once freed (Butler 1997: 31-61).

5   *En passant,* Makhanya was apologising for inaccurate reporting on the Transnet V & A Waterfront story in which the *Sunday Times* falsely accused Transnet of selling state assets to foreigners and used the opportunity to elucidate what he saw as the role of journalists.

5.

Freedom of expression: the case of Zapiro

Politics have changed. My principles have not changed.
I'm still very much for progressive values. I'm railing against
inconsistencies and contradictions. I have been sued.
The Human Rights Commission should have defended
my right to publish my cartoons, in the name of freedom
of expression.[1]

What does 'freedom of expression' mean in South Africa's democracy when
internationally recognised cartoonist, Jonathan Shapiro, who works under the
name Zapiro, had claims for damages against him for R7-million in 2008, by
President Jacob Zuma, over a cartoon? (This claim was reduced in 2011 and a
trial date set for October 2012.) This chapter examines the alterity, otherness
or radical difference of Zapiro through this cartoon and argues that the ideological interpellation, or name-calling, as 'enemy' and 'racist', coupled with the
lawsuit by the president, caused ambivalence and loss for Zapiro.[2] In addition,
he appeared to make a half turn towards the voice of power when he removed
the showerhead from the cartoons of the president, albeit temporarily. (Zapiro
has depicted Zuma with a showerhead since the president announced in his
rape trial that he took a shower after having sex with an HIV-positive woman.
In all fairness to Zuma, he has subsequently explained that he never said he
took a shower to prevent contracting HIV/AIDS. He said that when the judge
asked him what he did after he had sex he replied that he took a shower.)

Before a discussion of the Lady Justice cartoon and the furore that it caused, let us turn to Butler's explication of ambivalence and loss, for which she is indebted to Freud. While Žižek's thought derives much from Hegel's dialectical materialism, his philosophical offerings are also psychoanalytical, based on the Lacanian interpretation of Freud. However, as Lacan suggested, and Žižek agreed, 'one never goes beyond Freud; one uses him, one moves around him' (Kay 2003.18). In the same way, this analysis of the cartoon, the subjection of Zapiro through interpellation and his subsequent reaction move around Freud.

In explaining psychic turns, ambivalence, loss, melancholia and the subject, Butler says that, in Freud, the ego is said to turn back on itself, whether in the Nietzchean sense of turning (as in retracting) what has been done or said (in shame at what one has done) or in the Althusserian sense of the reflexive turn or the moment of becoming a subject when one turns towards the voice of interpellation. Using the example of love to explain Freud, Butler says that once love fails to find its object, it takes itself as not only an object of love, but of aggression and hate as well. 'The turn that marks the melancholic response appears to initiate the redoubling of the ego as an object ... not only is the attachment said to go from love to hate as it moves from object to ego, but the ego itself is produced as a psychic object' (1997: 168). She proceeds to suggest that the ego is a poor substitute for the lost object, leading to ambivalence. Loss and mourning does not have to be about the loss of a loved one – it can also be about 'the loss of some abstraction such as one's country, liberty, an ideal', and so on.

Bearing this framing in mind, and understanding Butler's interpretation of Freud, we can now proceed to unravel how and why the Lady Justice cartoon caused dislocation in society, and how Zapiro reacted. I must note, recalling Foucault,[3] that while Zapiro says that his principles have not changed – he is 'railing against inconsistencies' – we do see changes in him too. He depicted Zuma with a showerhead when Zuma had admitted to having a shower after sex with an HIV-positive woman. But once Zuma became president and there appeared to be widespread support for him, Zapiro removed the showerhead. However, he then replaced it when it emerged that the already polygamous Zuma had fathered yet another child out of wedlock. Zapiro was showing multiple subjectivities.

The Lady Justice cartoon caused dislocation

In this hard-hitting, stark, shocking – but also serious – image, Zuma is depicted as unbuckling his belt to 'rape' Lady Justice, whose hands are pinned down, while the ruling party, the ANC, and its alliance partners enthuse.

The enthusiasts are the Cosatu general secretary, Zwelinzima Vavi; the SACP secretary general, Blade Nzimande; the then ANC Youth League president, Julius Malema; and the ANC secretary general, Gwede Mantashe. After this cartoon was published, Zapiro was called a 'right-winger' by the then ANC spokesperson, Jessie Duarte, and a 'racist' by the then deputy president of the ANC, Baleka Mbete and Malema, outside the court after Zuma was acquitted of rape charges.

This chapter first analyses the furore over the cartoon, then deploys the theoretical concepts 'legitimate adversary', 'interpellation' and 'subjectivisation', and relates them to the outcry and labelling of Zapiro as a right-winger. The chapter will show, through an interview with Zapiro, the ambivalence, half-turns and loss experienced by the cartoonist over his label and lawsuit. It will also document civil society's reaction and its support for Zapiro. The aim of this chapter is to explore freedom of expression in order to identify the intersection between the floating signifier, democracy, and the freedom of the press. In doing this my objective is to delve into the contradiction between a cartoonist sued for millions of rands for exercising his right to express his opinion and a constitution protecting freedom of expression. (It is important to note that freedom of expression in the Constitution has limitations: it does not extend to propaganda for war, incitement to violence or advocacy of hatred that is based on race, ethnicity, gender or religion. It also provides for a balancing of rights: between free speech and free media and rights to equality, respect and dignity.)

The chapter will also deploy the psychoanalytical concepts of ambivalence and loss in relation to the changing subjectivities of Zapiro.

Misa explained the political context for the cartoon thus:

> The implication was clear; justice was being raped by the campaign the ANC and its allies were waging against the courts, which were trying Zuma on various corruption and racketeering charges. Published in the *Sunday Times* in September 2008, the cartoon caused a furore as it catalysed a debate on how far cartooning can go before it is defamatory. Zapiro faced a firestorm, even from supporters like political analysts Sipho Seepe and Xolela Mangcu who felt he had drawn too far. The ANC threatened to sue and the already fiery atmosphere blazed. The following Friday, Zapiro drew again in the *Mail & Guardian*. He drew a twin image and this time a word bubble from Zuma said: 'With respect …' The implication was clear again: all week, the ANC had protested that it respected the judiciary and the outcome of the judgements. On the same day that the second cartoon was published, the High Court judge Chris Nicholson threw out the charges against Zuma and claimed that he had been subject to a political conspiracy. The ANC was ecstatic and outside court, deputy president of the ANC Baleka Mbete attacked Zapiro and accused him of racism. The incident has hardened the cartoonist laureate whose work is often dark with anger now; it is a far cry from the role he played as court jester to a ruling party he has always supported. Cartoonists are meant to push the envelope and enjoy, arguably, a higher freedom of expression than other journalists, said media freedom advocates. It is a space worth watching especially as all signs point to Jacob Zuma becoming president in 2009. (Misa 2008: 81).

Zuma did indeed become president in April 2009. He subsequently issued claims for a total of R7 million against Zapiro (R5 million for defamation and R2 million for damage to dignity) for the Lady Justice cartoon. Ferial Haffajee, who was in 2008 editor of the *Mail & Guardian*, wrote the above summary of the events, noting that the most important points were: first, that while there was support for the independence of the judiciary, a campaign had been waged against the courts for trying Zuma for fraud and corruption (he was found by judge Hillary Squires to have a corrupt relationship with businessman Shabir Shaik) as well as for his alleged rape; second, the question of how far a cartoonist can go with freedom of expression; and, third, the 'firestorm' and debate that this cartoon set off.

Haffajee observed that it was the rape metaphor that stirred the emotions. The image of Zuma, together with the showerhead, makes reference to his rape trial. AIDS activists, as well as the media, denounced Zuma for the statement 'I took a shower', which they took to mean that after having had sex with an HIV-positive woman, he had a shower to prevent contracting HIV/AIDS (it would in fact have further weakened his resistance to contracting the disease). The criticisms also stemmed from his admitting having unprotected sex with an HIV-positive woman and that this occurred after he held positions as chair of the South African National Aids Council and of the Moral Regeneration Campaign. What message was he sending out to people in South Africa, which has one of the highest HIV/AIDS related incidences, and one of the highest levels of rape, in the world? Zapiro's image was deliberately ambiguous and played on the allusion to rape, of both the alleged rape of an HIV-positive woman and the potential rape of justice (I use the term 'ambiguity' in the Freudian sense here, not to mean vagueness but rather to mean more than one meaning, a layering of meanings, if you like). Certainly, the cartoon directly depicted the rape of justice, but the surplus it refers to indirectly is his alleged rape of an HIV-positive woman. In the cartoon, the justice system is powerless, held down by powerful political forces assisting Zuma. There is a fairly clear layering of meanings in the cartoon: the attack on the judiciary, the potential rape of justice, the alleged rape and showering after sex, and the support for Zuma by the alliance partners. These layerings, as well as the ambiguities and ambivalences, are shown in the discourse of some ANC leaders, alliance partners and members of the public.

The ANC and the public discourse over the Lady Justice cartoon

Julius Malema described the cartoon as 'racist', saying that it exposed Zapiro's attitude not only about black leaders in the tripartite alliance, but also about black leaders in general (*The Times*: 9 September 2008). He converted race into the Master-Signifier. Malema felt that Zapiro failed to understand that Zuma had not been found guilty of rape in the trial brought against him by 'Kwezi', the woman who had accused him of rape in 2005. In the same article, Cosatu's secretary general, Zwelinzima Vavi, usually a fan of Zapiro's, reacted to this particular cartoon saying that he was 'shocked, devastated and lost for words. Zapiro has equated us to rapists. There is no basis for this cartoon. What is he saying to the world? Is he saying Zuma is a rapist? This cartoon goes beyond acceptable levels of freedom of expression'. In a joint statement the ANC, ANC Youth League and SACP accused Zapiro and the editor of the *Sunday Times*, Mondli Makhanya, of abusing press freedom.

For Zapiro, the issue raised the essential question of 'cartoonist as watchdog, not lapdog' (*Sunday Independent*: 14 September 2008). In an interview with the journalist Maureen Isaacson, he defended his rights as a cartoonist:

> Gone too far? That has been said to me and to cartoonists all over the world for a long, long time. We are commentators. Yes, the cartoon is over the top – that does not mean I would not do it again. Cartoons work by putting together things that are unexpected, occasionally shocking, joining dots that did not look like they could be joined and making an image that looks like it was there all the time ... (*Sunday Independent*: 14 September 2008).

This explanation for the role of cartooning in a democracy was supported by a *Mail & Guardian* editorial (12-18 September 2008) which asserted that there was ignorance about the role of the cartoon in modern democratic societies such as South Africa. 'Cartoonists are the court jesters who make us laugh and then cry when we realise that what's been drawn is often the fundamental truth or a portent of what might come to pass if we are not vigilant', the editorial read. 'The cartoon is a sacred space and believing in media freedom is not a tap you can switch on and off, taming his pen here or encouraging him to sharpen it there ...the greater the freedom of the cartoonist, the higher the democratic quotient of a society.'

While Zapiro does not make reference, himself, to the rape allusion, the *Mail & Guardian*'s ombudsman, Franz Kruger, felt that the rape allusion was reading too much into the cartoon, while the reference to the actual rape case could not be missed:

> What Zapiro has drawn is a common metaphor, that of the rape of justice, itself well established in the persona of a blind-folded woman carrying scales ... it seems to me that the Zapiro cartoon has offended against sensitivities that are mainly political – as Malema says they are disrespectful of some political leaders. I don't think newspapers have to

be as careful about these kinds of sensitivities' *(Mail & Guardian*: 12-18 September 2008).

Kruger noted that 'sensitivities' were offended, but did not spell out what these sensitivities were. Through the following excerpt, I venture to argue that these 'sensitivities' are about being 'passionately attached' to wounds of the past, those of racism and colonialism. The political commentator, academic, and, at the time, a columnist for *The Weekender*, Xolela Mangcu, entered the debate by arguing that this was a race issue. He felt that Zapiro needed to show 'more respect'. 'Some of the writings about black people offend even the most reasonable defenders of press freedom in the black community.' He went on:

> And so I urge my white colleagues to take this as a report from the colonies – the 'natives' are restless. They are unhappy at the manner in which the 'masters' depict them. In exercising our freedoms, we also need to show greater sensitivity to the dignity of other people, even those we dislike. That is the essence of our constitutional democracy and its human rights culture. If we as journalists violate that basic principle, then why should anyone respect it?' (*The Weekender*: 13-14 September 2008).

It is significant that Mangcu turned a freedom of expression debate and a statement about the attacks on the judiciary, depicted in a cartoon, into a race issue, by referring to 'natives' and 'masters'. This can be interpreted as plain obfuscation and a clear example of how the floating signifier 'race' is being rigidified into the Master-Signifier. That 'race' was a floating signifier among ordinary South Africans is shown in examples of citizens who wrote to the papers. They were not divided on the basis of race. Some black people thought the cartoon was apposite in its message, while some white people found it an affront. What the gaze on the cartoon showed was a contest within democracy, a society that is fractured, and a cartoonist causing further dislocation. It showed that society was not unified along the lines of race, but was instead fluid and diverse – a state of being that can only be deemed to be good for the deepening of democracy.

The public's gaze on Zapiro

The following views expressed by readers in a few newspapers show that the issue raised debate on what freedom of expression meant and what press freedom is in a democracy, and they also showed that the South African public had diverse opinions across race and gender lines.

I have always considered Zapiro a great cartoonist, but his cartoons depicting Jacob Zuma are despicable. They are hurtful in the extreme. If this constitutes press freedom, we might as well condone any kind of abuse (Ndo Mangala, *Mail & Guardian*: 12-18 September 2008).

The cartoon is not offensive to females and it hit the nail on the head (Kirsten Zissimides, *Mail & Guardian*: 12-18 September 2008).

Like diagnostic surgery, it is invasive, damaging – and necessary (David Le Page, *Mail & Guardian*: 12-18 September 2008).

As a woman I am in no way affronted by the cartoon … rape is quite an apt metaphor for the sense of entitlement and 'might is right' that Zuma and his supporters are displaying (Evyl Shnukums, *Mail & Guardian*: 12-18 September 2008).

The ANC and its hagiographers are mad because someone is calling it as it is (Mokone Molete, *Mail & Guardian*: 12-18 September 2008).

I find the cartoon deeply disturbing (Krys Smith, *Mail & Guardian*: 12-18 September 2008).

After seeing Zapiro's latest masterpiece, I asked myself whether we need say more about what the ANC and its alliance partners are doing to our justice system. The bullying, verbal attacks and protests are doing great damage to our country in general. If you don't understand in words what they are doing, Zapiro captures it all in his cartoon (Thabelo Lebona, *Sunday Times*: 14 September 2008).

Like many South Africans, I am concerned about the unfair political pressure being exerted on our judicial system. However, I was shocked by Zapiro's cartoon, which equated a number of our democratically elected leaders with the dregs of society planning the most abhorrent crimes. Cartoons like this close the door on rational debate. It was not just a bridge too far, but many bridges too far (Peter Cownie, *Sunday Times*: 14 September 2008).

Some standpoints show free-floating views, not stuck to a Master-Signifier of either race or gender. They elucidate a lack of homogeneity and the impossibility of reconciliation in society, given the divided nature of subjects and subjectivities. The discourse also showed how the issue raised debate on what freedom of expression meant, and what press freedom was in a democracy. Freedom of speech was supported (except for the last quotation by Cownie), and the absence of unity of identity on the basis of race or gender was evident. One woman felt that this was not an anti-feminist cartoon (Snukums), a white person felt offended (Cownie), and some black people supported Zapiro. Before we move on to a theoretical understanding, I would now like to turn to an interview with Zapiro which, I contend, reveals several attachments: to principles of democracy as he understood them, to justice, and then to an experience of loss of an ideal and, finally, to ambivalence.

An interview with Zapiro[4]: the divided subject [5]

On lawsuits, Lady Justice, Zuma and the HRC:

I will defend the cartoon [Lady Justice]. I have no doubt I will win. I have my integrity intact. There is a huge contradiction in freedom of speech on the one hand, and those law suits against media institutions on the other. He is the president now. I don't want to see the country go down the tubes. I want to see the country succeed. I suspended the shower when he became president.

The Lady Justice cartoon caused a huge furore but they didn't sue for quite a while, about three months later. I made a submission to the Human Rights Commission. They have not made a finding.[6] I've not heard from them. I feel they should be defending my right to do that cartoon. There was no incitement to hurt, maim or kill. It is a metaphorical attack and is within the realm of freedom of speech. The HRC copped out. My submission was made on 20 December 2008.

On the role of the cartoonist

The role of the cartoonist is to knock the high and mighty off their pedestals. To be irreverent; to be a sceptic and not to be sycophantic; to make interesting and new connections between disparate things; to be hypothetical and hyperbolic; to exaggerate things in order to highlight a point of view; to use parody and satire, and humour is just one of the devices, but it's the best. Cartoons can be powerful and not all are funny. The Lady Justice one was very serious.

On the creative process:

I always go through a lot of angst. There is a fair amount of self-doubt. Am I hitting the right note? I would say that it is has been a decade and a half of enormous press freedom. I've been in the right place at the right time.

On Jessie Duarte:

She blusters like crazy. She said I should be prosecuted to the full extent of the law. She's bluffing. She is a terrible face of the ANC. She is unfailingly grumpy. Her reactions are knee-jerk. She has no understanding that divergent views in a democracy are important. She said my work was right-wing journalism. Her arguments are faulty and stupid in their brazenness.

In the interview Zapiro said that he does not merely ridicule for the sake of it. He pointed to the 'smear' tactics' of the ANC but also made a distinction between the two ANC presidents, Mbeki and Zuma. He said that Mbeki has never sued but, instead, used his 'online rantings' to make his views known, while Zuma's intervention, the lawsuit, was harsh and intimidating. He railed against several things: his 'targetting', his lawsuit, and the interpellation or labelling of his work by Duarte as 'right-wing journalism'. The question arises, then, about what space there is for journalistic action and agency when the contest is phrased in such bellicose terms. And then, when disagreements or criticisms are reflected in newspapers, through cartoons such as Lady Justice, a cartoonist is labelled an enemy, one who is anti-transformation and against the new democracy. From Zapiro's interview it is clear that he intended the opposite. He intended deepening democracy but he was seen as an affront to democracy. He caused dislocation in society, but indeed society was already dislocated.

Zapiro made a turn to an institution, and for the argument of this philosophical trajectory, one could call it a turn to the voice of authority, or the voice of the law, the state, or the Constitution when he dispatched a letter, dated 13 November 2008, to the SAHRC in defence of his cartoon. By August 2009, he had not received a response. Eventually, by July 2010, the Commission ruled in favour of freedom of speech, saying that Lady Justice did not constitute hate speech, unfair discrimination or a violation of human rights as enshrined in the Constitution. The SAHRC said that while the cartoon was 'probably offensive and distasteful', it expressed a level of 'free, open, robust and even unrestrained criticism of politicians by a journalist' and had stimulated 'valuable political debate' (*Mail & Guardian*: 25 June-1 July 2010). The finding by the SAHRC, an independent statutory body set up as a Chapter Nine institution in the Constitution to protect democracy and the Constitution itself, is an encouraging one, supporting the Mouffian view that robust fights and contestations are intrinsic to a democracy. There are many reasons why debate and conflict should be defended but the main reason is that they allow for a clash of ideas which can lead to the elusive truth and they can prevent tyranny and domination. This is not to say that finding common ground is an undesirable goal. It is not in principle a bad thing, nor is it impossible, but when homogeneity seems to be forced, disguised as 'national interest' or development goals', that's when we should be wary.

Legitimate adversaries and enemies of the people

Mouffe's concepts in several works distinguished between 'legitimate adversaries' and 'enemies'. The case of Zapiro raised the issue of the ANC's inability to distinguish between these two. Mouffe suggested that the failure to do so in any democratic system meant that democracy itself would be jeopardised. For example, she posited that

> democratic debate was not a deliberation aimed at reaching *the one* rational solution to be accepted, but a confrontation among adversaries ... The adversary is, in a sense an enemy, but a legitimate enemy with whom there exists common ground. Adversaries fight each other, but they do not put into question the legitimacy of their respective positions' (1999: 4).

The democratic paradox is that 'Antagonism is ineradicable and pluralistic democratic politics will never find a final solution' (2000: 139). In other words, and to apply this theory here, democracy was, and will always be, an unending disputatious process.

Zapiro represents a legitimate adversary, part of the 'agonistic pluralist' space. But he had been demonised and turned into more than an adversary: he was hailed as racist, enemy and right-winger although there was an outpouring of support for him from elements of civil society, by supporters of academic freedom, members of the media, and former activists against apartheid, as well as international supporters. However, there is ambivalence in the Constitution itself about freedom of expression. The Constitution merely stipulates, in Clause 16 (1), that 'freedom of speech' is protected as long as it does not promote hatred, racism and violence. It does not draw a clear line where criticism ends and hate speech begins.

It is worth digressing, at this stage, into some recent history to develop this point. In the same year that the Constitution was born, 1996, the deputy CEO of Independent Newspapers, Ivan Fallon, presented the 1996 Freedom of the Press Lecture at Rhodes University in which he commented that freedom of expression and freedom of the press meant different things to different people. He observed that the 'complaints by ministers are on the whole, in my experience at least, constructive and healthy. They have never touched on the freedom of the press, or involved any threats, even veiled ones' (Fallon: 1996). He continued that the criticisms had always stopped well short (at least from the political circles that matter), of any serious retreat from the freedom given to the press over the previous couple of years, and concluded:

> That, of course, may alter as the honeymoon period ends, the miracle of the Mandela era recedes and particularly as electioneering begins in the run-up to the 1999 elections. But I for one sincerely doubt it. I have never before come across a society which so appreciates and cherishes the benefits of its press freedom at all levels. It has been a long time in coming, it was hard won, and I don't for a second believe there is any threat to it.

These sentiments captured the mood of 1996, when the Constitution was ratified. The tone of Fallon's comments echoed the thinking in general in the media profession at the time. It seemed that the honeymoon period between the ANC and the media lasted for five years, during Nelson Mandela's presidency, but in fact Mandela was belligerent with Sanef over criticism in newspapers of the ANC (this is discussed in the next chapter). Nevertheless, from 1999, for ten years during Mbeki's presidency, a decidedly frostier relationship ensued. The journalist and commentator, Justice Malala, captured this in July 2009 when he looked back and reflected that 'since 1999 we have had a government that believed that only those words and edicts issued from the Union Buildings were right' (*The Times*: 3 August 2009). He went on:

> Those who dared utter anything contrary were hounded and ridiculed. Many were regarded as enemies of the state. The voice of South Africa died. Those who spoke out against our crazy approach to AIDS were victimised. And there was Zimbabwe. For years we aided, abetted and defended a dictator. Not once did the South African government condemn the brutality and madness of Robert Mugabe (*The Times*: 3 August 2009).

Yet the ANC was not consistent. Indeed Malala himself wrote about the international relations director general, Ayanda Ntsaluba, who said in July 2009 that if

Sudan's president, Omar al-Bashir, showed his face in South Africa he would be arrested: '... say what you will about Zuma's cabinet, this announcement makes me believe that, at the very least, this is a government not shutting itself off from the voices of the people. For the first time, in a long time, we have a government that responds to the words of civil society' (*The Times*: 3 August 2009).

It is not my purpose to chronicle the ANC's relationship with Zimbabwe and its foreign policy in general. What is important is that in August 2009 Malala believed that the Zuma regime held much promise for openness, that it was not a government that was shutting itself off from the people. He changed his mind when strident calls were made to curb the media's independence.

Just as there were contradictions within the ruling party, so too were there contradictions in society, among the citizenry, that abounded in debate around the Zapiro cartoon. Almost a year after the watershed 52nd ANC National Policy Conference, commonly referred to as the Polokwane Conference, in December 2007, Dominic Timothy Ruiters wrote that the cartoon raised a national furore. He said that the depiction of Zuma poised to rape Lady Justice had 'evoked an unprecedented national response. The cartoon's brazen interpretation of current political events has been met with both high praise and severe criticism from different sectors of the public sphere' (30 September 2008).

I agree with Ruiters: a challenge to the status quo is always necessary within a democracy, otherwise democracy cannot continue to realise its role. But democracy cannot have an ultimate goal, or a final realisation, as its role is to constantly pose a challenge to what become static views about who can and cannot speak and make decisions. This is a Mouffian way of explaining the contentions and contestations over the Lady Justice cartoon, especially with regard to the challenge to the status quo: the challenge must never end and the achievement of unity, and consensus would stunt democracy. These widely disparate and fluid views about what freedom of expression constitutes or does not constitute are important for negotiating new spaces for democratic deliberation. Let us take publisher of the *Mail & Guardian,* Trevor Ncube, for instance,. He stated, in an interview, in August 2008, that he was a fundamentalist on the issue of freedom of expression. For him, there was a constant conundrum over where – or whether – a line should be drawn in relation to the freedom of expression debate.

> The French philosopher Voltaire said: 'I might not agree with what you are saying but I defend your right to say it'. Invariably you have to deal with the public good versus the individual's rights versus public decency. We don't know what that balance is. Who you are, where you are coming from, what your context is, your value system, and your view of the

world, all these inform the parameters of what public decency is. Are there limits there? They are not easily definable. Zapiro pushed the envelope maybe with the sexual imagery. Some sections of the public are clearly uncomfortable with this. I have discomfort with saying he should be censored.

The crux of the matter for Ncube was to debate the issues rather than create untouchable sacred cows. The opposition Democratic Alliance's spokesperson for communications, Dene Smuts, argued in a similar fashion, but she was talking about the ANC Youth League leader, Julius Malema, not Zapiro. She also qualified her point to suggest a distinction between the fundamental right to speak your mind and old-fashioned incitement to do harm, saying that 'Julius Malema has as much right to shock us as cartoonist Zapiro does'. Smuts went on to say: 'When he [Julius Malema] boasted this week that the ANC Youth League and he are not afraid to break new ground on any subject and to say what they think, he sounded like a free-speech prophet in a land that had lately become too politically correct' (*Sunday Times*: 28 September 2008).

Smuts wrote that Malema had set himself up as an exponent of the key concept of free speech but the difference was that Malema's claim was to die for Zuma, not for free speech. Smuts's argument was subtle: let us support free speech, and Malema's right to it, but let us be aware of his tendency to incite violence. With the Lady Justice cartoon there was no evidence of any incitement to violence. However, that the debate took place and that Zapiro was not fired for being too controversial were testament to the multiplicity of democratic deliberative spaces and testified to the fact that freedom of expression was robust in South Africa. There were also nuances within the alliance's response. Vavi, for instance, did not accuse Zapiro of being a racist, a right-winger or an enemy of the people, but said he was 'shocked, devastated and lost for words' (*The Times*: 9 September 2008). His discourse was still within the ambit of democracy.

Unity in society stunts democracy

For Mouffe, who advocated 'agonistic pluralism' (2000: 139), social division was part of a radical democracy. The diversity of positive and negative opinions and ideologies in the responses to Zapiro represented an 'agonistic pluralism' in South Africa's transitional democracy, showed the diversity of a plural society, and were a means towards achieving a radical democracy.

Antagonism, in Mouffe's philosophy, was ineradicable and a pluralist democracy meant that there ought to be no dreams of impossible reconciliation or 'final solution'. The theory for a radical democracy was that a 'well function-ing democracy calls for a vibrant clash of political positions'. The attraction of Mouffe's position was her condemnation of deliberative democrats such as Habermas and Rawls for denying the dimension of undecidability and ineradi-cability of antagonism. She drew attention to the significance and mechanisms that constitute 'democracy'. For Mouffe, antagonism is an integral part of the political space. Deliberative democracy theorists, in her argument, negated the inherently conflictual nature of modern pluralism. Zapiro represented the multi-plicity of voices in a modern pluralistic society. His was a radical voice function-ing to deepen democracy. In Mouffe's argument, 'an agonistic approach to the political and the social acknowledges the real nature of frontiers and the forms of exclusion that they entail, instead of trying to disguise them under a veil of rationality or morality'. She argues that we have to come to terms with this, and resist the temptation to 'naturalise its frontiers' and 'essentialise its identities'.

In the *Challenge of Carl Schmitt*, Mouffe argued that liberal democratic theorists were proposing that left and right splits were passé since the fall of the Berlin Wall, and that it was time for a more consensual form of politics – that is, an inclusive consensus was now possible. But, for her, denying antagonisms did not make them disappear. Conflict, therefore, was necessary and must be welcomed. Thus Zapiro's challenge in the Lady Justice cartoon should be seen as a robust critique of the contradictory nature of politics in South Africa, and one that heralded the open-endedness of conflicts.

After the cartoon furore Zapiro made a documentary about cartooning for the television programme Special Assignment. The SABC meant to air it, but at the last minute it was cancelled. On 26 May 2009 a political satire documentary by Zapiro was due to be screened on SABC with much anticipation from an eager public, especially because the original screening, which was due to have taken place in April 2009 just before the general election, was cancelled. Hours before the show was due to go on air, it was pulled. The cancellation made head-lines in local and international news. The Special Assignment documentary was an examination of freedom of speech and cancelling it was another form of hail-ing or interpellation, trying to bring into line, causing dislocation. In discussing on the documentary, Jessie Duarte said that Zapiro had taken a comment in the court case about Zuma's alleged rape out of context, and then used a 'deroga-tory' image, a shower, 'and thought that that would be funny' (*Mail & Guardian Online*: 27 May 2009). This was what Duarte said in the documentary:

> I don't think he's a small fish in a small pond. I think he's a cog in a
> wheel ... of right-wing elementary journalism that looks at people from
> a very one-sided viewpoint and doesn't allow for the opposite views to

come through. I think Jonathan Shapiro should be taken to court where a court can hear his side of the view and Mr Zuma's side of the view and where it can be decided whether he should punitively pay for his race and class bias.

This is what Zapiro was talking about when he talked of how Duarte 'blusters, like crazy'. On a more theoretical note, however, labelling his work 'right-wing elementary journalism' is ideological interpellation *par excellance*, an attempt to try and create homogeneity, or fix the unfixed and fluid social, out of its irreducible heterogeneity. Dario Milo, a media law expert, said in the documentary that Zuma's case against Zapiro was 'problematic for our democracy' and was going to create a 'chilling effect on freedom of expression where there will be self-censorship by satirists and others when they are writing and expressing themselves because they're worried about lawsuits' (*Mail & Guardian Online*: 27 May 2009).

A letter asking how Zapiro could be right-wing pin-points the ideological obfuscation involved.

> Jessie Duarte thought that Zapiro was an element of 'right-wing elementary journalism'. Never before have I seen anybody's viewpoint so grossly misrepresented for the sake of political point-scoring, as Duarte obviously aimed to do … Zapiro is one of the most visible, consistent and influential left-wing critics of government, so it is understandable that they would like to frame him as a right-winger. They know that, in the South African context, the right wing will be a perpetual minority. In reality, the ANC is much more concerned with the dissatisfaction of people who are the beneficiaries of the planned transformation process and are becoming restless on the left (Erwin Sieben, Harrismith, *Mail & Guardian*: 29 May-5 June 2009).

As Sieben correctly pointed out, Zapiro is more of a left-wing commentator, given his social critiques, but 'framing' him as right wing and an outsider in the democracy suits the ANC's purposes, enabling it to occupy the moral high ground. This obfuscation has to be questioned.

One of the basic tenets of democracy is that it cannot exist without freedom of expression. Social antagonism is germane to democratic practice, debate and contestation. Žižek wrote that Laclau and Mouffe posited a series of particular subject positions – for example, feminist, ecologist, democrat and so forth – the signification of which was not fixed in advance but changed according to the way it was expressed.[7] Žižek said (2005:250)

Let us take, for example, the series feminism – democracy-peace movement-ecologism: insofar as the participant in the struggle for democracy 'finds out by "experience" that there is no real democracy without the emancipation of women, insofar as the participant in the ecological struggle finds out by experience that there is no real reconciliation with nature without abandoning the aggressive masculine attitude towards nature,' and so forth. In essence, his argument is that a unified subject position is being created, well and good, but we must not forget that such unity is radically contingent.

Žižek calls the subject position a mode of how we recognise our position in the social process. This is indeed describing the subject position of Zapiro. The ideological labelling and subjection of Zapiro failed. He refused the identity of right-winger and racist by continuing with hard-hitting cartoons, committed to his subject position as a 'democrat'. He saw himself as holding fast to his original principles, the same as those he adhered to when he fought against apartheid, as he said in the quotation opening this chapter. However, ambivalence and loss is also experienced, in the interview and as witnessed by the removal of the showerhead and in his turn towards the SAHRC for support. This will be discussed below, but first we turn to a friend of Zapiro's and a fellow cartoonist, Andy Mason, who expounds on the role of the cartoon in a democracy but who has also talked about why Zapiro removed the showerhead. Mason calls it a 'brilliant strategic move'. I contend that it shows ambivalence on Zapiro's part and, in fact, a half turn towards the voice of power – an Althusserian response to the ANC's injunction and interpellation of Zapiro as a 'right-winger' – which is part of the process of changing subjectivity.

The role of the cartoon in a democracy and half-turns

Mason, in an interview (7 August 2009), explained the role of cartoons in a democracy. He posited that cartoonists reflected the times in which we live: 'In recent times [in South Africa] the jester's space has been a bustling thoroughfare', and freedom of expression a contest between liberal values from the West and African values of dignity and respect (for Mouffe, such a 'clash' of ideas would be excellent for the deepening of a forever-open democracy). Mason observed: 'People want to know what the line is regarding freedom of expression. There isn't one'. Clearly, given Trevor Ncube's and Dene Smuts's views, discussed earlier, and Mason's perspective, freedom of expression is a negotiated space in a democracy, forever fluid, undecided and unfixed. On Zapiro and the showerhead, however, Mason made the following observation:

> Othering is what cartoonists do. He mercilessly and brilliantly satirised Zuma, and got positive feedback. Then Zuma became president of us all. So in that context, Zapiro didn't want to diss [insult] him and his country, he's proudly South African, so he removed the showerhead. For the first time Zuma was seen in a human light. This is the genius of Zapiro, this temporary suspension. It was a brilliant strategic move.

I consider it more than a 'brilliant strategic move'. While Zapiro resists the totalising and essentialising identity of a 'racist' and 'right-winger', he also shows ambivalence by the temporary suspension of the showerhead. If we bear in mind Butler's theory of subject formation – that subjection is paradoxical, that one is dependent on that very same power that subjects one, that the psyche turns against itself in a reflexive move and that ultimately, through the operation of conscience, there is ambivalence and loss (1997: 169-189), how are we to understand Zapiro's response as seen in extracts from the letter to the SAHRC in which he explained himself and in the interview when he said he experienced 'angst' and 'self-doubt'? This angst and self-doubt is not the same as deferring to Butler's theory that Zapiro had allowed himself to be subjected and that he had made a self-reflexive turn against himself. It is subtler than that. In his letter to the SAHRC, Zapiro emphasised the allegorical, symbolic nature of his cartoon about the rape of the justice system. He hardly referred to the layering of meanings except for the statement: 'I feel strongly that the real intimidation of the judiciary and of individual judges justifies my use of the potentially shocking rape metaphor' (letter to SAHRC: November 2008) and he said: 'The cartoon shows the abuse of the justice system, not of a real woman'. This is not to say that Zapiro was apologetic and made a full swing towards the voice of power. By no means. In fact, he stated categorically: 'I have no regrets at all about doing it'. But half-turns are evident.

Butler explained that turning back on oneself means different things in Hegel, Nietzsche, Freud and Althusser. In Hegel it marked the unhappy consciousness (Butler 1997: 168), in Nietzsche it suggested a retraction of what one has said or done, or recoiling in shame. In Althusser it was the turn of the pedestrian towards the voice of the police officer, or the law, when hailed ('hey you') which is simply self-subjugating. And in Freud, the ego was said to turn back against itself once love failed to find its object and instead take itself as not only an object of love, but of aggression and hate as well, the melancholic response to loss. Could the action of writing to the SAHRC constitute some form of turning? Could the temporary suspension of the showerhead from further cartoons once Zuma became president be a retraction? Yes and no, hence my argument for the ambivalence and half-turn of Zapiro. In any case, the suspension was very temporary. In 2012, Zapiro drew Zuma cartoons replete with showerheads.

Zapiro was at pains to point out in my interview with him that he was loyal to democracy as an ideal; he was committed to his country; he was not always confident about his work; he was unsure if he was 'hitting the right note'. Moreover, he said, 'I go through a lot of angst'. He also said: 'I was once considered to be part of the struggle. I'm now called an enemy and a right-winger'. In the light of Butler's trajectory, using Freud, Zapiro was mourning the loss of an ideal. This is exactly what my interview with Zapiro showed. While he did not allow himself to be subjected in the sense that he maintained the hard-hitting caricature of public figures, he showed ambivalence when he removed the showerhead, and most definitely displayed considerable melancholia at the loss of an ideal. He had been an anti-apartheid activist and, in that sense, at that time, turned fully towards the main struggle player, the ANC. In post-apartheid South Africa he was turning away from the ANC because he saw the organisation becoming undemocratic. He did not completely ignore the interpellation and lawsuits, and proceed with life as though they were irrelevant or had not happened. And he did make a turn to the SAHRC. Let us examine some of the extracts from this letter to the SAHRC of November 2009, which appeals to the institution to understand his rationale.

> In a recent magazine interview (*Leadership*, October 2008), Human Rights Commission chairperson, Jodi Kollapen was asked 'Where do you draw the line between hate speech and the right to freedom of expression and opinion?' He replied: 'We cherish the freedom of expression charter in the Constitution. People have the right to say things that other people may not like and that may offend or shock them. This is freedom of expression and it would be very difficult to classify opinionated utterances as hate speech per se' ... My point is that if this cartoon is demonstrably excluded from the class of speech that should be censured by the HRC, then the opinions expressed in the cartoon are protected by the Constitution ... The meaning of the cartoon is quite obviously metaphorical, not literal. That it is a metaphor is obvious because the central figure in the drawing is clearly not a real person, but rather the well-known symbolic figure, 'Lady Justice'. Personifying abstract aspects of society (Justice, Democracy, War, and Liberty etc.) is a tradition that began many centuries ago and is widely used in newspaper

cartoons. The Lady Justice personification has been around for over 2000 years since Roman times and is arguably the most famous of these allegorical figures. She is instantly recognisable by her blindfold (signifying that justice is 'blind', meaning impartial), her balance scale (representing the weighing of evidence and arguments) and to an extent by her Roman-style sandals. Sometimes, just to make absolutely sure for the reader, she has a sash labelled 'Justice' (or as in the case of my cartoon, 'Justice System') ... If the figure of justice is a symbolic figure, as is already established, then it follows that the cartoon itself can only be symbolic or metaphorical ...

It is in the public interest that cartoonists and other satirists are able to make such robust interventions in public discourse ... I have no regrets at all about doing it. It generated a huge amount of debate and large numbers of South Africans across the racial spectrum said the cartoon articulated their feelings ... The cartoon has even been credited by some analysts as having played at least some role in putting pressure on Zuma and his allies to distance themselves from the perception that they were threatening the judicial system. A couple of days after the cartoon appeared in the Sunday Times, both Zuma and Mantashe declared their respect for the judiciary. I am heartened that Sunday Times editor Mondli Makhanya supported the publication of this cartoon and has firmly stood by me when this resulted in verbal attacks on me by powerful people. And he too was vilified by some of these politicians ...

Respectfully yours

Jonathan Shapiro[8]

While Zapiro's letter is not apologetic, there are some gaps in his rationalisation of the cartoon. He does not offer too much on the HIV issue, or Zuma's alleged rape. He could be backtracking.

Ambivalence, Butler wrote, may be a characteristic feature of every love attachment that a particular ego makes (1997: 172-174). In this case, the love object could be the ideal of democracy or it may 'proceed precisely from those experiences that involved the threat of losing the object'. She uses Freud's terms entzogen, meaning withdrawn, an object-loss withdrawn from consciousness, until the outcome characteristic of melancholia has set in. In Zapiro's interview and in his letter to the SAHRC there seems to be some loss, loss of an ideal, worry about the future of democracy, angst, also a withdrawal.

Some concluding reflections: misrecognition, ambivalence and loss

It was through experience that Zapiro, learned that there was no freedom of expression without democracy, and there could be no democracy without freedom of expression. In a Mouffian sense, this chapter showed that Zapiro should be viewed as a legitimate adversary, not an enemy of the people. What some members of the public wrote showed how fluid and open-ended society actually is and how identity is socially constructed. Not all black people found the cartoon offensive, not all white people found it innocuous, and not all women thought it was the height of anti-feminism. It was a powerful anti-rape statement – rape of all forms. Zapiro's discourse and actions showed his own ambivalence and half turns towards the interpellations. My analysis, in a sense, contradicts how Zapiro sees himself standing 'steadfast'. He was, and he was not, at the same time. Yes, he stands firm to his commitment to democracy and freedom of expression. But, like all subjects with multiple and split subjectivities, he also changes. It is a progressive bent to change. As Foucault famously said, do not ask me who I am and do not ask me to remain the same (1969).

The role of cartoons in a democracy became apparent through the debate which stirred emotional responses and prompted thinking about the limits of freedom of expression. Was the cartoon offensive or was it a serious statement of the politics of the day? It was indeed reflective of the politics of the day and, as I have stated already, a functioning democracy calls for a vibrant clash of political positions (Mouffe 2000: 104). Agonistic pluralism provides a different way to establish antagonists, as in 'us and them'. But the Zapiro case showed how labelling him 'right wing' attempted the creation of an 'enemy' and attempted foreclosures. A radical pluralist democratic model needs to encompass the multiplicity of voices and various forms of expression, rather than consensus, unity, and harmony. In a sense, this was exactly what was reflected in society in South Africa, and signified, in 2008 and 2009, a society in which information, ideas and perspectives were free flowing. A great variety of heterogeneous voices came to the fore. However, what is clear, if one considers the voices of Malema's vulgar labelling of Zapiro as 'racist' and Duarte's equally vulgar inter-pellation of the cartoonist as 'right wing', was that the ruling party, the SACP and Youth League wished to hegemonise and essentialise the kind of plural society that existed, masking inconsistencies through social fantasy. Cosatu's Zwelinzima Vavi, on the other hand, spoke more honestly. He was 'shocked' and at a 'loss for words' (*The Times*: 9 September 2008). He was after all a fan of Zapiro and at the time, before 2010, an even bigger fan of Zuma. Vavi did not jump on the ideological obfuscation bandwagon of labelling Zapiro, he merely questioned what, precisely, the cartoonist was aiming at. He did not decide that Zapiro was an outsider to democracy, even though he was hurt and offended that Zuma could be depicted in such a harsh way.

So what, then, occurred in South Africa over the Lady Justice furore, the cancelling of Zapiro's documentary on political satire, and the subsequent labelling of his work as right wing journalism? It was clearly an attempt to shut down a potent critical space in the public sphere. The lawsuits were another such attempt, one which can be termed attempted subjectivisation, or calling him in to toe the line. I say 'attempt' because total subjectivisation did not occur. A totalitarian shut down would have entailed the jailing of Zapiro, yet by 2012 he was still at work. The next question, then, is what stops the ANC from total subjectivisation. The answer surely must lie within two possible scenarios. One is that there must be an ambivalence within the ANC itself, indeed within the 'many ANCs', meaning that there is no one centre holding the ANC together. The other is that it could also be that the ANC was forced into a negotiated settlement, and therefore forced into a constitutional democracy, so it finds itself with one foot in this constitutional democracy and another foot still in an authoritarian past. One could go further, to argue that the ruling alliance was showing its Stalinist past. Although there is no fixed tendency within the ANC there are many strands – of democracy, democratic centralism, Stalinism, and even liberalism.

The labelling as right wing is a sign of 'othering'. This is counter-democratic. Democracy is not about oneness, unity, and closures, but about acceptance of difference, debate and heterogeneity. Duarte was looking for rational consensus with the media, which was not possible given the divergent voices. For as long as the media is independent from political interference, consensus and oneness is impossible, and for as long as consensus in society is the objective, so the fluid, unfixable nature of a democracy in process and in progress will remain elusive. There were clearly many in South Africa's ruling alliance who became extremely insecure about openness and so for them the solution was more strident calls for the excesses of the media to be curbed. However, in South African society, finding its feet within a democratic framework, it was not possible to stabilise the meaning of democracy through rational consensus. In South Africa, during 2008 and 2009, there were no significant closures in our transitional democracy, but there were attempts at closures, for instance the suing of Zapiro; the ideological, injurious interpellations; and the cancelling of his documentary on freedom of speech. These were the warning signs that democracy needed protection. Zapiro is a legitimate adversary in a democracy. But powerful political forces, which constructed him as an enemy, questioned his legitimacy. The ANC has not silenced him; the constitutional democracy prevents this and the organisation's stated commitment to the constitutional democracy prevents it as well.

Michele Barrett said that ideology was a vain attempt to impose closure on a social world whose essential characteristic is the infinite play of differences and the impossibility of any ultimate fixing of meaning (cited in Žižek: 1994). The ideological interpellation of Zapiro failed, in the sense that he continued firing missiles directly into the hearts of the powerful, depicting in extreme form caricatures of the corrupt, greedy and racist – as is the nature of cartoons. He found out that democracy is not a process that has an end; it is fluid, with disparate twists and turns. The public found out, through experience, that freedom of expression is linked to democracy. Many members of civil society debated the cartoon and its implications, through letters to newspapers and calls to the radio. Zapiro lost an ideal. He also showed ambivalence, and the interpellation he experienced must be seen in the historical context: in the transitional democracy to be labelled a racist and a right winger is the equivalent of being an enemy just as in the apartheid era to be labelled a 'communist' was the ultimate insult from the perspective of the dominant power relations at the time. Donald Woods, former editor of the *Daily Dispatch* in East London and a fierce critic of the apartheid government, sued the minister of transport, Ben Schoeman, for calling him a communist from a public platform. A *Weekender* editorial made this point: 'the reputational damage of being considered a communist had real consequences – those tainted with the red brush faced social exclusion ...' (*The Weekender*: 26-27 September 2009).

There is contingency in labelling, there is contingency in subjectivities. At one point there was no greater damage than being called a communist and today, it would seem, there is no greater damage than to be called a right winger. Zapiro turned to a state institution, the SAHRC, which he hoped would protect his right to freedom of expression. By September 2009 he had made six unsuccessful attempts at a response from the SAHRC. It was only in June 2010 that a finding was made that his work was within the bounds of the Constitution, was not hateful and did not incite violence and racism.

This chapter has shown ambivalence in the subjectivities of Zapiro when he suspended the showerhead once Zuma became the president in April 2009. Butler would call this a state of being withdrawn, or *entzogen*, but not a 'cancellation' (1997: 176). While Butler talks of reflexive turns it appears that these turns are 180 degree, or even 360 degree turns. In other words, using Freud for instance, she talks about the turn from love to hate. This takes us back into a dichotomous binary opposition, for it does not allow for nuance. In this sense, then, I offer a more nuanced theoretical perspective in speaking of 'half turns'.

When Zapiro did not ignore the labelling and the injunctions against him but took them up with the HRC. It could be 'misrecognition', a refusal to accept the totalised identity conferred on him. I argue that it could be conceived as a 'half-turn' because he did not proceed 'cheerfully' with his cartoons, but acknowledged the interpellations (or labellings and attempted subjections) without accepting them. He tried to clear his name. At the same time he refused identification or misrecognition, hence my concept of the half-turn that allows for a more nuanced position. Interpellation is a social demand, a symbolic injunction, a performative effort through language, but there is always the risk of misrecognition – you could turn away and pretend you have not heard. Interpellation, Butler pointed out, can also be a social category. 'Black woman', for example, can be an insult or an affirmation, depending on the context. Schoeman intended to insult Woods by hailing him a communist during apartheid years, but hailing the former SACP leaders Chris Hani and Joe Slovo as communists was, in effect, hailing them as heroes.

In the context of post-apartheid South Africa, the labelling of Zapiro can be seen as a foreclosure as well as a totalising reduction and essentialising of his identity, but he would not accept or recognise this interpellation of himself as enemy and right winger, and nor would members of the public. The aim of the injunction was to rein him in. Zapiro's insistence on his rights as cartoonist in a democracy reveals a clear understanding of the radical nature of democracy as open-ended and full of antagonisms. Zapiro is an example of a social agonist and a legitimate adversary.

Ultimately, the courts will decide whether Zuma's rights to dignity were injured to the extent that suing over the Lady Justice cartoon is warranted. In pursuit of the lawsuit, Zuma's lawyers seem to be emphasising dignity in the Constitution, which is in concert with the discourse for a media appeals tribunal where the argument is that journalism is shoddy and sensationalist and has little concern for rights to dignity and equality. A trial date has been set for October 2012 and the case will heard in the South Gauteng High Court. The amount was reduced to R5 million. The case of Zapiro shows that freedom of expression cannot exist without democracy, and democracy cannot exist without freedom of expression. It shows that this was a fight internal to democracy itself but the president's and the ANC's attempts to create homogeneity and unnatural unity by shutting down dissenting spaces, such as a cartoonist's and a newspaper's freedom, render democracy fragile.

NOTES

1   Jonathan Shapiro, in an interview, 22 July 2009.

2   Ambivalence is a psychoanalytical concept explained by Freud as simultaneous love and hate of the same object. Ambivalence is also a pre-condition for melancholia together with the loss of an object, but this object can also be an abstraction or ideal, for example, liberty (see Butler 1997: 173-189).

3   In the introduction to *The Archaeology of Knowledge* Foucault famously said, in describing changing subjectivities, 'Do not ask me who I am and do not ask me to remain the same'. In other words, I am constantly changing, or reconstituting myself as subject (1969).

4   This was an interview which I conducted with Jonathan Shapiro by telephone on 22 July 2009.

5   The divided subject to Lacan is that subject which speaks, claiming primacy, and that subject of the unconscious, but is also not independent of linguistic structure (2008: 53-54).

6   Subsequent to this interview the SAHRC did make a finding, which was in Zapiro's favour. It found that his cartoon did not constitute hate speech (see *Mail & Guardian*: 25 June-1 July 2010).

7   But of course there was a change of subjectivities when Zapiro removed the showerhead later, only to re-install it.

8   Zapiro sent me a copy of this letter to the SAHRC in September 2009.

6.

Social fantasy: the ANC's gaze and the media appeals tribunal

We are aware that every Thursday night a group of journalists ... decide what stories they will go into. This is very clear when we do our analysis. What we see is a pack approach with a story that breaks in the *Saturday Star*, then is repeated in *Business Day* with a slightly different angle, and then in *The Citizen* with a ... slightly new perspective.[1]

'The gaze' is part of the 'social fantasy', 'a point at which the very frame (of my view) is already inscribed in the "content" of the picture viewed' (Žižek 1989: 105-127). Fantasy is the way antagonistic fissure is masked. Psychoanalytical Žižekean ontology is used in this chapter to deconstruct the ANC's gaze on the media.

In 2008, Jessie Duarte was one of the most hostile people in the ANC towards the media. The quotation here, opening this chapter, highlights her 'gaze' – inaccurate and fantasmic – on journalists and how she perceived the profession to operate. This chapter will elucidate the concepts of ideology and social fantasy, then the concept of the gaze, before it deconstructs the ANC's discourse through the words of the first three post-apartheid presidents, Nelson Mandela, Thabo Mbeki and Jacob Zuma; the ANC 'Letters from the President'; ANC online contributions to the public about the media; and the national spokespeople for the ruling party, Duarte in 2008 and Jackson Mthembu in 2010. This chapter focuses strongly on Mandela, and in the next two chapters there are specific case studies featuring Mbeki and Zuma respectively. The chapter discusses the proposal, put forward at the ANC's policy conference in Polokwane in December 2007, to investigate the possibility of a media appeals tribunal, the ostensible reasons for which were a lack of transformation and diversity in the media, that the self-regulatory mechanism was inadequate to curb 'the excesses' of the media that was a law unto itself, and there were many mistakes in the shabby journalism produced in the country. But I believe there was more to this than meets the eye.

In psychoanalysis, individuals are always split subjects (Lacan 2008; Laclau 1996; Žižek 1989). There is a split between what they consciously know and do, and what they unconsciously know and do. Fantasy is unconscious as in 'for they know not what they do', but Žižek suggests a more conscious position and goes further to say 'they know but they are doing it anyway' (2004).[2] I argue that the ANC is aware of what it is doing.[3] We do not live in a post-ideological world, where there is no longer a left or right, and Mouffe argues this too (2005: 1-16). Everything – language, text, and action – is ideological. Fantasy does not mean something that is opposed to reality. Quite the reverse. Fantasy is what structures what we call reality. It is the means whereby the psyche fixes its relation to enjoyment (Kay 2003: 163). The subject is already caught by some secret supposed to be in 'the other' and this is fantasy: Duarte is caught in her fantasy of the media as 'the big other' intent on plotting and planning against the ANC. In this sense, then, ideology and fantasy work together. Fantasy is the support that gives consistency to what we call reality. It is not an illusion, nor is it an escape from reality. It supports reality. So, for Duarte the media really is conspiring to undermine the ANC. She is creating a social fantasy of the media and, in so doing, is merely reaffirming the ANC's beliefs that require a particular expression of, or essence of, society that reflects its position on political unity. Its dogmatism on unity requires that the media postulates a similar dogmatic position or else suffers the consequences of being constructed as the antagonistic other. This is legitimised by the ANC's fantasy of a media conspiracy.

From what perspective was Duarte gazing at the world of journalists when she construed them as a unitary group, sitting together and collaborating on their next stories, despite coming from various newspapers? (From personal experience as a journalist, I know that groups do indeed often socialise over drinks but they are very cautious about letting on what stories they are working on, let alone collaborating on different angles with others from different newspapers – it is quite unheard of for journalists to share stories and let slip what they are working on. In fact, it's quite a comical thought.) However, where Duarte is correct is that when a story is broken in a newspaper, other newspapers try to get new perspectives on the same story and so keep it 'alive' – or 'run with it', to use the industry jargon. In other words, news makes news, although you can't merely repeat another newspaper's story, you have to find something new to say about the same thing or 'dig deeper'. Still, if you had to ask any journalist in South Africa whether they all get together to discuss what stories they will break in the week to come, and to share ideas and angles, they would be both bemused and amused. What we witness is Duarte's social fantasy, a fantasy that alters and influences perceptions of reality. Žižek describes this fostering of the delusion that there is always something out there pulling the strings, a conspiracy theory, in *The Ticklish Subject* (2000a: 362).

The value of a conspiracy theory is that it can account for all sorts of things, weapons of mass destruction or terrorists, all fostering the delusion of something 'out there'. In using the term 'pack approach', Duarte was seeing the media as a monolithic bloc. There is an indivisible remainder in her discourse, an excess and a paranoid construction of the media as a conspiracy. It could be argued that her words represent the extreme, the worst possible case put forward for the ANC's argument against the media. Is this so? My answer to this is 'yes and no'. In its stupid vulgarity, perhaps, this is an extreme example of how to understand the ANC's gaze on the media, but if one compares Duarte's views to those of Mandela, Mbeki and Zuma, we see versions of the same thing, articulated with varying degrees of elegance. Mandela wagged his finger at the editors saying he was unhappy with their lack of support for the transformation project; Mbeki was more vitriolic but did not attempt any interference in its independence. Motlanthe, whose brief stewardship as interim president was treated the most unfairly by the media, was the least confrontational. It was Zuma who took legal action against the media, and under whose leadership the ANC has been most threatening. In Zuma's discourse, as we will see, his words can be ambiguous but it is in terms of his legal and legislative actions, including his support for a media appeals tribunal in 2010, that the ANC has wreaked greater damage to media freedom and the idea of an open democracy. However, the ANC itself is not a unified subject. There are in effect many different 'ANCs'. There was the ANC pre-Polokwane and post-Polokwane. The ANC headed by Thabo Mbeki before December 2007 was the ANC of the patriotic bourgeoisie. The faction of the ANC which ousted Mbeki could be called the left-leaning faction headed by Cosatu, the SACP and the ANC Youth League. It is said that the ANC is now de-centred with no fixed point ideologically or in its programmatic action. In Chapter Two, the shifts in ANC media policy were discussed using the arguments of Ruth Tomaselli (1994) about the 'militants' and 'pragmatists'. In Zuma's ANC-led government of 2010 there were fundamental splits and fights over economic direction between the economic development minister, Ebrahim Patel, who hails from a trade union background, and the finance minister, Pravin Gordhan, who was the former South African Revenue

Service commissioner (see *Sunday Independent*: 'Ministers fight over economic direction': 25 July 2010).

There was the ANC of Mandela, the era of the rainbow nation and national reconciliation; there was the ANC of Mbeki, the era of secrecy and fear where all enemies were banished from the political mainstream; then there is the era of Zuma, where the ANC is at its most fractious. Among others, the division in 2012 was over 'the second transition'.

The gaze of the three presidents on the media

Nelson Mandela

At an address to the International Press Institute congress on 14 February 1994, Mandela said:

> A critical, independent and investigative press is the lifeblood of any democracy. The press must be free from state interference. It must have the economic strength to stand up to the blandishments of government officials. It must have sufficient independence from vested interests to be bold and inquiring without fear or favour. It must enjoy the protection of the constitution, so that it can protect our rights as citizens. It is only such a free press that can temper the appetite of any government to amass power at the expense of the citizen. It is only such a free press that can be the vigilant watchdog of the public interest against the temptation on the part of those who wield it to abuse that power. It is only such a free press that can have the capacity to relentlessly expose excesses and corruption on the part of government, state officials and other institutions that hold power in society. I have often said that the media are a mirror through which we can see ourselves as others perceive us, warts, blemishes and all. The African National Congress has nothing to fear from criticism. I can promise you, we will not wilt under close scrutiny. It is our considered view that such criticism can only help us to grow, by calling attention to those of our actions and omissions which do not measure up to our people's expectations and the democratic values to which we subscribe (Mandela 1994).

Mandela adopts here an outstandingly progressive view of the role of the media in a democracy. Within a relatively short time, however, his passionate attachment to the ANC blinds him to the democratic values he expressed in 1994. Mandela displayed ambivalence about the media when he addressed editors of newspapers a mere twenty-four months after this speech. But the ANC's view of the media did not begin with Mandela in 1994. The ANC established a Media Charter as early as 1991 and, it must be noted, there was no unitary view to start with (Tomaselli 1994). The 'militants' argued for more control of the media, while the 'pragmatists' advocated independent control for broadcast media and self-regulation for the newspaper industry. It appears as though, in the context of global media liberalisation the pragmatists won the day.

Mandela's social fantasy: black journalists are puppets

Notwithstanding Mandela's words of February 1994, which show exemplary notions of press independence in the new South Africa, in November 1996 he sought a more loyal contingent of journalists and accused the media of having a hidden agenda and being part of a conspiracy. During the apartheid era, the ANC's view of the media had been equally critical: that because the media did not adequately challenge the status quo it essentially supported apartheid. That this view did not change after the inception of the new democratic order is clear from meetings that Mandela held with Sanef. The first meeting took place on 1 November 1996 and was attended by Brian Pottinger (editor, *Sunday Times*), Anton Harber (editor, *Mail & Guardian*), Thami Mazwai (Sanef chairperson), Raymond Louw (editor, *Southern Africa Report*), Moegsien Williams (editor, *Cape Times*), Judy Sandison (editor, *Radio News*, KwaZulu-Natal) and Shaun Johnson (editor, *Cape Argus*). The discussions were reported in *Rhodes Journalism Review* No.13, 1996 and No.15, 1997. The following is an extract from an article: 'Media on the Menu' which showed Mandela's ambivalence about media freedom.

> We would like an independent ... press which can criticise freely and without fear – and be prepared if we criticise it. The press ... (and) the government ... have a joint responsibility to address the problems in the country ...There is a perception among the population that the mass media is controlled by a minority section of the population... Even those who have committed themselves to democratic values ... cannot accurately portray the aspirations of the majority because they do not live among them ... There is an attempt from traditionally white organisations ... to resist transformation. Some of the newspapers that used to support the apartheid regime ... give unqualified support for transformation. Generally speaking, though, I seem to feel that the conservative press is trying to preserve ... the status quo ... Because of this some

senior black journalists are not writing for their audiences, but ...
believe the only way to get ahead is to join a campaign against transformation (Mandela, cited in *Rhodes Journalism Review* 1996).

There are three points to note here. The first point is that while there appeared
to be an air of openness in his support for a free press, he criticised the press for
not supporting transformation in the way he understood it. And, while criticism goes both ways, the press was not reflecting the views of the majority. It
was also clear, from the sweeping statement he made that he felt there was a
'campaign against transformation', and that he desired unity with the press. The
way in which he described the role of the press must also be highlighted: he saw
a 'joint responsibility' of the press and the government to address the problems
in the country, although how the press was meant to solve problems of housing
delivery, crime, unemployment and corruption was not clear. Mia Swart, an
associate professor at the Wits Law Clinic, understood this when she wrote:
'The current levels of poverty and the widening gap between the haves and the
have nots in this country has nothing to do with the media. The responsibility
for the current high levels of poverty and unemployment can be placed squarely
on the shoulders of the ruling elite' (*Mail & Guardian*: 20-26 August 2010).

The second point is that Mandela asserted that the press was controlled by
a minority which 'was unacceptable in our vision'. What this reflects is an illogical assumption that if the press were controlled by the majority, this would
necessarily solve the problem as the ANC experienced it. The third point, and
arguably the most disturbing, was his reference to black journalists writing
not for their audiences but to 'get ahead' (meaning to gain promotion), and
the implication was that they were kowtowing to their white bosses. Race was
essentialised in Mandela's discourse. At that first meeting between Sanef and
Mandela, none of the editors present challenged Mandela on his views and
understanding of the role of the media in a democracy.

At the next meeting, in June 1997, there was an outright vitriolic attack on the
media. Writing in 2010, the group political editor of Independent Newspapers,
Moshoeshoe Monare reflected on the second meeting in 1997, suggesting that
the ANC had never trusted the mainstream press. He pointed out that the first
ANC leader to articulate the view that the media had set itself up as a fierce
opponent to the ANC was Nelson Mandela (*Sunday Independent*: 22 August
2010). In his opening speech to the ruling party's 50th National Conference in
Mafikeng, Mandela said:

> In a manner akin to what the National Party is doing in its sphere, this
> media exploits the dominant positions it achieved as a result of the

apartheid's system, to campaign against both real change and the real agents of change, as represented by our movement, led by the ANC … When it speaks against us, this represents freedom of thought, speech and the press – which the world must applaud … When we exercise our own right to freedom of thought and speech to criticise it for its failings, this represents an attempt to suppress the freedom of the press – for which the world would punish us.

The second meeting between Mandela and Sanef, in June 1997, was tense. In an article entitled 'Tough Talk from the President' (*Rhodes Journalism Review* 1997), Mandela suggested that black journalists were beholden to white editors, they had to 'earn a living' and thus were unable to reflect the aspirations of the majority. In this instance, Brian Pottinger did not hold back, and responded that this 'was insulting' to his black colleagues. The direct challenge to Mandela's racialised interpellation was a hopeful moment for democracy. Others, however, made half turns towards the voice of power, and some made full turns. An extract of the interchange in the *Rhodes Journalism Review* between Mandela and Pottinger follows:

> **Mandela:** There is no point in beating about the bush with problems. Whatever measures have been taken, the truth is that the media is still in control of whites, conservative whites, who are unable to reflect the aspirations of the majority … I was asked in Harare why black journalists are so hostile, especially to Zimbabwe and President Mugabe. … We do not have black journalists saying what they would like to say. They have to earn a living. While there are a few exceptional journalists, many like to please their white editors.

> **Pottinger responded:** It is insulting to my black colleagues to suggest that they kowtow to me …

> **Mandela:** The last time we met, I said how you had not behaved in the manner I expect of you. I invited you and gave you information. You thanked me. In the next editorial you made a statement accusing the ANC of dishonesty. If a journalist and a paper like the *Sunday Times* can accuse an organisation like ours of dishonesty, you destroy a relationship … We are dealing with a trend. The real problem is not black journalists, but conservative white journalists who are able to instruct their colleagues under them … You don't publish our articles. You don't want us to reply to your campaign.

Mandela's assumptions were that there was a campaign by the media against the ANC. The problem was the 'conservative white journalists' rather than the black journalists, who were seen as subjects without agency. Mandela's outlook could not envisage a more open critical journalism in a democracy. Instead, he caricatured the relationship of black to white journalists in apartheid-like terms. Moreover, in a predictable social fantasy tied to the logic of nationalist ideology, any criticism by the media of 'the liberation movement' was intolerable, as they were controlled by white bosses whereas the media should be reflecting the aspirations of the majority. As leader of the former liberation movement, he had the authority to interpellate in terms of the social fantasy that the ANC was the moral barometer, while the press was stepping out of line by 'accusing an organisation like ours of dishonesty'. In this social fantasy the ANC cannot be dishonest. The legitimate interpellating voice of moral authority speaks: 'The last time we met, I said how you had not behaved in the manner I expect of you'. This is a social injunction, in the Althusserian sense, and the aim is to bring the subject into line through a social demand. Hegemony in democratic politics is formed through exclusions (as seen in Mandela's exclusion from the democratic project of white editors). These exclusions return to haunt the politics based upon their absence. This haunting, in South Africa, returned in the form of black editors, who were no less critical than white editors of the shenanigans of the powerful.

Half-turns to Mandela's interpellation: the editors' reactions

Subjection is paradoxical, according to Butler (1997), a point that is central to this book. The paradox that Butler refers to is a complex idea which signifies the dominance by a power external to oneself. Yet one's formation as a subject is also dependent upon that very power. Butler's theory is that the figure of the psyche 'turns' against itself. Deploying Foucault, Althusser, Hegel, Nietzsche and Freud, she discusses subjections and asks why it happens. Is it about guilt, is it conscience, is it recognition of the interpellating name, or is it a love of the shackles – as in passionate attachments – to norms of the past which oppress? The following extracts showed the editors' reactions to the social injunctions that came from the ANC leaders (*Rhodes Journalism Review* 1997). Their views were diverse and did not show unity on the basis of race or on the basis of their profession. Some turned fully towards the voice of power, some made half turns and some made no turns at all, turning their backs on the injunctions, preferring to misrecognise the ideological hailing.

If you as president speak about senior black journalists being under the command of white editors, this has a demoralising effect on these journalists, and on the whole community (John Battersby).

To suggest malevolence is not a fair reflection (Jim Jones).

As far as the press is concerned, it is sad to see that there is generally a negative tone ... So when Mandela gets impatient in dealing with editors of newspapers that reflect this negativity, I strongly identify with him (Mike Tissong, night editor of the *Sowetan*).

Right now, black journalists are being questioned about their commitment to press freedom simply because the word patriotism features in their vocabulary. Because whites do not feel the same degree of loyalty to the new order, our bona fides are being questioned (Thami Mazwai).

Much of the disagreement reduced things to race in an almost simplistic way. It is not as if when you resolve the racial issue you resolve the problem of the press and its relation to government (Mike Siluma, editor of the *Sowetan*).

I was amazed at the anger and venom with which he raised his criticism ... By reacting the way he did, he also opens himself up to criticism that he is trying to manipulate the media through intimidation (and I challenge any editor who attended the meeting to tell me they did not feel intimidated) (Ryland Fisher, editor of the *Cape Times*).

I was surprised. Never did I expect President Mandela to react the way he did. I would have thought that we'd moved away from the old days when press bashing was a must for the National Party heads of state (Dennis Cruywagen).

Antagonism towards the media is certainly not restricted to the president. His views are shared by others in the cabinet, notably Deputy President Thabo Mbeki ... What about the question of black journalists wanting to please their white bosses? I have certainly not encountered this at Independent Newspapers KZN (Dennis Pather).

Battersby's response, that it had a 'demoralising effect on journalists', does not constitute any turn at all, as it does not respond directly to the issue at hand.

Jones's comment that Mandela's implying 'malevolence' was unfair was also not a turn either way, but it was a criticism of Mandela. Tissong's reaction to the hailing was to 'strongly identify' with Mandela – a complete turning against one's profession and towards the ideological interpellation. Mazwai's comment is one of the most interesting, where he reflects passionate attachment to an atavistic idea of race as the Master-Signifier, even under the new democratic order. His comment that 'we as black journalists are suffering because whites in the profession do not have the same amount of patriotism to the country' is a complete 360 degree turn towards the voice of power. Siluma, on the other hand, saw Mandela's interjection as ideological when he said that this was about essentialising race, and it was 'simplistic'. Fisher made no turn and, while admitting to being intimidated, he pointed out the obvious: that Mandela could be accused of trying to 'manipulate' the media. Cruywagen did not make a turn, but he too pointed out the obvious: that this had echoes of the National Party's interpellations of the media. Pather's statement that he had not encountered black journalists wanting to please their white bosses at Independent Newspapers corroborates my own experience, having worked at the same group, at *The Star* newspaper as a features writer in the mid to late 1990s. In fact, having worked at most of the newspaper houses in the country since 1990, I have not encountered any black journalist, including myself, wanting to please white bosses. It had never entered my mind to do so either.

Incidentally, Fisher, Tissong, Mazwai, Cruywagen and Pather are all black. They all differed in their reactions to Mandela's interpellation. Three out of five did not accept the hailings and did not turn towards the voice of power, or turn against themselves or their profession. Both Tissong and Mazwai, however, did make that turn. Siluma hit the nail on the head when he commented that the views about race were simplistic.

They were particularly so in 2008, when Duarte made her comments about a conspiracy in the media. By then, the colour of editors and owners had changed, and more than fifty per cent were black; the press remained critical and the ANC remained unhappy about the media's criticisms. As Fisher had pointed out, the ANCs response to criticism was 'manipulation' and 'intimidation'. For Butler, this would amount to subjectivisation. The outcome was a process of establishing the media as 'other', and signalled that if you were not with 'us' (the ANC), then you were not only the 'other', but an enemy rather than a legitimate adversary. As Raymond Louw, editor of the *Southern Africa Report*, observed about Mandela's interjections: 'There is an air of the schoolmaster bringing pupils to heel in the manner in which he uses the term "to correct" them'.

For Mandela 'the people' existed as one united whole, and the people's unique representative was the ANC. There are four points to be made here.

First, Mandela desired more unity with the media, meaning an uncritical and more favourable press. Second, he conflated the ANC's transformation project with the project of the media, shown in his words that 'we have a joint responsibility to address the problems in the country' (a serious misunderstanding of the role of the media). Third, there was a surplus attached to the media, meaning that there were extra qualities attached to it, for example that there was an agenda or conspiracy against transformation and the ANC. Fourth, the ANC believed that the media was one entity with a 'pack approach' to the ANC.

Thabo Mbeki's gaze on the media (1999-2009)

President Thabo Mbeki 'enjoyed' a particularly acrimonious relationship with the media and, like Mandela, would have preferred a more sycophantic press, one that was in unity with the ANC. In the biography of Mbeki by Mark Gevisser it was particularly enlightening to track the second democratic president's relationship with the media. 'There was but the slimmest folder of negative references to Mbeki prior to 1994', was how Gevisser described the media's view of Mbeki (2007: 643). In fact, he observed, that when Mbeki came to power in 1994, it was with the *Mail & Guardian*'s goodwill – and the *Mail & Guardian*, one of the fiercest critics of the apartheid regime, had kept up its fierce watchdog role over public figures after 1994. The then editor of the paper, Anton Harber, wrote that Mbeki was a 'suave and experienced diplomat' and a 'moderator and conciliator'. The same newspaper was later to become Mbeki's strongest detractor when, in April 2001, a headline screamed: 'Is this man fit to rule?' Gevisser cited Mbeki's 'first volley against the press' at the Cape Town Press Club when he accused the media of 'harbouring a tendency to look for crises and to look for faults and mistakes'. By 1995, Gevisser observed, Mbeki was branding any criticism of the ANC as racist.

Like Mandela before him,[4] Mbeki also made it clear what he expected of black journalists at an address to the FBJ when he told them to 'roll up your sleeves and stop whinging like a whitey.' From this point onwards, Gevisser commented, journalists accused Mbeki of wanting a sweetheart press, adding that even Mbeki admirers such as *The Star* newspaper's political editor at the time, Kaiser Nyatsumba, noted that Mbeki's views were a sign of 'over-arching ... paranoia'. The trend to paranoia, attempted subjectivisation and interpellation of the media continued throughout Mbeki's presidency. To counteract the effects of the hostile media, in 2001 Mbeki began something new in the ANC – writing online letters to the public. The rationale for this was that the organisation felt it did not have a voice. The following extract from the very first letter, 'Welcome to *ANC Today*', makes clear that the main reason for this online discourse with the public was that the ANC had 'no representation whatsoever in the mass media'.

> First of all I would like to congratulate the Communications Unit on its decision to publish *ANC Today*. It is of critical importance that the ANC develop its own vehicles to communicate news, information and views to as many people as possible, at home and abroad. Clearly, the Internet provides an added possibility to achieve this objective … Historically, the national and political constituency represented by the ANC has had very few and limited mass media throughout the 90 years of its existence. During this period, the commercial newspaper and magazine press representing the views, values and interests of the white minority has dominated the field of the mass media. This situation has changed only marginally in the period since we obtained our liberation in 1994 … We are faced with the virtually unique situation that, among the democracies, the overwhelming dominant tendency in South African politics, represented by the ANC, has no representation whatsoever in the mass media … With no access to its own media, this majority has had to depend on other means to equip itself with information and views to enable it to reach its own conclusions about important national and international matters … The world of ideas is also a world of struggle. *ANC Today* must be a combatant for the truth, for the liberation of the minds of our people, for the eradication of the colonial and apartheid legacy, for democracy, non-racism, non-sexism, prosperity and progress (*ANC Today*: 26 January-1 February 2001).

For Mbeki, as for Mandela, the mass media reflected white minority views and was unsupportive of the ANC; therefore he had a duty to communicate with everyone so that the majority's views could be heard. The logic appeared to be that if you were not supportive of the party, you were unsupportive of the national transformation project. It seemed that Mbeki regarded the airing of different ideas on transformation as a threat.

The following sentence from the online letter, on how unity of the nation can be achieved, implied that there was only one view of transformation and all of society had to have the same opinion on change: 'The only way this will happen is if we proceed from common positions about the nature of the problems our country faces'. It was a dogmatic position that placed political unity above all. This idea was also what Mouffe argued against in her analysis of Schmitt (1999: 5). In placing political unity above all else, she said, the space for pluralism, and therefore more tolerance in a democracy, was closed off. In this book, I argue that democracy is a floating signifier, in which identity should never be essentialised, and that 'common positions' are not possible in a democracy which supports pluralism. Mbeki's pattern of discourse on the media followed the same trajectory throughout the decade of his presidency, but it started in his deputy presidency.

The ANC, during Mbeki's presidency, also vilified the media as the following extracts show.

> An article that appeared in the local media this week, originating from the Agence France Presse (AFP) news agency and distributed by the South African Press Association (SAPA), revives the wearily familiar theme of the supposed decline of popular support for the ANC … With its former chief whip in prison, his successor accused of sexual harassment and deputy president under a cloud after his financial advisor was jailed, the party which has dominated power since the end of apartheid appears intent on dragging itself through the mud on a weekly basis … where do so many media institutions get their stories about South Africans' attitudes to the ANC? (*ANC Today*: 24-30 November 2006).

Here, the ANC constructs the media as one that imagines stories: 'Where do these media institutions get their views from?' The extracts below clearly spell out what the ANC's expectations of the press were.

> In this regard the opponents of our democratic revolution, who lack a significant political base among the masses of our people, have sought to use the domestic and international media as one of their principal offensive instruments, to turn it into an organised formation opposed to the national democratic revolution and its vanguard movement. Because of this objective reality, which is not of our making, this short series will, in part, rely on what some in the media say … Whatever the intentions of the authors of these articles, which we do not know and on which we cannot comment, obviously what the journal would achieve, first because of its cover page, would be to tell the story that once again, and as expected, yet another African country, South Africa, was sliding towards the dismal failure that necessarily characterises the African continent! (*ANC Today*: 24-30 August 2007).

Here the media is spoken of in war-like terminology, as an 'organised formation' that was an 'offensive' against the National Democratic Revolution. The central question for the media, according to the ANC, was whether 'our democracy will survive'. One way to describe this response from the ANC was that it was paranoid and defensive. Its hysteria was beginning to build. The media, the letter said, thrived on the negative and downplayed the positive. This was a theme, trend and pattern that persisted and dominated the nature of the ruling party's discourse. The ANC during the Mbeki administration was extremely disappointed in the media and how it portrayed the country. During Mbeki's era the African Renaissance was a theme around which he portrayed his administration. It was meant to be an era of hope for post-colonialism, and so for this reason criticisms of the media seemed to be deeply embedded in his attachment to race oppression. Mbeki was 'recalled' as president of the ANC by the party's National Executive Council on 19 September 2008, in an 'effort to heal and unite the ANC' according to the ANC general secretary, Gwede Mantashe (*The Weekender*: 20-21 September 2008). The recall occurred directly after Pietermaritzburg high court judge Chris Nicholson's ruling which implicated Mbeki in a probable conspiracy against Zuma. By the time of the recall, and the next day's announcement by Mbeki (20 September 2008) that he had resigned, Zuma had the support of the ANC Youth League, Cosatu and the SACP, while ANC branch and regional structures were split in their support between Mbeki and Zuma. Deputy President Kgalema Motlanthe served the country as an interim president until Zuma was officially inaugurated as president in April 2009.

Motlanthe: held back

Motlanthe hardly commented on the media, save for on one occasion (known to me). In a panel discussion at the International Media Forum South Africa in May 2008, held in Johannesburg, he told international and local journalists that the ANC was as committed to press freedom as it had been sixteen years previously. He then quoted the ANC's policy before it assumed power:

> South Africa has been a closed society, with many restrictions on the flow of information. Legislation ... the structure of media ownership, of media resources, skills ... have undermined the access of information for the majority of the population. The ANC believes that the transition to democracy in South Africa entails a movement from a closed society into one based on a free flow of information and a culture of open debate.

Motlanthe's discourse did not have the same ring to it as Mandela's or Mbeki's. Nor was he against the media in any injunction or ideological interpellation.

That there was no conspiracy theory or vitriol from Motlanthe is ironic because, in fact, he himself was a victim of the media either collaborating with sections of the ANC who wanted Motlanthe discredited or more likely, being careless about not checking sources when the *Sunday Independent* published a story under the headline 'All the President's Women' about Motlanthe's many lovers, one of whom was supposed to have been pregnant with his child (*Sunday Independent*: 25 January 2009). The source, the pregnant woman, later retracted the story in February 2009, and was found to be a liar. The newspaper group apologised to the interim president and he graciously accepted the apology without suing. In fact the newspaper's apology was small and tucked away compared to the front splash that the front-page untrue story was given. Motlanthe downplayed the disgraceful newspaper saga and said it was a matter for the Press Council and Sanef to pursue.

Zuma's discourse on the media

Zuma was elected president of the ANC at the 52nd ANC policy conference in Polokwane in December 2007, at which Mbeki was axed in what could be called a bloodless coup. The debate on the possibility of a media appeals tribunal to regulate the independent media culminated at the ANC's NGC meeting in September 2010 when there were more strident calls for a tribunal and a resolution was passed that Parliament should investigate its implementation (see Appendix 2 for the wording of the resolution). However, the following statement by the ANC, issued a month after the Polokwane conference in December 2007, already contains references to a media appeals tribunal.

> The Lekgotla confirmed that the ANC must intensify its engagement with all sectors to promote the transformation of the media to reflect the diversity, interests and perspectives of South African society; and to facilitate the free flow of ideas and information, with due respect to the rights and dignity of all South Africans ... Particular attention needs to be paid to the growth and development of a sustainable media sector. The meeting called for the development of a broad-based black economic empowerment charter for the print media industry ... The NEC Communications sub-committee will soon set up a task team to investigate the establishment of a media appeals tribunal, which would strengthen and complement and support existing institutions (ANC NEC: 20 January 2008).

This extract elucidates a somewhat vague rationale for more regulation, including a tribunal, but no details were spelled out as to what the specific mandate of the task team to 'investigate' the setting up of a tribunal would be, or how it would be constituted. Then, there were contradictions in the ANC's statements. In one letter it stated that free flow of ideas and information would be facilitated, while at the same time it proposed further regulation in the form of a charter and a tribunal. Both these kinds of regulations, constitutional law experts were quick to point out, would restrict a free flow of information and could be unconstitutional. For instance, the chief justice of the Constitutional Court, Pius Langa, stated in a speech at the Durban University of Technology: 'The courts do not want a media that is uncritical and overly respectful' (*The Star*: 31 March 2008). Both the judiciary and the media are of critical importance to the country because they play a central role in keeping our government in check and holding it accountable for the exercise of its mighty powers: 'The independence of the judiciary and freedom of expression are two pillars of an open and democratic society'.

The following is an extract from a long January 2008 letter from President Jacob Zuma, 'The Voice of the ANC Must be Heard':

> ... Every day brings fresh instances of a media that, in general terms, is politically and ideologically out of sync with the society in which it exists ... The media, viewed in its totality, should be as diverse as the society which it serves and reflects. This is clearly not the case in South Africa today. At times, the media functions as if they are an opposition party ... The freedom of the South African media is today undermined not by the state, but by various tendencies that arise from the commercial imperatives that drive the media. The concentration of ownership, particularly in the print sector, has a particularly restrictive effect on the freedom of the media. The process of consolidation and the drive to cut costs through, among other things, rationalisation of newsgathering operations, leads to homogenisation of content (*ANC Today*: 18-24 January 2008).

Zuma's view is that the media is not diverse and that the threat to press freedom is not from the political arena and the state but from commercial imperatives. However, it is argued here – analysing his discourse from a postmodernist, radical democracy and psychoanalytical framework – that Zuma, like Mandela and Mbeki, clearly dreams of unity or reconciliation with the media, although unlike Mandela and Mbeki he has not essentialised the floating signifier, race. How could the media be 'ideologically out of sync with a society', as though society was one? This was precisely what Mouffe developed in her thesis: there can be no unified society as such because of society's fractured, plural and diverse nature. Hence, 'the social' rather than 'society'. You can have a media, however, which reflects many diverse voices, and this is what the media should be striving towards. But the hidden text here is that Zuma seemed to be arguing for a media ideologically in sync with the ANC as the true representatives of 'the people'. Quite the reverse of diversity, ironically. After all, if the ANC is the true and only representative of 'the People' and 'the People' support the ANC, and the media is critical of the ANC, therefore the media is out of sync with 'the People'. It is a social fantasy. 'At times, the media function as if they are an opposition party.' Here, Zuma was referring to the media as a totality. In effect, this inaccuracy reflected the social fantasy, as neither the media as a whole, nor society 'as a whole' exist. Both are diverse, fluid and non-fixed.

In the end, Zuma's conclusion was that the 'commercial interests' of the media were to blame for homogenisation of content, and in the end newspapers were out of sync ideologically with 'the people'. The discourses of Mandela, Mbeki and Zuma were distinctive examples of how attempts are made to stabilise the ruling party's identity by creating 'the other', that is 'the media', as outsiders in a democracy and as antagonists rather than legitimate adversaries. Zuma was the first ANC president to call for a media appeals tribunal. Such a measure would signify the most repressive measure ever taken against the media, either during apartheid or in the democratic era in South Africa.

The media appeals tribunal

A new set of journalists and editors in 2008 were acutely aware of the ideological social fantasy of the ANC in wanting more regulation. In much the same vein as Žižek the media seek 'Che Vuoi', translated not so much as 'what do you want' but rather as 'what's really bugging you?' (1989: 87-128). What the interviews below reveal is that the journalists saw that a series of floating signifiers were quilted into the one Master-Signifier, 'transformation', which in the quilting signification meant loyalty to the ruling party. Žižek wrote of democracy:

> In the last resort, the only way to describe 'democracy' is to say that it contains all political movements and organisations which legitimise themselves, designate themselves 'democratic': the only way to define 'Marxism' is to say that this term designates all movements and theories which legitimise themselves through reference to Marx, and so on.

What the interviews with editors suggest is that the ANC expects the media, in its reporting, to consign democracy and its legitimacy to the signifier 'ANC'. The editors consider this to be at odds with their profession and with democracy itself. This is what is really 'bugging' the ANC.

Reflecting on regulation and press freedom, the then *Sunday Times* columnist and opinion page editor, Fred Khumalo, observed that Duarte's comments regarding more regulation were reminiscent of the old regime in South Africa. The commemoration of Black Wednesday in 2008, he wrote, brought into sharp relief the reality that freedom of the press is a contested terrain, even under a democratic dispensation.

> Indeed it is true that with freedom comes responsibility. Media practitioners do need to ... publish with due consideration for ordinary citizens' right to privacy and dignity. At the same time, the South African public deserves the right to information. Duarte ... said unequivocally that she was not comfortable with the current situation in which the media is self regulatory ... one has to conclude that the ANC wants a government tribunal vetting and passing judgment on media conduct ... It is indeed reminiscent of the 80s when, during the state of emergency, media organisations had to submit stories on violence to the then department of information for approval ... Once you interfere with the media's voice, you are effectively curtailing a necessary conversation between various sectors of our society. You are muzzling us. And that is the antithesis of the democratic values that lie at the heart of a nation we are building' (*Sunday Times*: 18 October 2008).

Drawing on the similarities between the new government and the old, Khumalo suggested that both had a vested interest in protecting themselves from stories that an independent media could and would tell.

Editors' gaze on a media appeals tribunal

I conducted the following interviews with editors, all of whom are black, over thirty-five years old, experienced, and have traversed the transition from apartheid. The interviews explore what 'turns' journalists made in the light of the ANC's desire to investigate a media appeals tribunal. The research question was: what is your view of the future independence of the media given the ANC's proposals for a media appeals tribunal? The most striking points to emerge from these interviews when they were conducted in 2008 were that most of the journalists felt that the ANC did not know how to implement a tribunal and therefore it was unlikely to happen; that should such a tribunal be instituted they would fight it at the Constitutional Court; and that the ANC was attempting closures of open spaces.

> There is a media boom here which is great; there is competition for readers and competition is good. The *M&G* today is more financially viable than it's ever been; that's because people are reading it. Today the *Sunday Times* has more black readers than white ... But the call for a tribunal is ominous and is an example of something the ANC has badly thought out. ... I don't think it will work; it will flounder, the same way that Essop Pahad said 'Let's pull advertising'; then didn't do it. The ANC is so divided; the new leadership itself is divided (Justice Malala: 23 January 2008).[5]

For Malala the future was unpredictable, showing indeterminacy in the unfolding democracy. Although he felt that the ANC had not thought through the media appeals tribunal enough and noted that the ANC was a divided organisation on this issue (as with many others), his discourse nevertheless shows concern about the possibility of a tribunal.

Rehana Rossouw also had doubts that such a tribunal could become a reality because it had not been thought through properly. Her doubts hinged on constitutional guarantees of press freedom.

> I don't think it will come to this. It is something that needs to be thought through to be established and they, the ANC, have not given it proper thought. ... I'm sceptical that such a thing as a tribunal can go through, given our Constitution that guarantees press freedom. The courts have consistently ruled within our legal framework that stipulates freedom of expression (Rehana Rossouw: 24 January 2008).[6]

Mondli Makhanya offered another reason as to why he believed that the Media appeals tribunal would not happen.

> I don't think that the tribunal will happen. It will present a terrible image of them. And if they try to do this, we will oppose them. We will go to the Constitutional Court with the matter (Mondli Makhanya: 24 January 2008).[7]

Hopewell Radebe went further than Malala, Rossouw and Makhanya in the sense that whether or not the issue was thought through, statutory regulation of the media was possible.

> Tribunals could happen. This will be fought by the editors' forum [Sanef]. Unfortunately journalists are not organised as they used to be. SAUJ does not exist any more, and Mwasa is almost non-existent. This, the tribunal issue, could be the thing that will bring journalists together. [Chief Justice of the Constitutional Court] Pius Langa has said that journalists must not wait for something to become a law before they fight it (Hopewell Radebe: 25 January 2008).[8]

Radebe made two salient points. He could see there was a possibility that it would happen and he had little faith in the profession's readiness for action. He speculated, optimistically, that should the media tribunal become more of a reality, it could be an impetus for a better-united journalist profession and more action (this action, to some degree, took place in 2010 when Sanef became actively involved in the Right2Know campaign which saw over 400 organisations and over 9 000 individuals sign up to oppose the Secrecy Bill). But by 2012, apathy ruled the day.

Similarly, Abdul Milazi, in the next interview, felt that agency on the part of journalists was the critical issue.

> It will all depend on the media itself, whether it lies down and plays dead or whether it stands up and fights the proposed controls. Embedded journalism has no future in any democracy. Freedoms need to be protected and governments cannot be trusted with that role. So the media will have to take up that role. But again the media also needs to be policed, but not by the government. An unchecked media can have similar outcomes as an unchecked government. The media also has stakeholders ... who have ... personal interests to promote. And that's the truth we cannot run away from (Abdul Milazi: 8 February 2008).[9]

For Milazi it would all depend on the media itself. He went further than the other journalists to observe and concede that the media industry should also gaze at itself and examine what interests it wished to promote.

The common thread in these responses was that the Constitution would protect the freedom to report without intimidation and that regulation in the form of a tribunal should be, and would be, fought. It should be noted however – and this was alluded to by Radebe – that organised once-active media lobby bodies were now dormant. Milazi's comments were salutary from two points of view. One was that the media should not believe it was a law unto itself, completely free to do as it pleased. The other was that it would depend on journalists' actions, or absence thereof. Milazi was arguing for a media that showed it was an important part of civil society and could and should exercise its agency. Butler's theory that subject formation takes place through a subject's turning towards the voice of authority, or making unpredictable turns, could be married with Milazi's view that what happened was contingent upon actors as agents of their own destinies.

Media experts, analysts and NGO players were, in 2008, less ambivalent than the editors about a media appeals tribunal. In fact, from the interviews below, it could be argued that they felt the tribunal could indeed happen. For the *Mail & Guardian* ombudsman, Franz Kruger, who has researched media tribunals across the world; for the media trainer and gender development activist in the media, Paula Fray; and for Tendayi Sithole of the FXI, a media appeals tribunal was far from unlikely in South Africa.[10] Kruger observed that while media appeals tribunals 'existed only at Polokwane', the ANC had not accepted what it meant to have a free and independent media and that 'it was not impossible tribunals could be instituted, and the ANC would couch it in terms of "development and transformation"'. Paula Fray concurred: 'The possibility of a media appeals tribunal exists. The warning signs are there. We should not be complacent about our democracy'. Tendayi Sithole, commented:

If the media becomes accountable to Parliament, that will compromise the independence of the media. The tribunal will be subject to executive abuse since Parliament is largely dominated by the ANC. Many events bear testimony to this – the arms deal, the SABC sagas, disbanding of the Scorpions. Not forgetting the fact that the print media and the ANC government are often at loggerheads in terms of their role in society and there are things that the government does not want the media to report on. The rhetoric of the ANC towards the media is often harsh and clearly shows intolerance as the media is also referred to as a 'liberal media' which is betraying the revolution. As such, the ANC would like a situation where the media is a mere lapdog that should blindly support the 'revolution'. Since there is no clear separation of the legislature and the executive, it is clear that the executive will bypass the legislature as in Mbeki's era. In sum, the institution of a media tribunal is hogwash, since the ANC is not clear how the body will work, but signs are clear that it wants to control the media.

In 2009 there was no evidence of the ANC's taking its December 2007 Polokwane conference proposal seriously. The idea seemed to have been in abeyance until preparation began for the ANC's NGC, which took place on 20-24 September 2010 in Durban. At the NGC the idea was reaffirmed.

The ANC's reasons for a media appeals tribunal: 2010

The ANC's main reasons for a media appeals tribunal include:

- the present self-regulation system does not work as it skews the decisions of the Press Council in favour of the media;
- there is insufficient protection given to those whose rights have been violated by the press;
- the Press Council is 'toothless' as it cannot levy fines and merely asks for apologies to be made; and when these are made they are insufficient in size and stature compared to the damaging article.

The ANC has also argued that independent regulation exists in broadcasting but has not resulted in censorship. Then, the retractions after mistakes have been hugely out of proportion to the mistake, and in less significant sections of the newspapers.

In its discussion paper *Media Transformation, Ownership and Diversity* (2010) the ANC provided the background to its renewed call for a tribunal. The paper said that at its 51st conference at Stellenbosch on 16-20 December 2002, the ANC had called for 'transformation' of the media: 'the ANC reaffirmed the importance of a free and diverse media to the democratic process and to the task of fundamental transformation'. The paper made the following points:

- It stated that its objective was 'to vigorously communicate the ANC's outlook and values (developmental state, collective rights, values of caring and sharing community, solidarity, *ubuntu*, non-sexism, working together) versus the current mainstream media's ideological outlook (neoliberalism, a weak and passive state, overemphasis on individual rights, market fundamentalism)'.
- 'The media needs to contribute towards the building of a new society and be accountable for its actions. Transformation in the media needs to target the entire value chain and investigate anti-competitive behaviour if any.'
- 'A cursory scan on the print media reveals an astonishing degree of dishonesty, lack of professional integrity and lack of independence.

Editorials distancing the paper from these acts and apologies which are never given due prominence and mostly which has to be forced through the press ombudsman are not sufficient in dealing with this ill..

- 'The abuse of positions of power, authority and public trust to promote narrow, selfish interests and political agendas inimical to our democracy' and 'this points to the fact that the problem of what is called 'brown envelope' journalism. This type of rot is a much more serious problem than the media is willing to admit.'

- 'Freedom of expression needs to be defended but freedom of expression can also be a refuge for journalist scoundrels, to hide mediocrity and glorify truly unprofessional conduct. Freedom of expression means that there should be objective reporting and analysis which is not coloured by prejudice and self interest.'

- 'The creation of a MAT would strengthen, complement and support the current self-regulatory institutions (Press Ombudsman/Press Council) in the public interest. Currently, citizens are subject to the decisions of the Press Ombudsman or taking the matter to courts if s/he is not satisfied with the ruling of the Press Ombudsman. As a result, matters take long to clear the names of the alleged wrongdoers by the media. Further, this is an expensive exercise for an ordinary citizen.'

- 'The 52nd National Conference Resolution tasked the ANC to investigate the desirability of setting up an independent statutory institution, established through an open, public and transparent process, and be made accountable to the parliament of South Africa.'

Before turning to the protests against statutory regulation from editors, civil society groupings and members of the public, as well as business, international media organisations, and a law society, I want to note a few points in the ANC's rationale for a media appeals tribunal.

First, the ANC's ideological social fantasy seems to be that there should be only one outlook in a democracy. The conception that the ANC has of democracy is of unity and consensus, hence the party finds it difficult to accept the different perspectives present in the media. Nor does the ANC substantiate its views that the media reflects a single oppositional perspective. Its social fantasy of a unitary 'outlook' means that it is unable to deal with criticism. Equating journalists' stories with the interests of owners of the media houses is a reductionist conflation of the relationships of relative autonomy enjoyed by journalists.

Second, that the media needs to be accountable for its actions to certain norms and values of professional conduct and to members of the public has never been in dispute within the media industry, but that it needs to be accountable to parliament – the majority of whose members are ANC – is what constitutes political control and an unprogressive hegemony. The ANC was not impressed with the self-regulatory mechanism of the media in which the veteran and well respected journalist, Joe Thloloe, hears disputes with a representative of the public and a media representative. Appeals are heard by a retired judge, Ralph Zulman, who sits with a media and a public representative. The ombudsman has issued a number of judgments against the media, often requiring the publication of prominent, and sometimes front page, apologies. As Mondli Makhanya said, 'The ombudsman has given some very harsh rulings against the media which, even though respective editors may not agree with, we abide by without fail' (*The Star:* 16 August 2010).

Third, the issue of 'dishonesty' in the profession arose recently only when the ANC attempted to tarnish the whole industry after an incident of bribery when journalist Ashley Smith of the *Cape Argus* accepted a bribe from the former Western Cape premier, Ebrahim Rasool. The ANC could not show how this was rife throughout the profession, nor did it have any argument to those who pointed out that Smith was widely condemned in his own industry and was fired from his job, while Rasool, who made the bribes, was promoted to ambassador to the United States *after* it was discovered that he had bribed a journalist. The bribery issue was used as a stick with which to beat the journalist profession, but the ANC did not examine its own actions when it promoted Rasool.

Fourth, the fact that apologies for inaccuracies in reporting were not always printed on the front page of the newspaper could have been discussed with the media industry, rather than the idea of imposing a draconian measure such as a tribunal. As the then executive director of FXI, Ayesha Kajee, observed in a press statement at the time, 'neither journalists nor politicians are above the law'. However, she also pointed out in the press statement that the FXI was 'gravely concerned that political interference in the South African media landscape seems to be increasing'. The call for a media appeals tribunal, she argued, arose from the ruling party's perception that major media companies in the country were 'hostile' towards it. Others shared the view that the proposal for a tribunal was based on a desire for political control over freedom of expression and over ownership of the media, and that the tribunal was aimed at intimidating journalists to stop them publishing embarrassing stories about government corruption (see, for example, Haffajee, quoted in *Business Day:* 19 August 2010).

Moreover, the planned legislation went against the various treaties to which South Africa was signatory, both 'internally recognised mechanisms of self-regulation, as well as other international tools' (*The Star:* 18 August 2010) including the Universal Declaration of Human Rights, the African Charter on Human and Peoples Rights, the Declaration of Principles on Freedom of Expression in Africa, and the Windhoek Declaration (a 1991 statement written in South Africa and endorsed by editors, journalists and publishers from South Africa). A media appeals tribunal would be a serious restriction on the right to freedom of expression enshrined in section 16 of the Constitution and would be a step backwards for accountability and transparency in the affairs of the public and private sectors.

Concluding reflections: 'You media are just hysterical'

Hysteria is one of the forms of neurosis, the other being obsession, according to Kay (2003: 164).[11] The media seemed to be united in its chorus around a common understanding of the stipulation in the Constitution in support of freedom of speech, a discourse that signals openings rather than closures. By contrast, the ideological interpellation of the media by the ANC and the ANC Youth League and the SACP, shows a 'surplus' and 'excess', which can be called rather hysterical. The idea of surplus and excess is indicative of ideology in operation. This raises the question Žižek (1989: 107) alluded to: what if evil resides in the very eyes of those perceiving evil? He gave the example of how children were portrayed in Charlie Chaplin films – teased and mocked, laughed at for their failures. The question to ask then is from which point or gaze must we look at children so that they appear to us as objects of bullying and teasing, not as gentle creatures in need of protection? Žižek answers that it should be from the point of view of children themselves. In an interview on 13 August 2010, Jackson Mthembu referred to the media as hysterical: 'You media are just hysterical. Why can't you just listen to what we are saying?' But one must turn the question around, as in the gaze, to ask whether he is the hysterical one. It was, after all, within his discourse in the run-up to the NGC that the surplus and excess is contained: 'If you have to go to prison let it be. If you have to pay millions for defamation, let it be. If journalists have to be fired because they don't contribute to the South Africa we want, let it be' (*Mail & Guardian*: 23-29 July 2010). The ideological fantasy of the nation and the role of the media in its creation are evident in this statement. There is an excess and surplus attached to the discourse that presupposes a particular kind of 'South Africa'. This, then, raises the question of what this might be and for whom? For the ANC there is clearly a conscious fantasy that South Africa should take the form of its own vision, which, though unsaid, is that which was articulated not so much in its own founding documents as in the 1955 Freedom Charter which grew out of the Congress alliance of that time. The vision was appropriated by the ruling party once it obtained hegemonic power after the failure of the Government of National Unity. The ANC then developed a conscious fantasy that the whole of 'the People' supports the party and therefore the whole of the media should support it as well – as is evident in the words of the secretary general of the ANC (elected to the position in 2007), Gwede Mantashe:

> A media tribunal is required to deal with the so-called 'dearth of media ethics' in South Africa. [It would] help to 'correct' the anti-ANC bias in the media. The media is driven by a dark conspiracy to discredit the National Democratic Revolution (*Biz Community*: 30 July 2010).

The conspiracy theory reflects a repetitive pattern in ANC leaders' discourse. The projection of its own inadequacies can also be seen in the following statement by the SACP leader and minister for higher education, Blade Nzimande, who said he 'would like to see a media tribunal used to stop the corruption in the media' (Nzimande 2010).

Mthembu reiterated:

> We strongly condemn the practice and promotion of the freedom of expression and freedom of the arts which knows no bounds and only sees itself as the most supreme freedom that supersedes and tramples other people's constitutional rights to dignity and privacy, and undermines our values. We therefore remain resolute and unmoved in our call for an independent arbiter in the form of a media appeals tribunal to monitor, regulate and chastise the kind of gutter, soulless and disrespectful journalism (*Biz Community*: 30 July 2010).

I argue that Mantashe, Nzimande and Mthembu showed significant hysteria. The split, Žižek wrote, between demand and desire is what defines the position of the hysterical subject (1989: 113). The ruling alliance, in the form of the ANC, the ANCYL and the SACP (but not Cosatu) have called the protests against the media appeals tribunal 'hysterical', but I argue that it is probably a projection of the ANC's own hysteria about what was being uncovered in the media. That the media reflects 'gutter, soulless, and disrespectful journalism' and that it is corrupt is, in itself, hysterical. Nzimande took the point further to suggest that the media was simply a reflection of its owners. Writing in Umsebenzi Online in June 2010, Nzimande said: 'I can hear some of my comrades saying 'It's the capitalist media bastard! What else do you expect of it!' So then, what is the ANC's hysterical discourse on the media really aiming at? Is it an attempt to deflect attention from itself? According to Ferial Haffajee, in an interview in August 2010, 'This is hegemonic control. Why do we have control over everyone else? We can regulate everything, but not you. This is more about the SACP losing power and the ANC worrying about its own power, rather than the media itself'.

Ideological social fantasy and enemies of the people

If the ideological interpellations, or labelling, such as 'capitalist media bastard', are considered, the media was 'the big other' with a surplus attached to it, in exactly the same way that Žižek described the anti-Semitic syndrome in Germany (1989). The media is labelled as hysterical, yet this hysteria was really a projection of a party in crisis, at odds with itself and its own power, its own splits and divisions. The ideological nature of the discourse could be seen in the 'surplus' that it produced and the tricks of displacement and obfuscation were part of a social ideological fantasy.

The media was the symptom for the ANC of all that was wrong with society. When confronted with its own shortcomings, reflected in the media, the ANC displaced – or projected onto the media – its own failures. In a classical displacement process the media becomes the cause of society's malaise. What was the 'surplus' in the discourse that made this super-ideology? Žižek cites Coca Cola (Coke) as not just a can of water and sugar but with a whole range of connotations around it, symbolising the 'freedom' of America and 'liberation' among other floating signifiers. There was something in Coke more than the object itself, more than sugar and water. In the ideological interpellations emanating from the ANC's hegemonic discourse, the media comprised the social fantasy of what was in the media – its journalistic role of telling the truth and being loyal to the public not the party – but in this displaced version, what it included was so much more: a conspiracy, an agenda, a capitalist plot, which was anti-transformation and hysterical. Underneath this tension there was a contest over the meanings of democracy.

But democracy can be saved. The only way to save democracy is to recognise the plurality of public spaces, the necessary antagonism in society, its incomplete nature and its fissures. To save democracy means taking into account its impossibility, its irreconcilable nature, that social division is constitutive, that antagonism is ineradicable and pluralist democratic politics will never find a final solution. There should, then, be no dreams of an impossible reconciliation between the ANC and the media for as long as the media remains independent from state control. From the comments of journalists interviewed in the latter part of this chapter – Makhanya, Malala, Rossouw, Milazi, and Radebe – there were no 'turns' against themselves, nor was there any heeding or succumbing to the powerful interpellations of the ANC.

This chapter has shown that the ANC did not regard the media as gate-openers and as a space which deepened democracy but, rather, as a conspiracy, with an agenda, the constitutive outsider or other, 'ideologically out of sync with the society in which it exists', to use Zuma's words. Journalists have, in the democratic transition in South Africa, kept the gate open, albeit in an imperfect way, as will be shown in the next chapter where I explore issues of ideology, excess, surplus and subjectivisation through the prism of the case of the *Sunday Times* versus the former health minister, Manto Tshabalala-Msimang.

NOTES

1 Jessie Duarte was quoted by Mandy de Waal in Moneyweb (3 September 2008). She resigned as the chief operating officer in the Presidency in April 2010 citing a smear campaign against her, rumour-mongering and gossip. Prior to this, she was spokesperson for the ANC, ambassador to Mozambique and, safety and security MEC in Gauteng in 1997 (when she was found guilty of driving a state vehicle without a licence and was fined R300).

2 See Žižek (2004) on Tony Blair in *Iraq: the Borrowed Kettle*. Blair knew there were no weapons of mass destruction but he nonetheless went through the social fantasy of believing that there were.

3 It became more apparent in 2010 that this was a conscious fantasy to rein in the media. See, for example, spokesperson of the ANC, Jackson Mthembu: 'If you have to go to prison, let it be. If you have to pay millions for defamation, let it be. If journalists have to be fired because they don't contribute to the South Africa we want, let it be' (*Mail & Guardian*: Big stick to beat 'errant' journalists: 23-29 July 2010).

4 It must, however, be said that Mandela's discourse here is only one of several other approaches to the media. For instance, Heidi Holland's analysis of Mandela and the media: 'Nelson Mandela has a soft spot for journalists ... When facing the death penalty he asked British journalist Anthony Sampson to write the speech he delivered from the dock. Thirty years on, at a private lunch ... he raised a glass to John Carlin to honour his journalistic excellence ... when asked by journalist David Beresford why he would serve only one term as president, he replied 'because the *Mail & Guardian* told me to.' She concluded: 'Sadly, today's rulers risk squandering the Mandela legacy of embracing journalists in the interests of a healthy democracy' (*The Star*: 8 February 2010).

5 In 2008, Malala was magazine publisher for Avusa, political commentator at ETV and columnist at *The Times*.

6 At the time of the interview, Rossouw was editor of *The Weekender*.

7   In 2008, Makhanya was editor of the *Sunday Times* (in 2010 he became Avusa editor-in-chief).

8   Radebe in 2008 was foreign editor at *Business Day*.

9   At the time of the interview Milazi was a senior journalist at the *Business Times/Sunday Times*. In 2010 he was news editor at *The Times*.

10   Franz Kruger was interviewed on 13 July 2009, Paula Fray on 21 July 2009, and Tendayi Sithole on 25 July 2009.

11   Of all the psychiatric disorders hysteria has the longest and most checkered history. It was until relatively recently assumed to be solely a dysfunction of women and caused by a 'wandering' uterus ... The symptoms most cited are: hallucinations, somnambulism, functional anesthesia, functional paralysis and dissociation, according to the *Penguin Dictionary of Psychology* (Reber 1985). See also Lacan: *My Teaching* (2008) on the obsessional, neurosis in its purest form, and hysteria. See also Kay: Žižek *A critical introduction*: 'Hysteria is one of the two forms of neurosis (the other being obsession) in which a subject resists integration into the symbolic order (2003: 164).

7.

The *Sunday Times* versus the health minister

True universalists are not those who preach global tolerance of differences and all-encompassing unity, but those
who engage in a passionate fight for the assertion of the
Truth that enthuses them.[1]

The aim of this chapter is to develop, through an analysis of the conflict in
2007 between the *Sunday Times* and the then minister of health, Dr Manto
Tshabalala-Msimang, a new theoretical perspective on the relationships
between three different kinds of subjects and subjections. The discussion is
about the loyal subject (Tshabalala-Msimang); the questioning subject (the
deputy health minister, Nozizwe Madlala-Routledge) who was fired for not
toeing the ideological line; and the *Sunday Times* newspaper.

'Subjectivisation' or subjection refers to the ANC-led government's attempt
to force the *Sunday Times* to its unitary view. This case study will show how the
relationships between government and media over the two subjects unfolded
during 2007; how the unfolding events highlight the way ideology works in trying
to create unity in a divided society; how there is an excess attached to the media
through its label 'enemy of the people', lacking in *ubuntu*;[2] and finally how the
attempted subjection of the *Sunday Times* failed, signalling a hopeful moment
for democracy. Reflecting on the Žižek quote above, the case study also discusses
how the media and the government dealt with their differences over the 'truth'

in two stories in the *Sunday Times*: 'Manto's hospital booze binge' (12 August 2007) and 'Manto: A drunk and a thief' (19 August 2007). The chapter explores how, on the one hand, *ubuntu* was used by the ANC to try and rein in journalists and, on the other, how journalists believed that they were engaged in a passionate fight for the truth, holding those in power to account for their behaviour and actions, while serving their profession and democracy. However, one must not forget that newspapers like sexy or juicy stories too, and this certainly was one.

While there was resistance to the ideological interpellation, or labelling, of *Sunday Times* journalists as 'enemies of the people', there was also ambivalence: half turns were made towards the interpellating voices. I have developed the concept 'half turn' from Butler's conceptualisation of the reflexive turn, which she developed from Althusser's concept of 'the turn' towards the interpellating voice of power (1997: 107-130).

The *Sunday Times* versus the minister of health: the events

In July 2007, an Eastern Cape newspaper the *Daily Dispatch* (owned by the company Avusa and in the same stable as the *Sunday Times*) began a series of reportage exposing an appalling set of conditions in the maternity wards at the Mount Frere hospital. Some of the front-page headlines included: 'Why Frere's babies die' (12 July 2007) and 'A mother's pain' (13 July 2007). The deputy minister of health, and women's rights' activist, Nozizwe Madlala-Routledge, also a member of the ANC and the SACP, was coincidentally in the Eastern Cape at the time of the news reports, for a conference. She made a spontaneous visit to Mount Frere hospital after reading the reports that newborn babies had died there owing to a lack of care and resources, and the next day she suggested that the situation was tantamount to a 'national emergency'. The report from the hospital showed that there was a dire shortage of medical equipment as well as clinical and support staff, inadequate infection control and a lack of management action on baby deaths. The ANC then placed an advertisement in a newspaper at a cost of R45 000, asserting that the media reports were a distortion of the facts, after the minister of health, Tshabalala-Msimang, herself visited the hospital on 22 July and found everything to be 'in order'. She duly declared that the *Daily Dispatch* reports were unfounded and that her deputy minister's comments were based on untruths (*Mail & Guardian*: 27 July-2 August 2007). Not only were the reports about conditions in the hospital construed as 'media lies', but Madlala-Routledge was fired on 7 August. The stated reason for her firing, according to President Mbeki, was that she was 'not able to work as part of a collective' (*Business Day*: 27 August 2007). Madlala-Routledge told reporters that she was fired for 'speaking out' and cited 'common denialism' as a key factor in explaining why Tshabalala-Msimang remained in the cabinet (*Sunday Times*: 2 September 2007). By 'common denialism', Madlala-Routledge meant Mbeki's AIDS denialism (that HIV did not cause AIDS), which was also echoed by the health minister. Mark Gevisser, author of Mbeki's unofficial biography, argued that this echoing was due to Tshabalala-Msimang's loyalty to Mbeki and her fervent belief in his position on AIDS (2007: 758). The journalist, Paddy Harper, agreed with Gevisser and quoted the political analyst Protas Madlala (no relation to Madlala-Routledge) who wrote, 'on HIV/AIDS the president dreams and Manto implements ... the common denialism is a very strong factor – they share this vision and she is very faithful to him and that is why she is getting this level of protection' (*Sunday Times*: 2 September 2007).

The reality was that the more people criticised the president's favourite appointees, 'the more he digs in his heels', Harper wrote, and, 'if you are a favoured appointee and in his good books, irrespective of how badly you mess up in your ministry, he will not remove you' (*Sunday Times*: 2 September 2007). It is worth taking a small digression to clarify what, in my view, was the central issue in Mbeki's denialist position on HIV/AIDS in order to understand the tension that arose after the *Sunday Times* exposé of the health minister, which led to the threat of arrest of the editor and his managing editor, and a threat by the then minister in the office of the presidency, Essop Pahad, to withdraw government advertising in the *Sunday Times* (*Mail & Guardian*: 7-13 September 2007). The denialist position on HIV/AIDS is encapsulated by Mbeki's now infamous comment in parliament in 2000: 'You see, if you ask the question does HIV cause AIDS ... the question is, does a virus cause a syndrome? How does a virus cause a syndrome? It can't.' (*Health-e*: 1 December 2009). He then called antiretrovirals, the treatment for HIV/AIDS sufferers, 'toxic'.

Thabo Mbeki: HIV/AIDS and race

> And thus does it happen that others who consider themselves to be our leaders take to the streets carrying their placards, to demand that because we are germ carriers, and human beings of a lower order that cannot subject its passions to reason, we must perforce adopt strange opinions, to save a depraved and diseased people from perishing from self-inflicted disease ... Convinced that we are but natural-born, promiscuous carriers of germs, unique in the world, they proclaim that our continent is doomed to an inevitable mortal end because of our unconquerable devotion to the sin of lust (Mbeki 2001, quoted in Daniels 2006).

In the above extract we see how Mbeki's discourse constitutes excess of meaning in relation to the concept of Africa, and of Africans, as lustful sinners. If you were to subtract the excess you would lose the enjoyment, in Lacanian theory. Enjoyment is attached to the surplus – in other words the added on, the extra, the unnecessary – (how necessary is it, for instance, for Mbeki to say that whites regard blacks as lustful sinners?). There is enjoyment but also pain and suffering. No other excerpt from the South African public discourse could be more apposite an example of how Mbeki himself was subject to his own social fantasy and Mbeki's words were the gaze from the outside that showed his own prejudices, and hysteria. The excerpt exposes what Žižek calls 'surplus enjoyment' (Žižek, 1989: 52-53). It is full of *jouissance*, the kind of pleasure that in Lacan is always sexualised. In other words, it is more than enjoyment, always transgressive, pain and suffering, at the limits of what subjects can talk about in public. In the way Mbeki speaks about AIDS one can see that for him both the excess and the enjoyment are coupled with the feeling of suffering and persecution, a kind of perverse *schadenfreude*, which is altogether too much to bear. Mbeki's stance on HIV/AIDS tied it to colonialism and poverty, and to race, the Master-Signifier, and had far-reaching implications for how he dealt with the pandemic in political and policy terms. Since 1999, HIV/AIDS had become one of the most politicised and racially-charged issues in the country, and a discourse rooted in his passionate attachment to the signifier 'race'. Rather than accepting the growing scientific evidence that HIV – emanating from the risky sexual behaviour of multiple concurrent partnerships – caused AIDS, he resorted to diatribes against prevailing views and to acceptance of dissident interpretations.

The Medical Research Council of South Africa and Statistics South Africa estimated that in 2005 over five million people in the country already had HIV or AIDS, while there were about 1 000 new infections daily, and about 600 people died of diseases caused by the virus every day (*The Sunday Independent*: 30 October 2005). The same article in the *Sunday Independent* reported that in 2005 the UN secretary general's special envoy for HIV/AIDS in Africa, Stephen Lewis, said that an estimated six million people were infected with the virus in South Africa, the highest proportion of any population in the world. In view of these statistics and the fact that Mbeki's former spokesperson Parks Mankahlana had almost certainly died of an AIDS-related illness in mid-2000, it was perplexing that Mbeki stated in a *Washington Post* interview in September 2003 that he personally did not know anybody who had died of AIDS. An investigation of the government's policy on HIV/AIDS showed how the issue had been characterised from inception by denial, ambiguity, a conflation of issues and prevarication. When Mbeki took the political centre stage in 1999, however, the issue also became racially charged.

In contextualising the politics of HIV/AIDS, Tim Quinlan and Samantha Willan (2005: 228) wrote that the professional staff of many ministries had given due consideration to the challenges facing the government, and that the national executive had this knowledge. However, they argued, the 'ambiguities and ambivalence on HIV/AIDS in major policy speeches of the president, as well as statements by the minister of health, indicated a lack of decisiveness about how to use that knowledge'. In 2009, after a change in leadership in the ANC, the official policy that antiretroviral drugs should be rolled out in all provinces began to be implemented with greater seriousness. Manto Tshabalala-Msimang was moved from her position as minister of health and sidelined to a relatively powerless administrative and management position in the office of the new president, Jacob Zuma.

Lacking in *ubuntu*

A month after the conditions at Mount Frere Hospital were exposed in the *Daily Dispatch*, the *Sunday Times* of 12 August 2007 ran a story under the headline 'Manto's hospital booze binge' about the alcohol abuse and tantrums of the health minister which took place in 2005 at the Cape Medi Clinic. The article said that red wine and whiskey were smuggled into her room before she underwent surgery, and that she had dispatched hospital staff to buy her food and alcohol. Then, on 19 August, the newspaper ran an 'exclusive' front-page story, whose headline read: 'MANTO: A DRUNK AND A THIEF – Exclusive: Shocking new revelations about the health minister' by senior investigative journalists Jocelyn Maker, Megan Power, Charles Molele and Buddy Naidu.

The story created uproar within the government. It stirred heated – and even vitriolic – debate within the journalist profession about whether publishing it was in the public interest, or whether it was just sensational vindictiveness and anti-*ubuntu*. It raised discussion about whether the publication of the investigation constituted freedom of expression in which the independent press was merely performing its duties to have public figures account for their actions, or whether it was an invasion of rights to privacy and lacking in respect. Finally, it led to the threatened arrest of the editor of the *Sunday Times*, Mondli Makhanya, and his managing editor, also senior investigator, Jocelyn Maker, for the theft of medical records from the Cape Medi-Clinic. Within weeks of both stories, some politicians and businessmen close to Mbeki formed a company, Koni Media, and made a R7 billion buyout bid for the *Sunday Times*. Some extracts from the newspaper:

Manto: A drunk and a thief

Health minister Manto Tshabalala-Msimang had alcoholic liver disease caused by years of excessive drinking when she had a transplant this year. Today the *Sunday Times* exposes a cover-up around the transplant by medical staff to hide her true condition — alcoholic liver cirrhosis — a disease synonymous with chronic alcoholism. The minister, despite getting the gift of life donated to her by a teenage suicide victim, is still drinking — damaging her new liver. And, in another explosive revelation, the paper can reveal that Tshabalala-Msimang was convicted of theft when she was a medical superintendent at the Athlone Hospital in Botswana in the mid 1970s. Hospital staff became suspicious as for months watches, jewellery, hats, handbags and even shoes were being stolen from patients. She was found guilty in the Lobatse Magistrate's Court of stealing a patient's watch, hospital blankets, linen, and heaters, and was declared a 'prohibited immigrant'.

On March 14 this year, just days after her controversial transplant at the Donald Gordon Medi-Clinic in Johannesburg, the minister's medical team stated publicly that their patient's liver had been damaged by auto-immune hepatitis – a long-term disease in which the body's immune system attacks liver cells. What they failed to tell the public was that the custodian of the country's health system was an alcoholic, which was why she needed a new liver. The *Sunday Times* has established that: Pressure was put on medical staff to keep secret her true condition. [...] The transplant and subsequent cover-up caused tension among doctors and staff involved in the minister's care who knew that Tshabalala-Msimang had been drinking before the procedure. Standard transplant criteria dictate that alcoholic patients stop drinking for between six and twelve months before surgery and permanently after surgery to protect the liver. Patients who do not comply are barred from transplant programmes. Experts said Tshabalala-Msimang only got the liver because she was the minister of health. Had it been any other patient in her condition they would not have qualified for the transplant and would have died. But witnesses have since come forward saying they've seen the minister drinking on numerous occasions since the transplant. In July she drank wine on a Sunday night flight from Durban to Johannesburg while she sat in business class. And in May, at a Pretoria birthday party she was drunk after drinking red wine. Just this week she was again seen drinking whisky. Medical experts, who refused to be named for fear of victimisation, said there had been other more deserving recipients on the liver transplant waiting list. They claimed that, given the circumstances, the allocation of a scarce donor liver to the Minister was inappropriate.

In Lobatse this week, a retired nurse, who gave evidence at Tshabalala-Msimang's theft trial, said she was found out after wearing a stolen patient's watch to work three weeks after it was reported missing. She said police later found other stolen items during a search at Tshabalala-Msimang's home. Contacted for comment on Friday, Gaborone High Court Judge Ian Kirby, who was Tshabalala-Msimang's lawyer at the time, confirmed he had represented her. [...]Other retired nurses and hospital staff also confirmed the incident. Current medical superinten-dent Dr M. Hirui refused to comment but an employee said Tshabalala-Msimang's antics were common knowledge among staff. 'Everyone here thinks it's hilarious that she is today a health minister in South Africa,' he said. These new revelations are part of a five-month investigation and come within a week of a *Sunday Times* exposé into how booze was smug-gled into her hospital room at the Cape Town Medi-Clinic in 2005. She was hospitalised for a shoulder operation performed by Dr Joe de Beer.

Staff at the clinic labelled her behaviour as 'appalling' and that she 'knew she had the power and misused it'. She also demanded food from Woolworths and lemons during the early hours of the morning. Hospital staff were dispatched to buy alcohol on a number of occasions by her bodyguards, a female friend and a senior staff member. Witnesses said the minister was drunk on a number of occasions. Today we can further reveal that in 2005 a hospital in Cape Town refused her entry for a shoulder operation because of her security demands. It was after this refusal that she was admitted to the Cape Town Medi-Clinic in Hof Street. Here, too, she insisted that all operations be cancelled on the Wednesday when was she was due to have her shoulder operation ... A 27-year old man, who was a patient just a room away from Tshabalala-Msimang, said on the Friday she was admitted he heard her 'screaming and shouting' at nurses. He said he also heard her ordering food and wine from Woolworths ... 'I thought at the time she must have been a psychiatric patient. Her treatment of the nursing staff was shocking. It was only later that night when a nurse came to take my blood pressure when I found out that it was actually the Minister of Health.'

(*Sunday Times*: 19 August 2007).

It was undisputed by the health minister herself that she was fond of alcohol, even after it was contra-indicated for her condition, cirrhosis of the liver. From the report it seems that she had been abusive to hospital staff – and that she was hopelessly lacking in judgement, having stolen a watch from a patient who was under anaesthetic, *nogal*. The reaction of the government was to launch a high-powered hunt for the person or persons who had broken the law by leaking copies of Tshabalala-Msimang's medical records. The then minister in the office of the president, Essop Pahad, condemned the story on the health minister as an outrageous invasion of privacy and threatened the withdrawal of government advertising from the *Sunday Times*. Mbeki wrote in his public offering, Letter from the President: 'Who are our heroes and heroines?':

> Some in our country and others elsewhere in the world, including the media, have acclaimed Ms Madlala-Routledge as a great heroine, before and after her dismissal on the basis that she seemed to demonstrate intellectual and personal 'courage' by defying the obligation to speak and act as part of a collective. In this regard, in her 10 August press conference … she made a point of emphasising her obligation to be accountable to the media … while the ANC serves as government … it will ensure that its members respect the principle and practice of collective responsibility. Time will tell what happened that gave the *Sunday Times* the right to tell the story it told, whether right or wrong, about what might have happened in our Minister Tshabalala-Msimang's private space in hospital. All of us, up to now, assumed that we had a constitutional and common sense entitlement to treat this 'hospital space' as being subject to the 'privacy and dignity' human right and privilege to which our citizens, including ministers, are constitutionally entitled (*ANC Today*: 18-23 August 2007).

The essence of the above letter was that Madlala-Routledge was far from a heroine. For Mbeki, Tshabalala-Msimang was the heroine (after all, her dignity and privacy had been violated, and she was a loyal subject). It is obvious that it did not suit Mbeki to have a questioning subject as his deputy health minister. His talk of 'collective responsibility' meant that he desired ideological unity, which had served him well with the health minister. His defence of Tshabalala-Msimang was based on what he called her constitutional right to privacy and dignity. The whole discussion, however, masked other issues: that conditions at Mount Frere hospital were shocking, and that this was under the watch of a health minister who toed the president's rather obstreperous and peculiar line that HIV did not cause AIDS. The scandal of Tshabalala-Msimang's earlier history was something of a digression, but Mbeki's was a false argument, an obfuscation of the real issues about the inability of the health department to manage deteriorating conditions in hospitals and a health minister found through the media's exposure to be unfit for office.

Mbeki, though, sought unquestioning loyalty from his cabinet, and the independent action of Madlala-Routledge led to her sacking. Mbeki saw her speaking out as an implicit criticism that went against the grain of cabinet loyalty. They had to be loyal team players to survive office. In essence, his ministers were his subjects *par excellence* and were not allowed to exercise their own judgments on any issue, whether appalling conditions at a public hospital or the crisis of HIV/AIDS.[3] Madlala-Routledge discovered this at great personal cost and lost her job. By declaring that the conditions at Mount Frere Hospital were tantamount to a 'national emergency', she played the role not just of a questioning subject but also of a defiant subject and by firing her Mbeki hoped to enforce hegemonic unity within the ANC by asserting his authority. Ironically, his actions set off a train of events that even alienated members of his own party, and the outcome was that the discourse of opposition in civil society grew, particularly when the press became subject to state vilification, harassment and even potential criminalisation.

Threatened arrest of the *Sunday Times* editor and his senior investigative reporter

On 14 October 2007 the *Sunday Times* lead story was 'Editor, journalist to be arrested'. Maker and Makhanya faced arrest for the illegal possession of medical records of the health minister, related to the story of 12 August 2007 about Tshablala-Msimang's stay at the Cape Medi-Clinic when she 'dispatched staff to buy her alcohol, threw drunken tantrums, abused nurses and washed down medication with wine and whiskey' according to the newspaper report (*Sunday Times:* 12 August 2007). The charges were related to contravention of Section 14 of the National Health Act (no 63 of 2003), which made it an offence to gain access to personal medical records and to publish them. It must be noted that the story about the health minister's behaviour at the Medi-Clinic did not reveal many specific details from her medical records, save that she had a serious liver condition yet was consuming alcohol. The story raised the question of whether she was fit to hold the office of health minister.

On 16 August 2007, Tshabalala-Msimang's legal team lodged an urgent application in the Johannesburg High Court to compel the *Sunday Times* to return copies of the minister's health records to the Cape Town Medi-Clinic.

Judge Mohamed Jajbhay ruled that the *Sunday Times* hand over copies of the medical records to the Medi-Clinic and pay the minister's legal costs. He also commented that there was a pressing need for the public to be informed, that the story was in the public interest, and that personal notes taken by journalists were not affected (*Sunday Times*: 2 September 2007) and thus freed the newspaper to write further on the matter of the health minister's fitness for office. The judge, however, also warned journalists to be cautious about using information that was tainted by criminal activity. The *Sunday Times* and Sanef claimed the judgment as a victory for freedom of the press, while the government claimed it as their victory: records had to be handed back to the Medi-Clinic, and the court ordered the *Sunday Times* to pay the legal fees. The judgement also criticised the *Sunday Times* for not affording the health minister enough time to respond to the allegations in the story (*Mail & Guardian:* 31 August-6 September 2007). It was clearly not an outright victory for either side: the judge gave with one hand, and took with the other. Indeed, not all media commentators found the judgement a victory for freedom of expression at all.

In my argument this saga exemplified the 'shoot the messenger' phenomenon. Both stories, the former health minister's drunken behaviour at the Cape Medi-Clinic and the later story about her being a drunk and a thief, were in the public interest – she was, after all, the health minister and this behaviour made her unfit for office. The fact that the *Sunday Times* had to pay the health minister's legal fees could not possibly constitute a victory for freedom of expression – it was punitive in legal terms, and in terms of the political philosophy of this book it was an attempt at subjection which aimed to create unity in society. Creating unity via social consensus constituted an unprogressive form of hegemony as it forecloses spaces for the uncovering of 'truths', or exposing abuse of power, and therefore curtails the space of a free media. After the stories were published, journalists at the *Sunday Times* and those who supported the newspaper's decision to run with the exposure were hailed as enemies of the people who lacked *ubuntu*.

The objective of this labelling, according to Butler's theories of power and subjection, was to bring the subject into line. The making of a subject was also not just about external power pressing upon a subject but was also about a subject making a reflexive turn, or a turn against him or herself. Throughout the Tshabalala-Msimang saga the media was labelled as enemy, supportive of Western, rather than African, notions of press freedom. How it responded to the attempted subjection and what this meant for the media's relationship to democracy, led to the question: was there resilience, resistance and agency; or a succumbing to the ideological interpellation; or ambivalence in its response? In the *Sunday Times* article of 14 October 2007, 'Editor, Journalist to be arrested', it was reported that Makhanya and Maker's phones were being tapped and intelligence operatives were trying to dig up dirt on them (*Sunday Times*: 14 October 2007). Then, the next day, Makhanya announced through his lawyer, Eric van den Berg, that he and Maker would hand themselves over to the police instead of waiting to be arrested. They would do this so that the matter could be dealt with as quickly as possible (*Business Day*: 15 October 2007). Makhanya had nothing to hide, so why was he then offering to make the police's work easier? This turn could be called a reflexive turn, and showing ambivalence.

The media: enemies of the people who have no *ubuntu*

The events brought to the fore contentions and contestations among journalists themselves, with some averring that the *Sunday Times* had gone beyond the realms of acceptable press freedom. It created debate about a Eurocentric and western mindset within journalism. For example, Thami Mazwai, a veteran journalist on economic affairs at the *Sowetan* and later head of Mafube, which published *Enterprise* magazine, in an article written a year after these events entitled 'What culture is press freedom?' asked whether, if the media must enjoy its constitutional independence and this right must be protected at all costs, it was time that it became 'more culturally literate in the context and interpretation of South African issues' (*Enterprise*, November 2008: 59). He wrote:

> ... Many black journalists who are graduates of the Model C system or white universities were trained by white colleagues and, through no fault of theirs, also see western thinking and ways of doing things as the orthodoxy. And, add to this, the power dynamics and relations in South Africa are pro-western and Afrocentrism is viewed with curiosity.[4]

Mazwai opposed the idea of universal press freedom and suggested, rather, that press freedom was contingent within its particular context, in this case South Africa – an 'African press freedom'. The ruling bloc calls this developmental journalism, which means that journalists should show support of the government's transformation project. Developmental journalism, as I discuss in the next chapter, is rigidly designated through the fixed meaning imposed on it. In effect, the rich variety of meanings in the polyphonic voices of the media are halted through the injunction to be loyal by highlighting the positives while having convenient amnesia about the negatives. This contest played out in the immediate aftermath of the exposé of the former health minister. On one side the then CEO of the SABC, Dali Mpofu, launched a tirade against the newspaper's journalists and then withdrew the SABC from Sanef membership. On the other side the then editor of the *Sowetan*, Thabo Leshilo, argued for universal press freedom. Mpofu announced on 31 August 2007, in a letter to Sanef, that he did not want to be associated with 'enemies of our freedom and of our people'.

> As editor-in-chief of the SABC it is my duty to inform you that we will no longer stand idle while we are being made a whipping boy and a scapegoat by the profit-driven media. Even less are we prepared to associate with the enemies of our freedom and our people. We cannot remain quiet while our mothers and our democratically chosen leaders are stripped naked for the sole reason of selling newspapers. This is women's month *nogal* ... When you ... justify criminal theft you must know that you are NOT speaking for the SABC and the majority of South Africans. The same people who at the beginning of the year were frothing in the mouth about how soft the government is on crime are now flag bearers for the theft of medical records, which might actually result in endangering a human being's life and her future treatment! How inhumane and how far removed from the basic value of *ubuntu*. Shame on all of you (SABC CEO in *Mail & Guardian*: 7-13 September 2007).

The hysteria is contained in phrases such as 'shame on all of you', and 'our democratically chosen leaders are stripped naked' by the 'profit-driven media'. Using political economy arguments, Mpofu conflated issues. His discourse ideologically interpellated the *Sunday Times* as an enemy. But he went further, for in talking about 'our people' he merged the ANC with 'the people'. Leshilo responded to Mpofu in a piece entitled 'Enemies of the People?' saying, 'We are, after all, savages incapable of comprehending the intricacies of such "foreign" universal values as press freedom in a free society"(*Mail & Guardian*: 7-13 September 2007) and adding that he had developed an 'uncanny ability to detect racist slurs and stereotyping very early in life'. And so, to him:

> ... the most demeaning caricature remains that of black Africans as subhuman savages who missed the evolutionary bus. Sadly, that stereotype persists to this day that black people are concerned only with fulfilling their daily needs. And, many black commentators perpetuate the backward notion that we black people should not be concerned with such esoteric and European issues such as global warming or media freedom.

Leshilo found Mpofu's letter to Sanef the 'most explicit display I have yet encountered of the racist notion that genuine concern about the erosion of press freedom is nothing but a bourgeois indulgence or a white pastime'. Mpofu had attacked the independent media and said that in a new democracy it is 'incumbent on all who treasure our freedom not to leave any uncontested space for those who seek to undermine or misrepresent it'. Leshilo countered this:

> In other words, all black journalists and editors should rally behind him in the SABC's imaginary war against black haters who hide behind press freedom to 'hijack our democracy' ... Sorry Dali, I'm unavailable for this intellectual buffoonery. Similarly, you have only yourself to blame for your inability to understand that Sanef could accept funding from the SABC and still criticise it. That is what happens in a democracy. Mpofu and his cronies want to ram down our throats their sycophantic brand of patriotic journalism. This non-journalism would have us extol the expertise of the surgeons who successfully implanted Manto Tshabalala-Msimang's new liver to show that we have world-class medical expertise. The *Sunday Times* today is the most hated newspaper in government circles because it dared to tell the public that she is a convicted thief whose ineptitude has ruined our public health system. Mpofu tells us that reporting in the public interest is inhumane and inimical to the values of *ubuntu*. He pours scorn on Sanef for defending the newspaper's right to bring us these stories ... We are after all, savages incapable of comprehending the intricacies of such 'foreign' universal values as press freedom in a free society.

Whereas for Mpofu the article exposing the former health minister as a drunk and a thief was inhumane, for Leshilo Mpofu's response showed a lack of understanding about the role of the media in a democracy. Leshilo considered that it was the likes of Mpofu who were hijacking democracy, through their sycophancy. For Leshilo, sycophancy was non-journalism. He was not kow-towing to 'white interests' – he felt the *Sunday Times* was just serving ethical codes in the profession – as well as democracy – by being a watchdog and holding power to account. The phrase 'universal values such as press freedom in a free society' is apposite and leads to the question of universalism versus particularism and the clash of traditional values (as proffered by Mpofu), with the liberal values in the Constitution and which found their way into the public discourse. The clash was an example of a healthy contest for the unfolding, unrealised, incomplete and radically indeterminate democracy, with no ultimate reconciliation possible. It was one of the most serious fights for democracy between the media and the ANC.

Let us return here to this book's concept of democracy, which is not a deliberation aimed at reaching the one rational solution to be accepted by all, but constitutes a confrontation among adversaries. However, in the master narrative formulated by the ANC and its supporters the media (in this case the *Sunday Times*) was not an adversary but an enemy – a hailing which showed the excess or surplus attached to the media. If you subtract the surplus you lose the enjoyment, and surplus is the last support of ideology (Žižek 1989: 124). In other words, if independent journalists were seen as legitimate adversaries there would be no excess. But they were conceptualised as enemy and positioned as outsiders to democracy. The displacement trick used here is that of heterogeneous antagonisms condensed into one entity. The heterogeneous antagonisms consisted of the labels, hailings or interpellations of anti-*ubuntu*, racist, enemies, that colonial creature,[5] anti-transformation and imitators of universal values of the west. There was a symbolic over-determination invested in the media, as seen in the discourse of Mpofu. The interpellation was clear: it was a social demand, a symbolic injunction in the discursive, aimed to bring critics back into line, to rein them in. Of course, there is always the risk of misrecognition, that the subject won't accept the label, as in the case of Leshilo who fought back against the totalising reduction of identity of the media being constructed as 'enemy'. He made no turn towards the voice of interpellation, nor against himself.

The plurality of voices in civil society

While, on the one hand, the president, his health minister, the Office of the President, and the ANC all tried to create unity through ideological interpellation, the plurality in society reared its head in a display of democratic dissension, showing fluidity not unity. The news of the firing of Madlala-Routledge generated international headlines. Locally, opposition parties and civil society groups, including the Treatment Action Campaign (TAC), Cosatu and the Aids Law Project (ALP), condemned the firing and circulated a petition to this effect. Fatima Hassan, senior attorney at the ALP and convenor of the Joint Civil Society Monitoring Forum, together with Mark Heywood, director of the ALP, commented:

> Everyone seems to have forgotten about section 195 of the Constitution, which sets out the basic principles that should govern politicians. It states that public officials have a duty to promote and maintain a high standard of professional ethics, to be accountable, transparent and to respond to people's needs. All politicians must provide the public with

timely, accessible and accurate information. Is this not what Madlala-Routledge did at Mount Frere hospital, and on other occasions? (*Mail & Guardian*: 17-23 August 2007).

Hassan and Heywood went on to the following observation on Tshabalala-Msimang: 'The minister's conduct can also be measured accurately against the Constitution. Despite several Constitutional Court findings against her, she has remained part of the team. Indeed, she is the quintessential "team player". 'Team player' was innocuous enough on the surface but in South African politics, and in particular the politics between the media and the ANC, its meaning was intrinsically interwoven into, and bound up with, ideology, and how to stop dissension from the voice of authority or power.

The government's side of the story

The spokesperson for the Department of Health in 2007, Sibani Mngadi, provided the reasons for Madlala-Routledge's firing. 'A self-proclaimed communist who became an idol of the opposition, the "bourgeois" media and global capital institutions, has ended up in conflict with the government she represented', he wrote.

> This is how one can sum up the three-year period of Nozizwe Madlala-Routledge as the deputy minister of health, which ended last week. She was dismissed for, among other things, flying to Spain with her son and a consultant despite her request to travel being disapproved by the president … When visiting Frere Hospital after a newspaper report alleged that it was experiencing a high level of maternal and infant mortality as a result of equipment and other problems, Madlala-Routledge declared a 'national emergency' to her invited media without consulting any other government authority. The effect of such a declaration on improving service delivery is yet to be felt. Her superior Tshabalala-Msimang used a different approach. She appointed a team of officials with expertise in maternal and child health to investigate, and their recommendations are being implemented by the national and provincial governments … Whatever her intentions were, Madlala-Routledge was loved by some international bodies that would like to change policies that are part of the government developmental agenda. She provided great opportunity for the opposition to attack health policies in particular, and she gave great sound bites to the media – but none of this was

helpful to the institution she represented – the government of the people of South Africa (*Mail & Guardian*: 17-23 August 2007).

Mngadi, in representing the view of Mbeki, showed here how dissensus from the government line was not to be tolerated. His deflection tactic was to talk about a trip to Spain. Madlala-Routledge had embarrassed the government. But essentially she was just doing her job, which was to highlight problems of delivery in order to tackle them. For the government though, she was not a 'team-player': she questioned and did not follow the rules of the game. The political analyst, Judith February, head of Idasa's Political Information and Monitoring Service, provided an analysis of the situation in an article 'How sick is our democracy in light of Frere Hospital?' She found that the response to the story was 'hardly one of a government that empathises' (*Business Day*: 27 August 2007):

> Instead it was one of obfuscation and nitpicking about statistics. In the process, too, Mbeki has chosen, all too predictably, to shoot the messenger. Critics are either racists or anti-ANC. Black analysts, commentators or journalists who find themselves critical of government action become unhelpfully labelled as lackeys of white colonialists. Once one frames the public debate on such issues in such crass and absolute terms, it becomes very difficult to have any sort of debate about SA's future. The reductionist logic of such labelling is, surely, insulting to black people as black critics are thereby perpetually viewed as unthinking. It also denies the complex reality of present day South African society where opinion has become far more nuanced and less influenced by race ... There are concerns that the Madlala-Routledge dismissal is symbolic of a further shrinkage of the public space to debate, differ and ultimately decide our future trajectory ... her dramatic dismissal has served to highlight several worrying examples of individuals either suspended or dismissed when they have tried to expose corrupt or wrongful action in the public sphere ... So, while the constitutional framework within which SA operates provides the legal space for citizens to engage, the political reality is increasingly being marked by at best, increasing defensiveness by the government and at worst, plain intolerance of dissent.

February's conclusion was instructive in the observation that agency, the participation of citizens and accountable governance were the lifeblood of democracy. Active citizenship, she felt, required that we continue to prise open the public space at all cost, or the consequences of passivity will be too great.

This is precisely what the *Sunday Times* did: it prised open the public space through the unsavoury story of the former health minister at whatever cost this might incur. It caused both dislocation and fracture in society. Journalists who supported the publication of the story argued that they performed their professional roles and their function in a democracy, which was to hold power to account. They felt they owed *ubuntu* to the people of South Africa who were suffering under a health minister who was inept and a drunk, and who refused to provide adequate HIV/AIDS care in a country which still had the highest HIV infection rate in the world.

Ironically, this was the anti-*ubuntu* legacy left by Mbeki and Tshabalala-Msimang. The gaze, however, can be turned on the media and its inadequacies, and the question arises as to why the media didn't investigate before 2007? After all, Tshabalala-Msimang became health minister in 1999, at the inception of Mbeki's presidency. Was it not the duty and responsibility of the media to investigate the past of every public figure? The media's role is to be loyal to citizens, act as a watchdog over the performance of government and civil society; its duty is to be vigilant and to expose malpractice in society and the state, even if it means having a robust fight. This deepens democracy.

Unity in society and ideology at work

In democratic discourse the media is widely acknowledged as a 'public space'. The trick of obfuscation that February alluded to was ideology at work. The point is that ideology deflects from the key issue and, in Žižek's words, 'works best on the stupid subject'. Stupidity, Žižek asserted, was a key category in ideology (2007a: 200-201). Žižek's theory of ideology stemmed from Lacan who was, in turn, influenced by Freud. Lacan said: 'My teaching is in fact quite simply language and absolutely nothing else' (2008: 26). While Lacan claimed to reduce his teaching to this simple statement, his central point was to emphasise how language shapes ideology. He said: 'A lot of people here probably believe that language is superstructure. Even Mr Stalin did not believe that'. Lacan then referred to Freud: 'Open the book on dreams,' he wrote, 'and you will see that he talks of nothing but things to do with words'. For Lacan, the subject performed a double function in language, as a divided self, a split subject. The postmodern subject was the split subject (we all, as postmodern subjects have multiple subjectivities – that of woman, feminist, mother, journalist, academic, author, black, middle class – so our loyalties are split between many different things). This is evident with the subjects discussed above: Mbeki's love and hatred for the people; Madlala-Routledge confronted by the conundrum of loyalty to the

ANC and government line on HIV/AIDS against her commitment and *ubuntu* in relation to people.

Žižek developed these notions further in his discussions on ideology and how it works best on the stupid subject, using Robert Zemeckis's film *Forrest Gump* to explain the point (2007a: 200). The film, he observed, 'offered as a point of identification, as the ideal ego, a simpleton and thus asserted stupidity as a key category of ideology'. The story is about the extraordinary life of a simple man who becomes a symbol of American heroism for his selfless attachment to his friends in Vietnam. Later, he is celebrated for his achievements. His girlfriend becomes a hippie, and later a stripper, and, for one night, his lover. The denouement: she dies from AIDS and leaves him to bring up their son. The symbolism in the story is that his stupidity makes him an unconscious participant in history, an automaton who executes orders. But ultimately he becomes a successful and wealthy man whereas his beloved fails despite being an active conscious agent. The film presents ideology at its purest, as non-ideological, an extra-ideological good-natured participation in social life, and its ultimate lesson is: 'Don't even try to understand; obey and you shall'. Gump ended up famous and a millionaire. His lover died of AIDS. The secret of ideology was revealed: its successful functioning involved the stupidity of its subjects.

There are parallels between this story and the relationship to power of Tshabalala-Msimang and Madlala-Routledge. The latter questioned, sought the truth, and was fired. The former followed the rules and kept her position (as did Gump). In this particular context, however, the subject was also an active agent, as hers was a strategic and instrumental deployment of stupidity to maximise her personal interests. She mouthed Mbeki's positions at every turn. It was poverty that caused disease in general, and HIV/AIDS in particular. She claimed that antiretrovirals were poisonous and advocated instead a healthy diet of beetroot, onions, garlic, the African potato and vitamins. Zwelinzima Vavi and Žižek would probably agree if they had to theorise the issue of the treatment of the two ministers by Mbeki. Vavi said of Madlala-Routledge:

> In the absence of any convincing explanation, we conclude that she was fired because of her views on HIV/AIDS, which were not shared by the president and Minister Manto Tshabalala-Msimang. It is very sad because this means the sheep mentality of following the leader will persist. It will deepen the culture of sycophancy among government ministers and officials (*Mail & Guardian Online*: 10 August 2007).

In this chapter, the issue of a 'sheep mentality' or sycophancy, of conflating disagreement with disloyalty, of obfuscation under the rubric of '*ubuntu*', was raised by many voices in South Africa's plural democracy. I have pointed to the diversity of dissenting voices. From different points on the civil society map we have heard voices, such as Leshilo's, from the journalist sector; such as the voice of February from an independent political monitoring organisation; such as the voices of Heywood and Hassan from the non-governmental and HIV/AIDS sector; and the voice of Vavi from the union movement – all signalling the plurality of civil society and refuting the attempts at subjectivisation and ideological interpellation by the dominant political party. The contest internal to democracy itself also shows the radical ambiguity of the term 'democracy'.

Universalism versus particularism: through the gaze of journalists

There is an enigma to universalism according to Žižek who asked: 'How is it that Homer's poem, *The Iliad*, even though it hailed from a particular historical context has retained its universal appeal today?' (2007a: 214). Applying the Hegelian approach to universalism as opposed to the standard historicist approach, he explained his contention thus: 'The universal appeal is founded upon a gap that is to say between their universality and their always imperfect realisation'. For him, it was precisely the issue of human rights that formed the basis for an ongoing appeal. He asked whether the appeal was universal or merely due to a specific western context.

This question, about universalisms and particularisms, was posed to editors too, concerning freedom of speech and the right of the newspaper to publish such a story. The journalists who were interviewed agreed that the *Sunday Times* should have published the exposé of the former health minister. They agreed that independence of the press was a 'universal' value in a democracy, thereby clashing with those who thought publication of the story demonstrated inhumanity. It was a clash of principles and ideas, although it could also be plausibly argued that the argument for the media lacking in *ubuntu* was merely an ideological deflection from the ruling party's own inadequacies and its desire to protect 'its own' (or one of Mbeki's own). Many of the journalists interviewed said that they did not buy into Mpofu's *ubuntu* argument, and by so doing showed what Butler called 'resignifications', or detachment from passionate attachments to the past which are injurious (being soft on those of the same race as oneself, or loyalty to the ANC because it was the party of liberation).

The interviews were conducted in January and February 2008.

Justice Malala said:

> This was a very scary development – a shooting the messenger phenomenon. There isn't a single fact about what was exposed about her that was disputed. The paper was accused of trespassing on her dignity and her privacy but this is a public figure. Her drinking and kleptomania affected her work. I didn't see what the problem was in exposing her except the ANC wanted to protect her. The SABC in its statements was then just an extension of the ANC. They accused the *Sunday Times* of a lack of *ubuntu*, among things, but what about the hundreds of thousands of lives lost because of this minister's policies of not rolling out ARVs? There was also in the *ubuntu* argument an implication that we must protect this minister because she was black but the thousands of poor that have died from receiving no ARVs, were they not black? The *Sunday Times* did admirably well on the Manto issue and it showed up the government's paranoia.

He mentioned the government's 'paranoia' signalling that, in his view, there was an excess and surplus attached to the media by the ANC-led government.

Rehana Rossouw felt:

> Independence of the media is a universal principle to me, closely tied to the principle of freedom of expression. Without a doubt the *Sunday Times* story on Manto Tshabalala-Msimang was in the public interest. I await eagerly the next instalment.

For Rossouw the issue was clear: the story was in the interest of the public and had to be covered.

Mondli Makhanya argued:

> Independence of the media is a universal, no-compromise principle. It should be one hundred per cent a principle not contingent on particular stages of democracy. There is an argument that we shouldn't see ourselves as an advanced democracy of the world, but then there are these countries that have made compromises; take the Zimbabwe media and where they ended up after being respectful to Zanu PF for too long. I have no regrets about the Manto Tshabalala-Msimang story. It was an important moment in South African media and in journalism because

we took something that everyone was whispering about behind the scenes and brought it out in the open. It provoked; the government had never been shaken like that. The letters from the public and phone calls of support, even from ANC members who said 'well done' and 'carry on', were just great. They said thank you to me, and 'you guys are brave and courageous'. Imagine that! ANC guys themselves were saying this. Sales went up which showed the credibility of the news item. People said this story was definitely in the interest of the public. The point is that when you put yourself in positions of leadership you have to behave in a certain way. I, Mondli Makhanya, as editor of the *Sunday Times* should be held to exactly the same standards being in a leadership position. I can't just do certain things. You have to have that responsibility that comes with power.

Makhanya said that in retrospect he would publish the story all over again. He did not turn his back on the story, and showed no ambiguity. He was loyal to the public and to his profession.

Hopewell Radebe reflected:

Independence of the media is a principle that must be embraced but in the end it is as free as the ruling party allows it to be. The Manto story was in the public interest, because of her public stature. She abused her position and it was despicable. The newspaper was absolutely correct to get those documents – how else will we get some stories unless people give us documents? The documents prove that she was there at that clinic at that time. There was no invasion of privacy because none of the medical details about her particular condition were revealed in the stories. Fortunately, the court ruled that it was in the public interest. The court appreciated that her medical history was not revealed but that she was getting nurses to buy her booze and undermine their integrity and that she was a thief in her past was in the public interest. All cases of fraud and corruption are in the public interest, so with this stealing issue it's the same thing. The media cannot be blamed for this story; we are part of the fight against corruption. The way the newspaper was treated was indeed a case of shoot the messenger.

Radebe's words against the former minister were strong: exposing corruption was the media's task in a democracy.

Abdul Milazi expressed:

Media freedom is a universal value to me. It is the oil that keeps the wheels of any democracy turning. I see no difference in the Manto Tshabalala-Msimang issue to that of the former US president Bill Clinton and Monica Lewinsky scandal, except that the former did not involve any sexual act. A government official who abuses power or acts in a manner unbecoming of someone holding public office should be exposed. The *Sunday Times* tackled the story, as any other newspaper anywhere in the world would have. I do not see why the *Sunday Times* coverage became such a big issue.

Milazi was also crystal clear that his role as a journalist was not to be loyal to the powerful but to hold powerful figures to account.

All the respondents felt that independence of the media and a free press were in the interests of democracy and formed a 'universal' value that should not be dependent or contingent on any particular stage of democracy. They were resisting being labelled enemies who lacked *ubuntu* and preferred not to recognise the calling and to adhere to the codes and principles of their profession. Theirs was a commitment to universal values which echoed Žižek's in the quote that opens this chapter: 'True universalists are not those who preach global tolerance of differences and all-encompassing unity, but those who engage in a passionate fight for the assertion of the Truth that enthuses them' (2000a: 226). For Žižek, the conundrum of human rights forms is whether they are embedded in a specific western context or whether they are universal. He tries to recognise the universal appeal of human rights rather than dismiss them as imposed western values, a position with which I agree. Žižek noted in an interview in the *Left Observer* in February 2002 that certain values should not summarily be dismissed merely because of where they hail from.

This may sound racist, but I don't think it is. Even when third world countries appeal to freedom and democracy, when they formulate their struggle against European imperialism, they are at a more radical level endorsing the European principle of universalism. You may remember that in the struggle against apartheid in South Africa, the ANC always appealed to universal enlightenment values ... (Žižek 2002b).

Ironic, then, that after apartheid, some unenlightened views were emerging within the ANC, as reflected in the debate over the former health minister's exposure in the media. I agree with Žižek that to dismiss universalism would be 'left conservatism'. At the same time, the discourse of journalists supporting the publication of the story, despite harsh ideological interpellations from the ruling bloc, showed the universalism of freedom of speech in action and the rich plurality and multiplicity of voices, all of which contribute towards deepening spaces for democracy. It also showed a turning away from and refusal to recognise the ideological interpellations, rather than a turning towards the voice of power. No reflexive turns were witnessed.

Further subjection: the attempted Koni Media buyout

Further attempted subjection of the *Sunday Times* occurred when political connections of Mbeki established a company to buy out the country's biggest independent newspaper. The story broke in the *Sunday Times* in a headline 'Mbeki Men in R7-bn bid to own *Sunday Times*' (*Sunday Times*: 4 November 2007). *Did Somebody Say Totalitarianism?*[6] Not yet, but the Koni buyout bid for the company that owned the *Sunday Times* was alarming. Why? Because the timing was suspect; it came shortly after the exposés in the *Daily Dispatch* and the *Sunday Times*. Mbeki's advisor, Titus Mafolo; the foreign affairs communications spokesperson, Ronnie Mamoepa; the retired chief of state protocol, Billy Modise; and businessman, Groovin Nchabeleng – all partners in Koni – made a R7 billion takeover bid (later reduced to R5 billion) for Johncom[7] in November 2007, within a few months of the events detailed above. Nchabeleng denied that the company was a front for the ANC and Mbeki. He denied that Koni Media was a threat to media freedom. The bid raised questions about the ANC's commitment to the independence of the media, and brought to the fore the organisation's plans to take the proposal for a media appeals tribunal to its December 2007 policy conference in Polokwane. However, while there was no proof that the Koni bid consisted of Mbeki's friends it still raised the question of political interference in editorial content. The chairperson of Sanef at the time, Raymond Louw, agreed: 'This is deeply alarming, as the company [Koni] is composed of prominent civil servants, and this may be an attempt to bring their own opinions to the *Sunday Times*' (*Sunday Times*: 4 February 2008). He continued: 'We are not suggesting that they are out to suppress press freedom but, as civil servants, they represent government's viewpoint and they could use the publications as a platform for government propaganda'. Louw made an instructive point: 'I cannot imagine how Mafolo, for instance, would allow a newspaper to publish stories like those on health minister Manto Tshabalala-Msimang'. The attempted buyout created heated debate and put the ANC on the defensive. Pallo Jordan (at the time an ANC national executive member and chairperson of its communications subcommittee) argued:

> There is always resistance when people who support the ruling party want to buy a newspaper. Why should it be seen as something dubious? Is it being suggested that people who support the ANC should not have a voice in the media? (*The Star*: 11 February 2008)

Arguing for diversification of media ownership, as the ANC had done on numerous occasions, was one issue, but owning newspapers and then calling this 'diversification' is quite another and to conflate the two was rather disingenuous. A former ambassador and chief of state protocol, Billy Modise, argued that his interest was 'purely business' (*Sunday Times*: 11 November 2007). When questioned about the high price of the bid when the company was probably worth R3.5 billion he responded: 'I'm sorry, I am not able to argue back and forth on this. We are still waiting to see what other bids are and where our bid will stand' (*The Star*: 11 February 2008). Mbeki dismissed the allegations that a government front company was involved in a takeover bid. Speaking at a gathering of the International Investment Council on 11 November 2007, he scoffed: 'Let's stop the propaganda. The media should not be raising 'scarecrows' but should do its homework first and study the company [Koni]' (*The Star*: 11 February 2008).

There were some in the national political discourse over the Koni bid, close allies of Mbeki, who saw the development as a positive one, with no sinister or cynical Machiavellian motives behind it. The businessman, Onkgopotse JJ Tabane, wrote:

> Last week's bid for the ownership of Johncom by the Mvelaphanda group, as well as another possible bid by Koni Media Holdings, is a positive sign of the future diversity of one of the most influential groups in media landscape. Somebody has seen the light ... In a country where more than 70% of the electorate have voted for the ANC, it should come as no surprise that many deals will be linked with people who have some kind of connection to the ANC or government ... This link, however, cannot be used to prejudice these people and dismiss them immediately as surrogates of government. ... We live in interesting times. And so we watch as the cookie crumbles and arguments for the status quo in media monopolies remain, now dressed in the borrowed robes of concern for freedom of expression and the imagined threat to press freedom (*The Star*: 12 November 2007).

For Tabane, a government monopoly would be better than a capitalist monopoly Thami Mazwai was also supportive of the buyout and he racialised the issue: while he found the uproar 'fascinating and typically South African', upon a 'closer look at the basis of the outrage', he found 'the usual suspects' which he reckoned to be the country's 'right-wing dynasty masquerading as liberals, as Suresh Roberts has poignantly observed' (*The Star*: 12 November 2007).

Suresh Roberts continued:

> Of course they are joined by their black fellow travellers, whom Christine Qunta graciously refers to as Askaris ... There is nothing wrong with liberalism as it represents lofty ideals worldwide; however as pointed out, South Africa's liberal constituency consists of dyed in the wool right wingers whose sole purpose is to ensure that blacks do not mess up this democracy, which is defined in their terms ...

Professor Guy Berger entered the fray, observing that race had become the all-consuming issue. Berger felt that to function fully in democratic governance, the media should stay separate from the state and that 'political ownership by anyone is not good for democracy' (*Mail & Guardian*: 16-22 November 2007). A simple and apposite point.

A *Business Day* editorial entitled, 'The passion counts', reflected in a light tone on the Koni bid:

> There's not a print journalist worth his or her salt who doesn't dream of owning a newspaper one day. So we understand how a group of bright South Africans might dream of owning the *Sunday Times* and its many sister newspapers in the Johncom group ... Perhaps the entry of a group of Mbeki loyalists into the press would be no catastrophe. But if they don't win the *Sunday Times*, will they still dream of newspapers? We doubt it. You don't bid for Johncom at a huge premium and without a business plan unless you don't care about how you're going to make a profit. And if you're not in it for the money, then your bid's political and, ultimately, a sham. The passion counts (*Business Day*: 7 November 2007).

There was no passion for journalism in the Koni bidders. Bruce's editorial made sense. Since the bid was unsuccessful, there were no further 'dreams of owning newspapers' that found expression in Koni or any other consortium until *The New Age* newspaper venture in 2010.

Before concluding these postmodern/psychoanalytical reflections on the situation of the *Sunday Times* and its attempted subjectivisation, I want to suggest that these events constituted a negative turning point in ANC-media relations. At the ANC's National Policy Conference in Polokwane in December 2007, four months after the former health minister's exposure began, a resolution was passed for a media appeals tribunal to be investigated. Such a tribunal would, in effect, herald state control of the media.

Failed subjection, resignifications and half-turns

How are we to blend this empirical case study and interviews with the theoretical concepts delineated at the outset: ideology, subjection, excess, surplus and the three kinds of subjects, subjectivities, and subjectivisation? First, there is the ideological subjection of Tshabalala-Msimang by Mbeki: she was the loyal, unquestioning subject but one who was also an active agent in promoting the former president's denialist AIDS policies. Second, we had the questioning subject, Madlala-Routledge, who was fired for not toeing the ideological line. Third, there was attempted subjection of the *Sunday Times*, through the threatened arrest of the editor and his senior journalist; the threat from minister in the presidency, Essop Pahad, that the government should consider withdrawing its advertising; and the attempted buyout of the *Sunday Times* by Koni.

The Master-Signifier was race in the cases of the exposure of the former health minister and the buyout bid. Those who were against the publication of the story – Mazwai, Mpofu and Suresh Roberts – hailed journalists in varied ways (for example, Makhanya was called that 'colonial creature' in the *Mail & Guardian Online* of 15 June 2007). The journalists were unfairly labelled as racist enemies pandering to western notions of a free press and with no understanding of what transformation entailed. But the real reason for the labelling was that they were not bowing down to the master narrative of the ANC. Those in support of the story being published argued in the name of exposing the abuse of power, the unfit nature of the health minister to hold that particular portfolio, professional ethics, and loyalty to citizenry and democracy. Loyalty to democracy, as editors' said, meant loyalty to the public, irrespective of race, class, gender or political affiliation. The populist intervention (if you expose corruption but it is 'one of our own' you are exposing, then you are anti-transformation, you are anti-black, and therefore you are an enemy of the people) was illogical, a reductionist master narrative and a rigidifying of the meaning of transformation and of democracy. The radical ambiguity of the term 'democracy' was shown: everyone was fighting in its name.

Then, we have the subject formation of Madlala-Routledge. For asserting herself and speaking out about conditions at the Mount Frere Hospital and for criticising the 'beetroot policies' of Tshabalala-Msimang, she was labelled as a 'non-team player', who was courting the international media. She caused dislocation in the imagined united social, and she was fired from her job. It would also seem that she 'lost'. But democracy in South Africa is a constantly negotiated, fluid, open-ended space, radically ambiguous, as stated earlier. This is reflected in the events at Polokwane in December 2007, where Mbeki was axed in a most humiliating but bloodless coup, by a narrow margin, which saw the populist favourite, Jacob Zuma, become president. Madlala-Routledge returned when the ANC appointed her as deputy speaker of the House of Assembly after the 2008 elections.

Besides the multiple subjectivities and subjections, this fight between the *Sunday Times* and the former minister of health showed that South Africa was a fluid society, undecidable in nature and unessentialised, as characterised by the post-modern condition, with robust fights and contestations. However, there were clear attempts by many within the ruling bloc to hegemonise the social by creating unity and foreclosures. This was done through ideological interpellations and the attempted buyout of the company which publishes the *Sunday Times* in an attempt to rein journalists in. The media played the role of watchdog by attempting to hold power to account and speaking truth to power, but did not recognise the ideological labellings. The newspaper and especially its editor, Makhanya's brave resistance to the attempted subjectivisation signalled an optimistic moment for its role in a democracy.

NOTES

1   (Žižek 2000a: 226). Žižek used the example of unconditional Christian universalism, where everyone can be redeemed, since in the eyes of Christ there are no Jews, Greeks, no men, no women. However, in this chapter I argue that the true universalists were, for example, Leshilo, who was fighting against the particularisms of journalists such as Thami Mazwai and Dali Mpofu who themselves argued that *Sunday Times* journalists were lifting values not intrinsic to Africa - as in freedom of speech - and were then lacking in 'ubuntu' or human kindness and compassion.

2   Ubuntu is an isiZulu word meaning the essence of humanity, compassion and kindness or 'I am what I am because of who we all are'.

3   Professor Kader Asmal, who was Mbeki's minister of education, confirmed this. He was a keynote speaker at the University of the Witwatersrand on the occasion of the commemoration of Black Wednesday, 19 October 2010, on the topic 'Free speech

is life itself'. He said during the discussion time: 'We were not allowed to voice our opposition to certain policies such as HIV/AIDS and Zimbabwe' (Asmal 2010).

4   While Mazwai, in this article, was talking directly to the issue of Zapiro's Lady Justice cartoon in 2008, the question of freedom of speech and culture and traditional values was raised in South Africa in earnest after the *Sunday Times* stories on the health minister in 2007.

5   This was a gem from Ronald Suresh Roberts, an ardent Mbeki supporter, who called Makhanya 'colonial creature' in the article 'Ronald Suresh Roberts's ode to Mbeki' (*Mail & Guardian Online:* 15 June 2007).

6   *Did Somebody Say Totalitarianism* is a book by Žižek (2002a) in which he says the minute one accepts the term 'totalitarianism' then one is already in the liberal democratic horizon.

7   Johncom became Avusa at the end of 2007 and is the company that owns the *Sunday Times*, the country's largest newspaper. It also owns the *Sowetan, Sunday World, Daily Dispatch* and has a fifty per cent stake in *Business Day* and *Financial Mail*.

8.

What is developmental journalism?

[The media] has no respect for our people ... It has no time to tell people what really is going on. It ignores government programmes and focuses on scandals and issues that are private. This media, this media, this media ... The media in this country want to insult us. They publish only points of view that they agree with, points of view that paint the ANC in a bad light. I'm angry. Angry because people who sacrificed their lives for this country are being treated with contempt. And I'm not the only angry one. The comrades are angry... [I want to] lead the charge to restrict the media in this country. The media needs to be controlled.[1]

This chapter focusses on how attempts were made by the ANC to hegemonise society through the construct of 'developmental journalism' in post-apartheid South Africa. The argument is that if you stitch the floating signifier 'development' to the transformation project as the ANC understood it, then developmental journalism takes on a fixed signification. This is a populist intervention, an unprogressive kind of hegemony, as in the quotation by the ANC member 'Mthunzi' who was 'angry' because the ANC was painted 'in a bad light' by the media, whereas it was ANC members who had sacrificed themselves for the country. In other words, because the ANC had led the liberation struggle, the media should support it in government. The dangerous implication is that the media must step out of its professional role. However, with this kind of 'logic' – and it is not an isolated view – the lines between party, state and the role of the media become blurred.[2]

The four sections of this chapter deploy the concepts of hegemony, *point de capiton*, excess, and surplus enjoyment. I first discuss how 'developmental journalism' is a floating signifier but how attempts at foreclosures are made. It must be emphasised, however, that the ANC does not hold a single unified view of the media or the idea that it must be controlled. There are more nuanced positions such as that of ANC NEC and SACP member, Jeremy Cronin, from 2009 the deputy minister of transport, and also a writer and poet and an anti-apartheid activist for many years. Second, I scrutinise how journalists understand developmental journalism, and how in their discourses it seems to be a floating signifier, unfixed, and untied to one particular meaning. Third, I discuss the significant developmental role played by journalists when they covered service delivery protests in Sakhile, Mpumalanga, in October 2009. Finally, I turn to the role of the media in the controversy surrounding President Zuma's private life in 2010, which I have termed 'Babygate' (this entailed an examination of the public versus the private and the role journalism played), reflecting on whether the role of the media could be 'developmental journalism' or scandal-driven and sensationalist, perhaps even full of *jouissance* – and enjoyment of the juicy story.

Hegemony, developmental journalism and *jouissance*

'Hegemony', as discussed in a much earlier work by Laclau and Mouffe entitled *Hegemony and Socialist Strategy* (1985), was focussed on the dangers of totalising and essentialising class. However, they also pointed to the dangers of attempting to essentialise identities and meanings. I have adapted this argument in this chapter. A radical political project is irreducible to the demands of one particular issue, be this race, gender, environment or class. In this case, it is irreducible to the demands of the ANC's understanding of developmental journalism. I have integrated this view of a radical pluralist democracy with how 'developmental journalism' has been used in an unprogressive hegemonic way against the media. The argument is that the ANC and the SACP seem to assert that they have the ultimate moral and political authority as to what should constitute developmental journalism and they tie this in with the transformation and democracy project as they understand it. Their aim is to assert and sustain control, and this desire for consensus constitutes an unprogressive hegemony via the ruling party's ideological interpellation of journalists as 'anti-transformation' outsiders to democracy unless they express approval of ANC policies and actions. In its desire for common understandings of what development, democracy and transformation mean, the ruling party forecloses spaces for debate.

To assist in defining developmental journalism, I turn first to an international example. The following extract from an article by Craig LaMay (2004), shows how developmental journalism is related to the role of the media in civil society. In the article, LaMay argues that the embrace of civil society is now ubiquitous in the field of democracy promotion, and that no matter how one understands the role of the media in a democracy its primary purpose is to inform the public on issues of importance and thus to make civil society's political participation meaningful. He notes that of the many challenges journalists face virtually everywhere, in developed and developing countries alike, one that they share is a political and social environment that they perceive to be, in one way or another, hostile to independent, professional journalism. Using the power of their voices, journalists potentially have the ability to change that environment through their engagement with, and support of, civil society associations. In short, the media and civil society are both forms of pressure from below that affect the decisions and activities of governments. LaMay wrote:

> In democratic theory, civil society is also the essential element in mobilising opposition to authoritarian or totalitarian regimes. Civil society, in short, gives democracy what the law, with its rules and sanctions, cannot … Ultimately, how journalism fits into the mix of institutions that compose civil society depends on how one understands journalism's core purpose in a democracy … civil society's job is to 'blow the whistle' when the government acts in ways that are repressive or irresponsible … the Western 'fourth estate' or 'liberal' view of journalism … sees journalism as institutionalising the expressive freedoms that provide a moderating influence on sources of power … Put another way, in the fourth estate formulation, the journalist 'blows the whistle' and civil society acts on the information. Finally, civil society also fits with a conception of journalism that is essentially developmental, which understands its role as promoting socio-economic change through education, economic expansion, and growth.

Of significance in LaMay's view was how theorising the issues of the media, democracy and development were similar in different countries. In South Africa too, the independent media and civil society act as 'pressure from below', and as whistle-blowers. LaMay concluded that nominally democratic governments continue to justify strict controls over the news media in the name of socioeconomic development and political stability. In South Africa, the difference was that while there was no strict control of news, there was a strong push from sections within the powerful ruling party that journalists should be ideologically more in tandem with it and be more loyal to the transformation project in the name of 'developmental journalism.' This was the fundamental basis for wanting a media appeals tribunal.

The quilting point, the *point de capiton*, or the nodal point or knot, in Žižek's political philosophy, are the terms used to describe how a given field takes on a fixed identity from the operation of naming. In other words, naming is like an upholstery button which ties meaning in a knot, to prevent slipping and sliding. Mthunzi's view of the media was a hostile one, embedded in populist rhetoric, and fixing the meaning of transformation to loyalty to the ANC. He drew an antagonistic frontier showing totalisation, which included exclusion: that is, of the media, in an 'us' and 'them' formulation. 'Our people', in other words, belonged to the ANC, and the 'other' was the media. This was a discursive totalisation because of the exclusion. As Laclau asserted, 'Populism requires the dichotomic division of society into two camps: one presenting itself as a part which claims to be the whole', and that, 'this dichotomy involves the antagonistic division of the social field' (2005: 83). Žižek's approach to the question of popular identities (in this case 'our people' and 'this media') was grounded, according to Laclau, in the performative dimension of naming in which Mthunzi created totalisation through exclusion of the media within society – and he went further, to say that he would like to lead the charge to restrict the media in the country. He said it in 2007; by 2010 it was no longer an isolated charge for there were many in the ruling alliance who wanted to restrict the freedom of the media. We see it in the desire for a media appeals tribunal by the leader of the ANC and president of the country, Jacob Zuma; by the SACP general secretary, Blade Nzimande; and by the ANC Youth League leader, Julius Malema. We have also seen it in the form of those in the cabinet – for example, the minister of state security, Siyabonga Cwele, who wished to push through the Protection of State Information Bill despite submissions from civil society and the media's protest that without a public interest defence it would create a society of secrets and would hinder the work of investigative journalism.[3]

The voices of Cronin, Sokuto and Mthunzi

To examine what developmental journalism means from the point of view of the ruling bloc, three positions will be analysed: those of Mthunzi, Cronin, and ANC spokesperson Brian Sokutu. I have chosen these three views because they expound differences in the same concept of development.

Compared to the hysteria from Nzimande and Malema, there were more nuanced views on the media's 'developmental' role from Cronin and Sokutu. Cronin explained in an interview in October 2009 that there was a section within the ruling alliance that viewed the media as the enemy, but he did not view it that way. To understand 'developmental journalism', he commented, the notion of the 'developmental state' was a 'useful reference or starting point':

> The developmental state was introduced into the South African discourse from the left part of the alliance. Cosatu and the SACP during the 90s challenged GEAR's neoliberal perspective of things. What we wanted was a different path from the Asian tigers and contrary to what was being pushed down our throats. We wanted a strong state role for coordination rather than just being driven by market forces. It is a swing to put the state back into the picture.

For Cronin, developmental journalism 'existed in the 1980s, with a proliferation of newspapers, such as *Grassroots* in Cape Town and *New Nation* in Johannesburg, which enabled communities to achieve identity, debate, discuss issues and learn from each other, and for anti-apartheid organisations to popularise boycotts'. He continued:

> Then in the 90s, talk radio played a role in discussions of the stories emanating from the Truth and Reconciliation Commission. National conversations were happening. My father-in-law, who was in denial about what happened during apartheid, had the scales fall from his eyes. By the end of that year, he said how could we have lied to ourselves? Media like this created a space for victims in our society. Today, journalism is shallow, sensationalist and personalised a lot of the time. It's scandal-driven. I'm not saying scandals should not be covered but journalism should not be driven by them. That's not 'developmental journalism'. Scandal-driven journalism makes people spectators in a spectacle, for instance, watching a spectacle of youth league leaders prancing around doing ridiculous things. The reaction to this journalism is that you are picking on us. Journalists as watchdogs have located themselves or positioned themselves in the same way as the opposition party, the DA. The opposition's take on things is that the country is going to the dogs, about to become Zimbabwe. Many politicians see this as 'Afro-pessimism'. So you've had the ANC always talking about starting its own newspaper. We don't want a tame media but we want a media that contributes to nation-building. We do want a diversity of views but it is necessary to

achieve a set of common understandings, focusing on the developmental challenges. It requires introspection on both sides – maybe more on the side of the ANC but also on the side of the media.

Several issues emerge from Cronin's understanding of developmental journalism. It could be encapsulated in the term 'common understanding' within which different ideas and disparate beliefs were foreclosed. It was in essence a tying into a knot, a tying of a variety of meanings into one, to prevent slippages and sliding. It was the work of a *point de capiton*. Cronin is suggesting a desire for unity in society, within which there is consensus rather than dissensus. The rationale for equating the media with the opposition seems to be that the media was critical of the ruling alliance. This conflation is a misunderstanding of the role of disagreement, critique and deliberation – and indeed the role of the media in deepening democracy.

Cronin's perspective focused on the idea that the media was shallow, superficial and driven by scandal-mongering that personalised politics rather than adopting an approach that assisted in nation-building. It is ironic that at approximately the same time as Cronin was interviewed, his comrade, Nzimande, made headlines in September 2009 for purchasing a luxury vehicle at state expense (*Mail & Guardian Online*: 13 July 2007). The press pointed to the gross materialism and elitism of political leadership purportedly fighting the capitalist system. It could be the focus on these contradictions that offends Cronin and so he labels journalism in South Africa as 'scandal-driven' and 'personalised'. To say that 'scandal-driven journalism makes people spectators in a spectacle' turns the issue around from the reality, which is that journalism was not actually the creator of the spectacle, but was merely reporting on the spectacle itself, so the real issue here is whether this kind of scandal – buying luxury cars at state expense – should be reported.

Nonetheless, Cronin's discourse was more nuanced than that of Mthunzi whose words 'this media, this media, this media', represented a rather hysterical position akin to Lacan's *jouissance*. While '*jouissance*' means enjoyment, ecstasy, sexual excitation, it also implies its opposite: suffering, persecution, and paranoia. In *How to Read Lacan*, Žižek explained Lacan's best-known formula, that the unconscious is structured as a language, and is thus not the preserve of wild drives that have to be tamed by the ego, but the site where a traumatic truth speaks out (2006b: 3). The discourse of Mthunzi showed this traumatic 'truth'. For Mthunzi there is a big other (the media) pulling the strings. Žižek explains this 'big other' in Lacan to be 'God' or 'communism' watching, as, in this case, for Mthunzi, the big other, the media, is watching over the ANC. The important point here is that the big other 'exists only insofar as subjects *act as if it exists*'.

While Žižek discussed the subjection to communism and God, in the case of Mthunzi subjection refers to the media on behalf of his organisation. It is not that the media does not exist, but the question whether it exists in the way that Mthunzi says it does, with such excess and surplus enjoyment attached.

While there was no evidence of hysteria in the voices of Cronin and Sokutu, it could be argued that all three voices – Cronin's, Sokutu's and Mthunzi's – displayed an attempt to close off spaces for dissension, albeit to different degrees, by trying to pin meaning down to one thing or to bring the meaning to a halt via the *point de capiton* – in other words, to prevent the floating meanings of development and transformation from sliding away from loyalty to the ANC. Mthunzi's views could not, and do not, reflect those of the whole organisation, widely known to hold a variety of positions and opinions. Spokesperson, Sokuto, for instance, explained in an interview in October 2009 how he saw the situation:

> Journalists have to understand where we came from, and where we are going. We don't expect them to take our statements and write them as is. Of course, journalists have to expose corruption; after all we are talking about taxpayers' money. But the development agenda needs to be looked at; this means you can't just write the negative stuff. There is lots of good news and the positives are not highlighted.

Sokutu's views could be juxtaposed with Mthunzi's surplus excitation within which the ideology was encapsulated. His statement that, 'journalists have to understand where we come from' shows contingency. Because we have come from a repressive apartheid past, and we now have a progressive government leading us, we must therefore be a bit softer on the ruling political elite. In addition, he voiced one of the commonly held views in the ANC, that the good news was not told. Reporting on the good news would be part of the developmental role journalists could and should be playing.

These voices in the ruling bloc try to mask antagonism in society by attempting to create more unity, but this can only work if there is a harmonious society. As in the Mouffian theory, borrowing from Derrida's 'democracy to come', this unity and harmony does not exist. Cronin said that there should be a 'common understanding', but in reality there can never be a fixed 'common understanding' in a radical plural democracy because identities are always 'becoming' and are not *a priori* fixed. How unfixed and how untotalised the nature of journalism is in the country is a sign of the open, unfixed nature of the fluid, undecided post-apartheid society itself.

The word 'freedom' in Žižekean political philosophy holds different meanings depending on the context, but what pins it down is the ideological field of left wing or right wing. In South Africa, 'development' exists in one field, the 'democracy' field, but the meaning still remains contested. The attempts to pin it down by journalists on the one hand and the ruling party on the other did not succeed in rigidifying its meaning. The above conceptual analysis was supported by the journalist, Issa Sikithi Da Silva:

> Some observers urge the media to not only concentrate on profit-making, but also embrace a reconciliatory, humanitarian and developmental approach and to stop acting as a 'prosecutor' and 'witch-hunter'. On one or more occasions, some influential members of the ruling African National Congress (ANC) wary of the media's historical loyalties – have accused the media of ignoring issues of social development and focusing instead on the government's shortcomings, all as they put it, in the aim of undermining the democratically-elected black government and boosting circulation (Da Silva 2009).

Openness and fluidity: the voices from civil society and journalism

The media disrupts the meaning of developmental journalism in the way the ruling alliance understands it. I asked respondents from NGOs and editors what their understanding of 'developmental journalism' was, and my analysis now turns to voices within civil society and the discourse of journalists, which are a stark contrast to the views of some within the ruling alliance. The interviews show how developmental journalism is not tied to the project of liberation or loyalty to the ruling party. The fluidity of the views encapsulated in civil society, I suggest, is an example of how a deepening of democracy could take place. Tendayi Sithole, then a researcher from FXI, expressed how he perceived the ANC's gaze on developmental journalism. For the ANC, he reflected, media reports should include only 'the good' of the government. He said:

> According to this framework the media is supposed to be the agent of development; then coverage of issues like police brutality, corruption, accountability are regarded as anti-developmental. This means they should not be reported since they are not on the national developmental agenda. The watchdog role of the media is curtailed.

In a similar vein, Paula Fray, head of the Inter Press Service News Agency (IPS), a global developmental journalism institute with a focus on Africa, commented that non-governmental organisations such as the FXI, as well as IPS, play important roles in promoting developmental journalism and bridging the gap between media and civil society:

> The IPS trains journalists, is involved in good governance issues, informing and educating the citizenry, bringing more women into the profession while performing a watchdog role. For me, a great concern is to build the relationship between the general media and the consumers of media. We also call on our reporters to ask questions they don't normally ask, across the continent. South Africa has a good media environment; we tend to take this for granted.

Through her organisation, Fray plays a developmental role in society and in journalism by, for example, the dissemination of information and involvement in good governance. Part of this developmental role is being conscious of gender imbalance. The voices of Fray and Sithole emanated from civil society. Sithole highlighted the terms of reference applied by the ruling party in respect of 'developmental journalism'. Fray emphasised the watchdog role and the need to ask questions. This section shows the intersection, or cross fertilisation, between civil society and the media. It explores how ideology works, and why Althusser's theory of interpellation still has relevance in explaining relationships in the context of South African transitional democracy. Althusser's thesis is reflected in Žižek's *The Sublime Object of Ideology,* in his insistence that 'a certain cleft, a certain fissure, or misrecognition characterises the human condition' and that the subject is constituted through misrecognition in the process of ideological interpellation, which happens through language. But this did not add up to closure. Rather, through the concept of misrecognition, there were possibilities for resistance, or in Butlerian terms, 'resignifications'.

Ideologically in tandem, or the more dissension the better?

The reflections below from journalists on how they understand developmental journalism elucidate a rather Mouffian concept of radical democracy: in essence the more dissension, the less consensus, the better for the deepening of democracy. There appears to be an understanding that society is fractured and that an irreducible heterogeneity exists, and that reconciliation between the ANC and an independent media is impossible. The way in which journalists understand developmental journalism is at odds with the way in which it is understood by the alliance. All of them state, in a variety of ways, that the ANC's discourse shows an unfortunate conflation: that patriotism means loyalty to the ANC and not to the country. The editors understand developmental journalism to mean playing an educative, informative role and holding power to account through the exercise of their profession, but they are also loyal to the Constitution and to democracy. They do not believe that being soft on the ANC because South Africa is still in a transitional stage of democracy is in the best interests of the country or the democratic project. The *Avusa* magazine publisher and *The Times* columnist, Justice Malala, supported a particular view of developmental journalism which is tied to education:

> Developmental journalism means empowering readers, for example, with basic information on finance. You get this in the *Sowetan*. It includes exposing corruption. The ANC would like us not to show up its deficiencies. They conflate patriotism with being loyal to the ANC. I love my country, that's why I write critically. There is a total disjuncture between the ANC and the ideals of the Constitution. Many of us feel betrayed by what the ANC wants today. It is so different from the ANC that we fought for. The SABC, for the ANC, is what transformation of the media and development journalism is about. The ANC feels that because it has been elected by the majority of South Africans, its deficiencies must not be shown up. Because it has a two-thirds majority support it thinks we should kow-tow to its understanding of what developmental journalism means. This is rubbish, for me. The ANC can't make certain distinctions; they feel development means being soft on the elected ones, and they conflate patriotism with being loyal to the ANC, a conflation of party and country.

Mondli Makhanya concurred with Malala:

> They [the ANC] want us to focus on the positives, what they have done for the country, delivered houses etc. We must be a conduit for this information. Yes, there is a place for that, but we also need to be critical. They would like us to be there when a minister cuts a ribbon. They would like us to be ideologically in tandem.

Makhanya's frustration lay with the ANC's inability to 'see' that it is not the role of the media to be 'ideologically in tandem' with the ruling party. For him, society consisted of a plurality of struggles, a plurality of demands and a decided lack of unity. He felt that the media should indeed cover the positives aspects of government, but there should also be criticism.

Rehana Rossouw struck at a critical issue when she said she was no longer sure what the developmental project of the ANC was:

> The ANC is trying to say we must be part of the developmental project but right now I'm not sure what their development programme is any more. They want us to be supportive of government's role; the problem is the ANC doesn't see the difference between ANC and government. My understanding of development journalism is what I learnt in community newspapers. Journalists could and should educate people, could politicise, educate and mobilise. When South Africa became a democracy we had to ask what democracy meant. We take up issues, for instance, the importance of Eskom providing electricity. Even newspapers such as *Business Day*, aimed at an elite readership, have debates on its Opinion pages which are educational, for example, we ran for six weeks what it is to be a developmental state.

Similarly, Hopewell Radebe pointed to the wide chasm in understanding, between independent journalists and the ANC, on the role of the media in development and transformation:

> To me it's about looking at all the different issues that affect society and how the government responds: rural issues, access to markets, roads, lack of infrastructure. But the ANC wants us to look at what has been done and feel we are not clapping our hands enough. The Fourth Estate acts as a watchdog. There will always be debate between governments and the media. But they say why should we listen to you? Who elected you; we are elected by 'the People'. Civil society is important for democracy so if you take Treatment Action Campaign or rates and services issues, who brings all these together and makes public the issues? It's the media. And it's not only about the bad stuff that's happening; it's also about the good. The government wants us to just talk about the good that's happening but we have to bring all aspects together, the positive and the negative.

Radebe's comment honed in on the ANC's unprogressive hegemonic stance when it asks the media: 'Who elected you?'[4] The reflections of Malala, Makhanya, Rossouw and Radebe showed that they were aware of an 'us' and 'them' formulation that had developed in post apartheid South Africa.

Similarly, Abdul Milazi said:

Developmental journalism to me means the media must get involved in the promotion of delivery with the same vigilance it tackles corruption. When the government fails to deliver on the people's mandate, the media should raise the alarm. In the same vein we must report on the positives. The media should shine the spotlight on the plight of the voiceless and never relent until something is done about it.

The journalists chose to misrecognise the interpellation of the ANC, refusing to accept the negative labelling terms. When Malala said: 'They conflate patriotism with being loyal to the ANC. I love my country, that's why I write critically', he was refusing to accept that his critical writing meant he was anti-democratic or anti-transformation. He saw his critical perspective as quite the reverse, as his developmental role.

An interpellation: journalism is 'shallow', 'sensational' and 'scandal-driven'

From the ANC and the SACP's point of view, journalism in the country is shallow, scandal-driven and sensational, as we saw in the Cronin interview. The question is: is it journalism that is shallow, sensational and scandal-driven or is it the characters and the behaviour from within the ruling elite that are shallow, sensational and scandalous? My point is that it is difficult to have sober or reflective headlines when some of the stories and characters about the political elite are so sensational and scandalous.

For many in the ruling alliance, when the media uncovers fraud and corruption in 'sensational' stories it functions as an opposition party and their reaction is 'you are picking on us', but to say that the media picks on the ruling alliance and functions as an opposition party does not pass the test of logic. When the media highlights the plight of the poor, or uncovers corruption, it is not functioning as an opposition party, it is just doing its job, even though in a sometimes imperfect way.

Sakhile in Mpumalanga

Let us turn to an example of the media highlighting service delivery. The media in all its main forms (radio, television and newspapers) covered service delivery protests in the township of Sakhile in Mpumalanga in October 2009. The protests garnered headlines nearly every day for three weeks. In this poor community, people who had little access to basic sanitation, water and housing, were shown on television and in pictures and stories in newspapers, burning tyres, stoning police vehicles and toyi-toying in protest against their local municipality for the lack of basic services. The story must surely have embarrassed the ANC, locally and internationally, for it reflected administrative failure. Some might have regarded this coverage as 'sensational'. There was an interesting outcome. After three weeks of protests and three weeks of headline-making, on 21 October 2009 Mayor Juliette Radebe-Khumalo and her executive committee were fired by the Zuma government. Besides the lack of service delivery, the residents were protesting against a municipal finance report which showed that R30 million in municipal funds could not be accounted for (*The Times*: 22 October 2009). After the firing, a resident, Thabo Selepe, was reported to have said: 'We are so happy and delighted that democracy has won. It showed that community structures work'. It might be argued that, besides the protest action taken by the Sakhile community, it was indeed also the media's covering of the protests which brought pressure on the government to take action against the corrupt and inefficient mayor and her committee. If the protests had not made head-lines, sensational though they might have been, without them action might not have been taken. It was ironic that the media were not regarded as heroes for highlighting the plight of the service-less residents of Sakhile. The day on which the firing took place, it was the leader of the ANC Youth League, Julius Malema, who was hailed as a hero. He visited the township and was carried high on the shoulders of the residents, while people sang freedom songs in his honour.

I am not suggesting that the media should have been regarded as heroes for merely doing their job, but the Youth League's leader being hailed as the hero could be read in two ways: that 'the people' were duped into believing that Malema had rescued them; or that their frustration was relieved by the presence of someone in power who thought their plight was serious enough for a visit to the township. The main point, however, is that the media was performing its role in a democracy by highlighting the struggle of residents in Sakhile. This concurs with the view of LaMay (2004) that in the fourth estate formulation the journalist 'blows the whistle' and civil society acts on the information. Finally, civil society also agrees with a conception of journalism that is essentially developmental, which understands its role as promoting socio-economic change through education, economic expansion, and growth, according to LaMay.

In this situation, it was the ANC itself which acted to fire the mayor. A set of forces came together to make a difference to the plight of the people of Sakhile: the community structures, the whistle-blower who gave informa-tion to the media about the missing municipal funds, the violent protests, and the month-long coverage by different forms of media. In October 2009 the ANC announced a plan to place the township under the provincial government administration for a year, while the fraud, corruption and mismanagement of the local council were addressed (News24.com: 22 October 2009).

However, while the media played a developmental role, it did not follow through. A year later, in October 2010, I looked through media reports to find answers to questions: have the residents received basic services, such as water and sanitation? Is the new system which placed the municipality under the administration of the Mpumalanga provincial government effective? Is there more transparency over municipal funds? Are there consultations between the provincial government and the residents about the needs of the community? There were no answers. This leads one to reflect that although the media plays its role in deepening democracy through developmental journalism it often does so inadequately. In November 2010, more than a year later, there were no reports in the newspapers, radio or television about what was happening in the township of Sakhile. Is this just carelessness on the part of the media, or callousness, or perhaps insufficient commitment to development? As a journalist myself I can only be candid enough to say that I think it's a case of there being so many stories to cover that one is always working towards a deadline for the next story and one forgets far too quickly what happened last year. But there is also a bit of each of those things – including carelessness. Radical democracy emphasised a vibrant, dynamic conception of politics that ensured that the object of analysis was never settled, uncontested or essentialised (Little and Lloyd 2009: 199). If journalists are to be radical actors in a democracy, or even actors in deepening democracy, they have to ensure follow-ups on stories such as that of Sakhile as issues are never settled and uncontested in a democracy and struggles are ongoing.

When the media plays a developmental role it is also, by the nature of its job, reflecting agonisms, dislocation and dissensus in society. To try to enforce homogeneity on these polyphonic voices for as long as there is no political control of the media would be impossible. There was no privileged element to developmental journalism for the media. There was a privileged element to developmental journalism for the ruling alliance and that was loyalty to the party which had liberated South Africa.

The final section of this chapter attests to this irreducible heterogeneity, to the fractured society, to the undecided democracy, and finally to developmental journalism in action. In February 2010, just before Zuma's state of the nation address, the press broke a story that Zuma, a polygamist who already had three wives and a fiancée, had fathered another child, but out of wedlock with a woman who was the daughter of a prominent public figure, and purportedly one of his friends, Irwin Khoza. Sections of the public who had previously been sympathetic to the president and his polygamous practices turned against him in this instance. The situation raised several concerns: public versus private; that the private was political; the chasms within the ANC; the liberal western constitution and customary marriage; not using a condom during the scourge of HIV/AIDS while preaching the practice; and sexism, patriarchy and gender equality. He did not use a condom, yet he had already suffered embarrassment previously, in 2006, during his rape trial, when it was revealed that he had not used one then either. The debates raged in the country through the press. It could be argued that this was ultimately what developmental journalism was supposed to be. The section that follows scrutinises the judgments that were made, not only from civil society, but also from the leaders within the alliance itself who eventually pressured Zuma into apologising to South Africa. My argument is that the covering of the scandal, rather than the covering up of the story, was a good example of developmental journalism in action.

Babygate: developmental journalism and a bit of *jouissance*

On 31 January 2010, the *Sunday Times* broke a story under the headline: 'Zuma fathers baby with Irwin Khoza's daughter'. The article revealed that a woman, Sonono Khoza, gave birth to a baby girl in October 2009, fathered by Zuma. This was three months before the polygamist president married for the fifth time and it brought the number of children Zuma had fathered to twenty. The revelation highlighted to the public that, yet again, Zuma had had unprotected sex with a woman who was not one of his wives. The first time that Zuma's philandering had been exposed was in December 2005, when he was charged with rape. He was then acquitted in the Johannesburg High Court in May 2006 and subsequently apologised to South Africans: 'I wish to state categorically and place on record that I erred in having unprotected sex ... I should have known better and I should have acted with greater responsibility ... I unconditionally apologise to all South Africans' (ANC Media statement: 9 May 2006). Yet, four years later, this scandal broke attesting to Zuma's risky sexual behaviour and lack of fidelity to his wives, in the age of AIDS.

The revelation of the birth of Zuma's twentieth child took place in the same week as the World Economic Forum's annual meeting in Davos, Switzerland. While all other leaders were questioned about serious issues such as world poverty, climate change and how to reduce inequality, Zuma was forced to answer questions about his private life and his polygamy. The report in the paper (*Sunday Times*: 31 January 2010) under a headline 'Zuma's child no 20' was sensational for an appropriately sensational story. It informed the newspaper-reading public that each of Zuma's wives was entitled to a personal assistant, a post worth R145 920 a year, and that medical expenses, air travel and security costs of the spouses were borne by the state. This, of course, raised questions among taxpayers about how public money was being spent.

The media's interpellation of Zuma enabled the public to subject its president to deep scrutiny: was this man morally fit to be leading the nation? What example was the president setting for the citizenry when his government was campaigning for monogamy or one partner at a time, and the use of condoms to prevent the spread of HIV/AIDS? Was he adhering to his own government policies? In addition, the public was reminded through the press that Zuma, as deputy president of the country, headed the 'Moral Regeneration' campaign in 2003, which was meant to stamp onto the consciousness of citizens the values and mores of living with integrity, not being promiscuous and having one partner at a time. The obvious contradictions in the conduct of the president were pointed out. There were two responses from the ANC to the story. The initial reaction of the ANC to Zuma's fathering his twentieth child out of wedlock was that this was a private matter and not of public interest. On 1 February 2010, ANC spokesperson Jackson Mthembu issued a statement declaring that the president had done nothing wrong and that this was a private matter between two consenting adults.

> The African National Congress (ANC) would like to set records straight that the matter between the ANC President and his personal relationship with anyone remains a personal matter … Our view is that the matter between any two consenting adults remains their own personal affair, not in the interest of anyone. That goes for some individuals and some media institutions. For the record, President Zuma has gone on record sharing his belief in polygamy and has demonstrated his responsibilities and his responsiveness that comes with any of the relationships. As the ANC, we have always made a distinction between people's personal affairs and their public responsibilities. In so far as we are concerned, the alleged relationship of the President and anyone should be treated as such. We do not see the correlation between the ANC policies on HIV and Aids and the President's personal relationships … Why should a relationship between two adults be made an issue? Why should it make headlines? Why is it characterised by some media as a 'Shame to the nation'? … We are of the view that the media and some political commentators are making a mountain out of nothing … This unjustified attack to the President is disingenuous. There is nothing wrong that the President had done. There is nothing 'shameful' when two adults have a relationship. How

does a relationship between two adults become 'shameful' to the people? Such headlines are alarmist and create unnecessary tensions and confusion ... (ANC Media Statement: 1 February 2010).

Mthembu's statement was a classic example of the tricks of ideological deflection or displacement. The questions raised by the statement were significant. In the context of a country riven by risky sexual behaviour that increases the incidence of HIV infection, how could personal behaviour of politicians meant to set an example not be of significance? Thus there is the pertinent question of whether the press was prying beyond the mandate of watchdog. Was the matter a private one, considering that Zuma was not only a public figure but also the president? What kind of example was Zuma, as the head of state and of the ANC, setting to South African citizens in the context of the high prevalence of HIV/AIDS related to sexual promiscuity? Were such headlines alarmist, creating unnecessary tensions and confusions, or were they directly in the public interest? These were the questions the story raised, yet Mthembu asked: 'Why should this make headlines?' While he placed the blame on the media for being disingenuous, one could argue that he himself was being disingenuous. In principle, there was indeed nothing shameful about having a private, consensual sexual relationship. But the context of a married man having unprotected sex outside of wedlock (and the president had three wives and a fiancée already) appeared to fly in the face of the norms of fidelity that marriage entails – even in a polygamous household. There was also something deeply disingenuous, dishonest and hypocritical about preaching to young people about condom usage to prevent the spread of HIV/AIDS and then not using one yourself. This was one of the reasons that the story should have made headlines, however scandalous and sensational those headlines appeared to be.

The newspapers did not drop the issue in spite of the set-down from the ANC. The sensational headlines fulfilled a role by informing the public about the various tangents and implications of the Zuma 'Babygate' crisis. For example, the then *Business Times* editor, Phylicia Oppelt, wrote the following in her column 'My Day', in a piece entitled 'The error of Zuma's ways':

If this was anyone but the president of the Republic of South Africa, I would have just shrugged my shoulders and written him off as a dirty old man who has more sperm than brain cells ... It certainly makes me ask what lessons he has learnt from the disgrace of testifying in 2006 that he had unprotected sex with a woman who was HIV-positive and that he had thought a shower might lessen the chances of contracting the disease ... So what happened to Zuma's role as a moral regeneration agent? Does our president think about the message he sends out to young people across this country about unprotected sex? Or is he so filled with a sense of invincibility that he has no cause to fear what the rest of us mortals do – unwanted pregnancies, sexual diseases and HIV/AIDS? As a woman and a South African, I am outraged (*The Times*: 2 February 2010).

In the act of writing such a piece Oppelt was an example of how the press performs a critical and independent role in a democracy, the developmental role of journalism in action. The 'Babygate' scandal provided some platform for open public debate but also provided the ANC with the space to air its side of the story and the space to Zuma to defend himself or apologise. Given Mthembu's statement that this was a private matter, the ANC then made a self-reflexive turn, when sections of the party pressured Zuma to 'come clean', to talk about it and to apologise to the nation (*The Star*: 3 February 2010).

Twenty babies in a mass Zuma baby shower (printed in the *Mail & Guardian*: 5-11 February 2010)

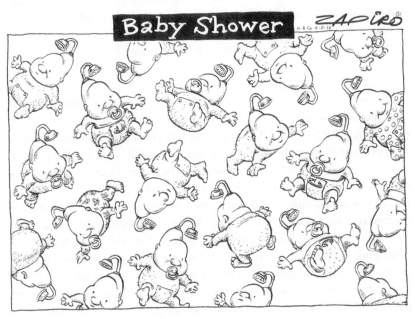

On 7 February 2010, Zuma, subjected to pressure from some ANC leaders and probably also through the press coverage and letters from the public in newspapers, made an apology to the nation for his behaviour. A *Sunday Times* headline told us 'Zuma: I'm sorry for the pain I've caused you' (7 February 2010).

Dissensus: in civil society, within the ANC itself and in the alliance

It was not only journalists such as Oppelt and Zapiro voicing their opinion on the matter and showing the cracks and dislocation in society. The matter raised dissensus within the Zuma administration and within the ruling alliance. And then there were voices from civil society. A cacophony of voices expressed themselves through the media. From a feminist perspective, the director of the NGO Gender Links, Colleen Lowe Morna, wrote a newspaper article entitled: 'This sets us back decades: Zuma's behaviour insults the ANC's progressive policies' (*The Times*: 9 February 2010). She argued that 2010 opened with a frenzy of reports about Zuma's third wife – his fifth marriage – peppered with letters and opinion pieces justifying polygamy on the grounds that it was not illegal or unconstitutional; that it was better to be transparent about relationships than have concubines hidden away; and that liberalism demanded tolerance of all lifestyles. 'The love child shattered this sycophantic barrage. It showed that contrary to Zuma's own claims about openness within his polygamous circle, the president philanders at will outside this circle'. Lowe Morna had identified the turning point against Zuma. Besides newspapers, letters to the editors, views from civil society organisations, and the official opposition's protests, other parties, for instance the African Christian Democratic Party (ACDP), the Congress of the People (Cope) and the Independent Democrats, called for Zuma's resignation on the basis that he was not morally fit to run the country.

On the eve of his state of the nation address, there was another sensational headline: 'More Zuma Kids!' (*The Star*: 11 February 2010).[5] Zuma delivered his address on the same day, and it seemed as though he had lost confidence, evidenced in an eighty-minute, dull and lacklustre address which did not meet expectations – and it was not only newspapers that said Zuma fell short of expectations. Zuma's ally, Cosatu's Zwelinzima Vavi, was also disappointed. Within a week of the state of the nation address, the finance minister, Pravin Gordhan, delivered the budget speech on 17 February 2010. It was hailed by the business sector as a good one. The inflation-targeting monetary strategy was, however, maintained. Cosatu was dissatisfied and felt betrayed: 'There's not even an attempt to meet us half way' (*Times Live*: 22 February 2010). Vavi said he would not put faith in individuals again, referring to Zuma, whom he had backed before the December 2007 National Policy Conference in Polokwane. In 2006-2007, Vavi called the bid for Zuma's presidency an 'unstoppable tsunami'. In 2010, he did an about turn and said that in future the federation would focus on policy rather than personalities (*Mail & Guardian*: 19-25 February 2010). Zuma's response was lame: Cosatu should have read the finance minister's speech more closely.

The populist alliance between Zuma and Cosatu seemed to be falling apart. As Laclau argued in *On Populist Reason* (2005: 180), the dimensions of populism consist of an aggregation of heterogeneous forces and demands. After the 'enemy' Mbeki was defeated at Polokwane in December 2007, new populist demands were crystallised in a new force or figure: Zuma. The hopes from the left were slowly falling apart. On 23 February 2010, Zuma dashed Cosatu's hopes again when he said that the lifestyle audit, which the federation was demanding to investigate corruption, would not take place. Zuma said those who thought that the budget speech was a declaration of war on the ANC's left-wing allies, had not read the document well enough to recognise that it was 'unapologetically pro-poor' (*The Times*: 23 February 2010). Cosatu was beginning to see that putting all its eggs in the 'Zuma basket' was dangerous. The populist alliance was unravelling, indicative of the open, fractured social in the undecided democracy. If firm and undying unity and loyalty were not possible between Vavi and Zuma, how could they be between the media and the ANC?

The media's role: developmental or sensationalist?

In this chapter I have argued that attempts were made to hegemonise society, as in trying to create more consensuses between the media and the ANC through the construct of 'development journalism'. But the term 'developmental journalism' was, for the ANC, tied into a rigid knot of meaning that limited it to loyalty to the ANC's perspectives and the media was viewed as the constitutive outsider in this 'democratic' matrix. Surplus enjoyment characterised the discourse against the media by some in the ANC, for example Mthunzi, while for others like Cronin the desire for more unity was reflected in his statement that there needed to be more 'common understandings'. It has been argued here that it was through journalists' understanding of what developmental journalism meant, and through its educative and informative role, that the creation of the space for debate of controversial issues was made possible.

The issue of Babygate allowed people to debate monogamy versus polygamy, to question why there was no known incidence of polyandry in the country, to debate the HIV/AIDS issue, and to expose the hypocrisy of the president, who was preaching the use of condoms while not using them himself. This speaks directly to the media's role of holding the powerful to account for their policies and their actions – and the chasms between them.

I have highlighted just how quickly a new administration, which came into power through populist demands, could be de-centred and split. Public opinion turned against Zuma but popularity within his own ranks began to dwindle too. There were cracks within the ANC's new populist wing. It was indeed Laclau's theory on populism in action: as quickly as popular demands become crystallised in a figure, so quickly can they disappear. Through the deployment of Butler's thesis of reflexivity we saw that journalists turned their back on the ANC's notions of development journalism, in active misappropriation of subjugating signifiers. We witnessed in the discourse of journalists that they saw the ideological interpellation to be a conflation of party, state and government. They asserted their independence, denying the interpellation and call to homogeneity. We also witnessed misappropriations of subjugating terms such as 'enemies of the people', as in Mthunzi's hysteria and demonisation of the media. The journalists did not accept these terms. Finally, we saw resignifications taking place as Vavi detached himself from the figure, Zuma, within whom all their demands were crystallised. It was an important example of the contingency and radical ambiguity intrinsic to democracy. The media's role was exceptionally developmental but it also enjoyed sensationalism, such as the baby-shower cartoon, where there was some *jouissance* attached – that is, this was a really 'juicy' story and there was excitement about it, just as it was with the Manto story in the *Sunday Times*.

NOTES

1   ANC member 'Mthunzi', *Daily News*: 21 August 2007.

2   In July 2010 this same view emanated from an ANC MP in a parliament hearing on submissions by civil society groupings, including the *Mail & Guardian,* against the broad clauses in the Protection of State Information Bill which could see journalists jailed for being in possession of classified information. ANC MP Cecil Burgess, chairperson of the parliamentary ad hoc committee heading the submissions, asked Nic Dawes, editor of the *Mail & Guardian,* 'As they would have said in the days of the struggle: are you with the struggle or are you against the struggle, Sir?' (See Paul Hoffman, 'Yes, we have trust issues': *The Times*: 28 July 2010).

3   It could be argued that this is an isolated view of the media, too random to be selected. However, by July 2010 the ANC had released a document for its NGC meeting: *Media, Transformation, Ownership and Diversity,* where a media appeals tribunal was to be discussed. Other voices against the media's independence as a self-regulating institution emanated from Blade Nzimande (*Business Day*: 30 July 2010; Jackson Mthembu (*Mail & Guardian*: Big stick to beat errant journalists: 23-29 July 2010); the ANC MP, Cecil Burgess (*The Times*: 28 July 2010); and Siphiwe Nyanda (*Sunday Times*: 1 August 2010).

4   Radebe was interviewed in 2008, but as late as 2010 President Zuma intimated that the media was not elected by the people. He also asked whether it has a role to play in nation-building, in the promotion of the country's prosperity and the stability and wellbeing of its people. The media, he said, had put itself on the pedestal guardianship. 'We therefore have the right to ask: who is guarding the guardian?' (*The Times*: 16 August 2010).

5   According to the story, it appeared that Zuma had two children, aged twelve and seven, with a prominent Pietermaritzburg businesswoman. However, as one read further into the story, it emerges that these children were among the twenty who had thus far been counted. Even though the headline was disingenuous, these children were not from one of the official wives. A presidential aide commented in the story that there was 'nothing new' about Nonkululeko Mhlongo and her children. When the press contacted Mhlongo she denied knowing Zuma and denied that he was the father (*The Star*: 11 February 2010).

9.

Concluding reflections: where is democracy headed?

Perfect democracy would indeed destroy itself. This is why it should be conceived as a good that exists as good only as long as it cannot be reached.[1]

Torfing said that we must accept a world of politics full of antagonism. Once we accept this, we need to then envisage *how it is possible under those conditions* to create or maintain a pluralistic democratic order, with a distinction between 'enemy' and 'adversary' (1999: 121). One of my main premises is that 'democracy' is secured precisely through its resistance to perfect or final realisation, and it is characterised ultimately by indeterminacy. My conceptual starting point, then, is that the tension between the media and the ANC is internal to democracy itself. One of my conclusions is that, through populist interventions such as ideological labelling, disparate antagonisms are condensed into one figure, 'the media'. Antagonistic interpellations against the media include that it is a body which is anti-transformation, that it lacks diversity, is profit-driven, is an enemy of the people, lacks *ubuntu* and is hysterical. In trying to control the media in South Africa, the ANC and some of its alliance partners have not accepted that a fractured society cannot exist without contestations or that there is a distinction between enemy and adversary in a pluralistic democratic order. The ideological labelling is a case of obfuscation.

My argument throughout this book is that the independent media is an agonistic, adversarial space and journalists are legitimate adversaries who have a significant role to play in the creation of, and the deepening of, a pluralistic democratic order. It is therefore inappropriate, but also unfair, to gaze on them as enemies, anti-transformation and unpatriotic. To constitute the media as an 'us and them' is to make it an outsider to the democratic space. Through the use of psychoanalytical concepts of ideological interpellation, Master-Signifiers and floating signifiers, social fantasy, and the gaze, I suggest that the ANC is unmasked as having regressive tendencies, and through its paranoia and hysteria is itself, rather than the media, blocking transformation. The ANC has turned the issue around to brand the media as the regressive force, indulging in ideological interpellation of critical voices in the media, hailing them through the performative of naming. It has summoned the intervention of a media appeals tribunal as a means of control.

One of my concluding reflections is that unity in society is not possible (not within the ANC nor between the ANC and the media) and attempts at unity suggest foreclosures of democratic spaces. Voices in the ANC and its alliance partners have, to different degrees, attempted to close these open spaces through ideological interpellations, lawsuits, interdicts against publishing, the Protection of State Information Bill and the proposed media appeals tribunal.

Butler's concepts of passionate attachments, misrecognition and refused identification, witnessed particularly in 'turns' away from – and sometimes towards – the ideologically interpellating voices, were useful in providing an understanding of the multiple subjectivities of journalists in South Africa. By the stories they published and the opinions they voiced, the editors showed that they turned their backs on the interpellating voices of power, misrecognising the labels. Those editors who were interviewed did not, for example, attach to race as a Master-Signifier, and nor was loyalty to the party of liberation a Master-Signifier. It is possible then that there was little conscious ideology at work in the disparate worlds of journalists, contrary to the suggestion by Jessie Duarte and others that there was an anti-ANC conspiracy in the media. While a few journalists made reflexive turns to the voice of power when they heeded a call for more loyalty and attempted to re-launch the FBJ, reiterating norms of the past, the majority did not.

The ANC threw the signifiers race and capitalism into the equation, assuming that the media is one big bloc controlled by 'white capitalists'. In my experience as a journalist in South Africa since 1990, I have not once been told that I could not cover a story or write from a particular angle because it would upset the advertisers, or that the 'white capitalists' would not be happy with this or that story (other journalists may have had other experiences, so I cannot speak for them).

The point is that the nuance of what is reported and debated, and the diversity of voices that do indeed exist, is missing from this kind of knee-jerk generalisation.

Notwithstanding the ANC's, ANC Youth League's and SACP's diatribe against the 'capitalist media', the capitalist system itself (while of course deeply embroiled in the spoils of capitalism) has in fact wreaked havoc on traditional media globally, as seen in the global economic recession of 2008-2010 coupled with the growing dependence of the wealthy on the Internet for news. This is how the intersection of commercial interests and capitalism entered into the fray of democracy and the media in this book, but it was not the focus.

For all her criticisms of the media in general, an important point that Mouffe made was that, even though the media were not all that powerful, there should be more pluralism in the media, and while journalists were not there to tell people what to think, they should be providing different views. 'Ideally, the role of the media should precisely be to contribute to the creation of these agonistic public spaces in which there is possibility for dissensus to be expressed or alternatives to be put forward' (Mouffe 2006: 974). In my discussion of the independent media in South Africa I have shown that journalists have been guided by this same vision. Mouffe theorised journalists as legitimate adversaries in a democracy, and I have done this for the case of South African journalists in particular.

The media caught in a deep slumber

I started this work on the media's role in a democracy, and the fight between the ANC and the media, with a particular view, an optimistic one, of how the media fight for democracy and independence, using English-language newspapers as examples. I have ended with a rather more open-ended view. The continued relative independence of the media is undecided. It was clear by 2010, when I conducted my research, that the media would challenge repressive legislative proposals in the Constitutional Court. In South Africa, prior to 2010, there was reliance on recourse to the parliamentary process in the form of 'submissions', rather than activism, among journalists. The deputy chief justice, Dikgang Moseneke, made reference to this speaking of South African politics in general: '"Lawfare" occurs,' he said in 2010, 'when politics is played out in the court. The layman's understanding is that this is political warfare that converts into legal warfare. In the past twenty-four months 'our society has had a fair share of political contestations that have played themselves out in our courts and in the Constitutional Court in particular' (*Mail & Guardian*: 29 January-4 February 2010).

Journalists did not always make use of the opportunities available to them, such as that on Media Freedom Day in October 2009, to use their own spaces, newspapers, to expose that their freedoms were being whittled away. It could be argued that the media, in particular the traditional media, had been caught in a 'deep slumber', to use the phrase of Stefaans Brümmer at the M&G Centre for Investigative Journalism. The resolution to investigate the establishment of a media appeals tribunal took place at the ANC's policy conference in Polokwane in December 2007, and was reinforced at the ANC's NGC in Durban in September 2010. It was clear that the independent media world was faced with intense pressure from the ruling party to toe the ideological line. The proposed regulatory instruments suggested closures which are not in tandem with an open society. What possibilities for action or agency existed? Brümmer has said, in an interview, that 'unless we engage and make ourselves heard, these consequences may well become part of the legal arsenal available to public figures who do not like the media's probing attention'. He thought that if these repressive measures had taken place during the apartheid era there would have been more of an outcry.

The democratic space was being shut down and journalists had been 'caught in a deep slumber'. I agree that there seemed to be far too much faith and trust in the new government because it was democratically elected. In the interviews with the editors on whether the media appeals tribunal might become a reality, most of them said it would not happen because the Constitution would 'protect us'. But surely it depended on which judges were sitting in the Constitutional Court at a particular time, and how they interpreted the law. Franz Kruger concurred with this when he said that 'one should be careful not to be absolute about the Constitutional Court. It could change in character and composition', and he explained, in an interview, that 'it is not impossible that a formulation could be found for this media tribunal. They would couch it in terms of transformation and development. The ANC has for a long time been unhappy about the media, and wants to prevent its "excesses" and "reactionary" behaviour.'

In 2010, it appeared that the media had awoken from its deep slumber when the Protection of State Information Bill was still on the table in Parliament and the media appeals tribunal was back for discussion at the ANC's September 2010 NGC. Sanef held a meeting with journalists at the *Sunday Times* offices in Johannesburg on 4 August 2010 at which it was decided that 'engagement' would take place with the ANC over their actions to curtail media freedom. A campaign would be launched to protest the proposed media appeals tribunal and the Protection of State Information Bill. Finally, if all these civil society actions failed, there would be a constitutional challenge. Although the environment pointed to a closing in of the spaces, there was still a turning against the ANC by the media rather than a turning towards its interpellating calls, and this signalled an optimistic moment for democracy. Ironically, while this meeting was taking place seven plain-clothes policemen arrived at the *Sunday Times* offices in Rosebank and arrested investigative journalist Mzilikazi wa Afrika for 'fraud' and 'defeating the ends of justice' (*Mail & Guardian*: 13-19 August 2010). It subsequently emerged that the ANC was unhappy about the exposure of divisions and fractures in the party's leadership in Mpumalanga and the arrest was part of a strategy to stop Wa Afrika from investigative reporting. Having been part of the meeting, I witnessed the arrest. It was a surreal experience as the rough manhandling of Wa Afrika by so many policemen was reminiscent of apartheid days. There were several cars lined up around *Sunday Times* offices, and when photographers tried to take pictures the police shoved their cameras away. When journalists asked questions about what the charges were and where they were taking Wa Afrika, just two words were offered in response: 'fraud' and 'Nelspruit'. A month later the charges were dropped and Wa Afrika instituted charges against the police for wrongful arrest.

Optimistic moments for democracy

Although there was some inertia among journalists about media independence vis-à-vis the regulatory environment, other evidence suggested pockets of optimistic moments cross-cutting these pessimistic moments. First, the failure of the FBJ to re-launch showed that the attempt to make a Master-Signifier of race had failed and, instead, a new non-racial journalists' body, Projourn, was launched at the end of 2009. Although this organisation has been pretty low profile 2010–2012. Race remained a floating signifier in the world of journalism. It had no fixed or full meaning and was not linked to another signifier.

Second, the protests of a poor rural community in Mpumalanga received a wave of media attention daily for a whole month in 2009, resulting in the firing of the mayor and executive committee for stealing the funds in a local municipality. This was an example of the media's exercising its professional role as watchdog, checking the abuse of power and attempting to hold power to account. It could not then be so easily dismissed as the 'bourgeoisie press'. However, the media fell down in not revisiting the issue once the fire of the burning tyres had died down.

Third, the ANC's efforts to interpellate Zapiro ideologically failed as he refused identification as 'right winger', 'racist' and 'enemy of the people'. He preferred to misrecognise the calling, or hailing, and continued with hard-hitting and irreverent cartoons of the powerful – and in 2009 he won the Vodacom journalist of the year award.

Fourth, the discourse of editors Rossouw, Radebe, Makhanya, Malala and Milazi on what 'developmental journalism' meant to them showed that they were committed to professional roles and would not succumb to the ideologically interpellating voice of the ANC or the injunctions to toe the line and show more loyalty. They recognised and saw the conflation and frequent elision between state and party, and resisted.

Fifth, the subjectivisation of the *Sunday Times* through the ideological interpellations of the paper's journalists as 'enemies of the people' who were lacking *ubuntu* failed in the sense that the newspaper did not turn towards becoming a sweetheart press.

An optimistic moment: attempts to make race the Master-Signifier in the world of journalists failed

The South African Human Rights Commission (SAHRC) ruled against the FBJ in 2008, declaring that blacks-only gatherings of journalists were unconstitutional. The forum then dwindled into 'nothing', according to several black journalists contacted. Some of them had joined the forum. Many more said they were 'not interested', that this was 'a backward move', 'behind the times', 'unprogressive', and that it was just 'crude racism' and not appropriate to the new South Africa. Were there issues that could affect black journalists only? Does one write 'black' stories and were newsrooms so full of whites that blacks did not get their chance to 'develop'? The majority of journalists interviewed commented that this was not the case and those who believed it to be so were operating in a social fantasy of what the media was, as there were very few white editors in the country by 2010 and the majority of reporters in newsrooms were black. Phylicia Oppelt noted: 'Most newspapers across this country are edited by black South Africans; senior positions across the different media platforms are occupied by black journalists' (*Daily Dispatch*: 31 August 2009). Race was tied to the transformation project in the discourse of successive presidents in the democratic era, but for many journalists race was a floating signifier without full meaning.

The failure of the FBJ to re-launch signalled an optimistic moment for democracy as it attested to the fact that there was no one view, nor a single unified identity, on the part of journalists, and certainly not on the basis of race. It showed that the attempt to rigidify the signifier, race, and turn it into a Master-Signifier, failed – meaning simply that race was not the be all and end all. The second optimistic moment was the formation in 2010 of a new non-racial organisation, Projourn, with the aim of addressing both political and non-political issues faced by journalists in South Africa. The third optimistic moment was that, even though the majority of journalists in newsrooms today are black they are not essentialising race or identifying purely on race terms, and they are not kowtowing to the ruling party's desire for a more loyal media. The floating signifier, race, was not fixed, not the main signifier to which all other meanings were attached or linked. The FBJ attempted to convert race, or 'black', into a Master-Signifier and it was a testament to most black journalists – in not identifying with one thing, in this case, race – that the call from authority failed. This then raises the question whether journalists have political identities. They do, but these identities are multiple and free floating, characterised, in Lacanian parlance, by 'a lack'.

A further optimistic moment: Zapiro's ideological interpellation failed

Signalling both optimistic and pessimistic moments, but mainly the former, was the furore over Zapiro's cartooning. The optimistic moment resided in the fact that Zapiro was not intimidated to the extent that he stopped drawing irreverent cartoons. His cartoons, he stated in an interview, were intended to 'knock the high and mighty off their pedestals', and they have not 'softened' since the law suit.

The pessimistic moment for democracy existed in the fact that a cartoonist could be subjected to a lawsuit at all, given a constitution which protects freedom of expression. Even more disturbing is the fact that it is the president of the country, Jacob Zuma who maintains this lawsuit against him. The action was an attempt to intimidate Zapiro into becoming a more loyal subject, to be more ideologically in tandem with the ANC, to be less critical. It was an illogical attempt to creat unity with the media through intimidatory tactics and a way of foreclosing the existing space for highly political and irreverent cartooning.

While I have argued that the ideological interpellation of Zapiro by the ANC failed in the sense that he did not heed the calling by accepting the label, he did, however, make a 'turn' when he suspended the showerhead. This could be interpreted as ambivalence, although he could also have merely been acting in a spirt of generosity or fairness, giving Zuma another chance. In balancing these 'turns', however, ultimately Zapiro 'talked back' with his cartoons, he did not embrace the injurious terms meant to subjugate and he remains a legitimate adversary in the unrealised democracy. 'Talking back' is a rejection of the injurious term, and Zapiro's cartoon after Babygate exemplifies talking back.

The failed subjectivisation of the *Sunday Times*

The case study of the *Sunday Times* versus the former health minister is an optimistic instance of the role of the media in a democracy. Three kinds of subjects and subjectivisations were examined. In the first, we saw the loyal and unquestioning subject of the former president Thabo Mbeki in the former health minister, Dr Manto Tshabalala-Msimang, nicknamed Dr Beetroot for advocating garlic, beetroot, onions and potatoes as a diet to cure AIDS. The second was the questioning, non-conforming subject, the deputy health minister Nozizwe Madlala-Routledge, who was fired for not toeing the party line. The third subjectivisation was against the *Sunday Times*, through the threatened arrest of the editor and one of his senior journalists, the threat from the government to withdraw its advertising and the attempted buyout by Koni.

Those who wanted to protect the former health minister used race as the Master-Signifier while those in support of the story being published argued in the name of the public interest and of democracy. Those against the story being published also argued in the name of democracy. This rendered 'democracy' a floating signifier: meaning completely different things to different parties as it was not fixed to any one full meaning. The chain of illogic was: if you expose corruption but you are exposing 'one of our own' then you are anti-transformation, and therefore you are anti-black, you are an outsider to democracy, and therefore you are an enemy of the people – or you are 'that colonial creature', as Robert Suresh Roberts called Makhanya.

We also witnessed the ambivalent effect of power, in the form of the psyche that turned against itself, which could be a turn of conscience, or consciousness, or the split psyche. The reaction to subjection by Makhanya could be viewed in a similar way to that of Zapiro. Both made half turns, showing ambivalence. In Makhanya's case, he said he would hand himself over to the police, even though he felt he had done nothing wrong. He said he would do this to hasten the process of getting to the truth, but as he had indeed done nothing wrong there was no need for such an action. In the theory of this book, he could be viewed as the typical postmodern split subject, partially subjecting himself to interpellation when he said he would hand himself over to the police. Or else it could have just been a tactical move, and it was only a half turn in the sense that he did not succumb completely to the voice of power. His newspaper continued in critical mode, and has continued to experience attempted subjectivisation and intimidation. In July 2010, Makhanya was elected chairperson of Sanef and was in August 2010 an important leader against the impending media repressions.

The subject formation of Madlala-Routledge was different. She was embedded within the ranks of the ANC-led government, yet broke these ranks and made a turn away from the voice of power, for which she was interpellated as a 'non team player' who was 'courting the international media' and she was fired from her job. It would also seem that she 'lost', but this was not so. The subsequent political events showed how democracy in South Africa is a constantly negotiated, fluid, open-ended space, indeterminate and ambiguous in character. At the ANC's Polokwane conference in December 2007, Mbeki was axed and Jacob Zuma became president. Madlala-Routledge, who had backed Zuma, was then brought back into the political space.

More optimistic moments: the discourse of editors

The discourse of the editors showed little or no 'turning' to the ideological hailing or to norms of the past. In reply to questions about the nature of democracy and the independence of the media, all the editors stated that an independent media was needed in South Africa's democracy because it served as a check on the abuse of power that could hold the powerful to account for their actions. The editors held varied opinions on development journalism but all referred to its significance in playing an educative role so that informed decisions could be made by the country's citizenry. The editors said that the independence of the media was a universal principle and intrinsic to a democracy. Most of the editors dismissed the possibility of a media appeals tribunal, some citing the Constitution that protected media freedom.

If the editors had said that they felt the publication of the stories about the health minister ought not to have been published, it would have shown that they were still attached to the ANC as a liberation party, but they did not reiterate the norms of the past and said that independence of the media was not contingent upon what stage of democracy the county was in. The relevance of this point is that in the logic of the ANC, because the country is a 'transitional' democracy, it must be protected from scandal. So if corruption was uncovered and spread across the newspapers it showed the ANC in a negative light, whereas in a young democracy the media should be giving the new government a chance and not be so hard on the new leaders. Mondli Makhanya aptly explained the view of the ANC on the media to me: 'We are now enemies of the people. Most of the people in the ANC were used to being on the right side of history. They then didn't expect to be taken on by the media. They wanted a honeymoon period.' He didn't add 'but for how long can a honeymoon last?', and he remarked that 'they would like us to attend more ribbon cutting events'. Also in an interview, Hopewell Radebe said that the ANC 'would like us to clap our hands more often'. There was no compulsion from among the editors to be loyal to the ANC although there is a sense of disquiet, when the interviews are analysed, in that the majority felt that the media appeals tribunal would probably not happen because the Constitution would protect them. Radebe warned that the tribunal *could* happen. He thought that the journalist profession was unorganised and that 'maybe we need something to bring us together; maybe it will be this issue'. And Abdul Milazi observed: 'It will all depend on the media itself, whether it lies down and plays dead or whether it stands up to fight the proposed controls'. The editors were all conscious of a growing unprogressive hegemony in the attempt at creating social consensus with the press. They were aware of the ideological interpellation of 'enemy' rather than legitimate adversary, and chose to misrecognise the hailing.

Pessimistic moments: the social fantasy of the ANC

I have drawn several patterns and conclusions from the ANC's gaze on the media. There was an over-investment by the ANC, and a surplus attached, in its discourse on the media. In other words, it attached more to the media than was necessary. The ANC's ideological social fantasy was that the media was a single, unified entity rather than an amorphous, fluid and undecided one. It desired unity and consensus with the media and when it could not get this it proposed controlling measures. It viewed the media as the enemy rather than a legitimate adversary. Its ideological interpellations were aimed at subjection and it rigidly fixed certain concepts such as development journalism to mean loyalty. I have called this hegemony in the guise of development. It forecloses spaces for openness.

Let us now return to Lacan's *jouissance* to understand the ANC's gaze. *Jouissance* is surplus excitation. It may imply enjoyment as we understand it, but ninety-nine percent of the time it is experienced as pain or suffering, as paranoia or persecution, according to Leader and Groves (1995: 128). They also explained that fantasy is a sort of magnet which will attract those memories to itself which suit it: 'If you have only a few memories from your childhood, you could ask yourself why you remember only those elements and not others'. The simple answer to this question is because it best suits your fantasy.

The social and ideological fantasy of the ANC about the media resided precisely in the excess attached to it, seen for example in the Letters from the President and the online contributions from presidents Thabo Mbeki and Jacob Zuma. The ANC and its alliance partners do not know how the media works but imagine and fantasise that they do, conferring certain identities and properties to it. For example, the ANC imagined that white editors were telling black reporters what to write, that commercial imperatives completely control what stories go into newspapers, and that black journalists and editors who were critical were 'coconuts', black on the outside and white inside, among other ideological interpellations and injurious gazes. This is Lacanian *jouissance* in operation.

The ANC's ideological interpellation of Zapiro as racist, enemy and right-winger, showed that it saw no distinction between enemy and legitimate adversary. Exposures of corruption and abuse of power, in the ANC's gaze, were plots hatched against it by the media. Duarte's statement: 'We are aware that every Thursday night a group of journalists ... decide what stories they will go into' is the ultimate example of this phantasmic gaze. The ANC's construction of the media has been a singularly paranoid one, a fantasy based on projection. In a typical Lacanian inversion, then, I've argued that the ANC must recognise, in the excesses attributed to the media, the truth about itself. Believing as it does, or says it does, in pluralism and social democracy, the ANC ought to make this move towards viewing the media as legitimate adversaries or friendly enemies, rather than enemies with whom it is at war, and with whom it has nothing in common.

Floating signifiers and Master-Signifiers

The ANC has converted floating signifiers into Master-Signifiers. For instance, in its understanding of developmental journalism we saw some artful ideological manipulation and obfuscation at work, rigidifying a floating signifier by means of a *point de capiton*. In other words, in order to halt the many rich and varied meanings of 'development' the ANC instead conferred on it one totalised and fixed meaning – loyalty to the ruling party. Editors understood the term developmental journalism to mean playing an educative role, being a provider of reliable information, but also being a powerful watchdog: exposing lack of service delivery and corruption and holding power to account. Radebe described the 'othering' of the media thus: 'They think of us as the enemies of the people. That's taking the media as not being part of the people, yet we come out of this society. But they think we are not enemies when we are praise singers. We are enemies when we criticise.'

The unpredictable and undecidable future turns for democracy

One of the important psychoanalytical contributions in this work is the deployment of the concepts of 'subjectivisation' and how the figure of the psyche can turn against itself, showing how subjection is paradoxical. 'Resignifications' are about how one can detach from norms of the past – for some liberation – as norms of the past, when repeated, can oppress. I have shown that the media world was under subjection in different ways. The focus was on political subjection, as in interpellations. A further arena of subjectivisation took place through conflation of state and party in the form of legislation, for example the ANC's support for the Protection of State Information Bill, which would hinder the free flow of information and therefore injure democracy. The absence of public interest defence means that journalists cannot argue that they possessed a classified document and published it in the public interest. The Bill trumps the Promotion of Access to Information Act, so that if there is a conflict between the promotion of access to information and the protection of information, the latter wins. The Bill includes almost unlimited power for the ministry of state security, which ensures that South Africa moves backwards to days of old – a security state.

In subject formation, power at first appears to be external, 'pressed upon the subject, pressing the subject into subordination that constitutes a subject's self-identity' (Butler 1997: 3). That was internal subjection. The subjections in the Protection of State Information Bill were external subjection, which is power from the outside of oneself. That you ought to have reasonably known that the document you possessed was a danger to national security, is an external subjection. But power also takes other forms, as I have described in the chapter on the Forum for Black Journalists. What about the figure of turning, a turning back on oneself or turning *on* oneself, a form of twisting so to speak? In 2010, journalists made many twists and turns. Editors did not know how to react to the ANC's call to discuss the media appeals tribunal. Should they engage? Should they ignore the call? *Business Day*'s editor, Peter Bruce said he would not participate in the call for a discussion on the tribunal. This could be viewed as a turn against the voice of power:

> I am just not prepared to give any credibility or comfort to the kind of Star Chamber that the ANC and its allies appear to have in mind … I recognise fully that my absence will have no effect whatsoever in the decision that the ruling alliance finally makes. It simply disgusts me and I want no part of it (*The Times*: 6 August 2010).

For the others in Sanef, there was ambivalence. However, it must be said that not all the editors and journalists present at the Sanef meeting on 4 August 2010 at the *Sunday Times* office were 'ambivalent'. Some had already resigned from their newspapers and had joined the new ANC-supporting newspaper, *The New Age*.

So it is also clear that the twists and turns did not emanate from the government, the ANC ruling alliance and the state alone. In the media industry itself there was evidence of reflexivity and fluidity. *The New Age*, owned by the Gupta Group, which was due to be launched on 20 October 2010, failed to appear. Five key editorial staffers made an awkward turn by moving to *The New Age*, and then made another reflexive turn and resigned on 19 October 2010, Black Wednesday, on the eve of the launch. The launch did not take place. The journalists did not provide reasons for their resignations but, reading between the lines, it appeared to be because they were subjected to or bullied by the Guptas into launching the newspaper when they were not ready. There were reports that the newspaper was understaffed and under-resourced (*The Times*: 21 October 2010; *The Star*: 20 October 2010; *Mail & Guardian*: 29 October-4 November 2010). This was probably not the full story, and by 2012 we had still not heard the full story, except that one journalist who had left the *The New Age* in 2011 told me that they had not expected 'so much management interference' in their editorial work. In a further twist, it was announced on 29 October 2010 that Henry Jeffreys, a former editor of *Die Burger*, who had only weeks earlier criticised *The New Age,* had taken over the editorship of the paper (*The Times*: 29 October 2010). He was once deputy chairperson of Sanef during the period 2007 to 2008. After a few false starts *The New Age* was launched on 6 December 2010. Jeffreys said in his first editorial that the paper 'held no brief for any political party', but 'we will generally support the government of the day, at all levels' (*The New Age*: 6 December 2010). This was obviously a contradiction.

The ANC's ideological labellings are all part of its naming trajectory, self-serving and intended to deflect from the ANC's own problems. I have highlighted a rich pluralist tradition that had developed in South Africa's democracy, where 'the people' are not one, but multiple and divided, as is 'the media'. I have also highlighted how the ANC turned against the media for shining the torch on failings which affect the poor of the country most of all.

Given the evidence and these reflections, I am led to conclude that the democratic path is open and undecided in a very typical postmodern fluid state, but free spaces such as that of the media are closing down. I have used the terms 'democracy' 'the media', and 'independence', in an affirmative deconstructive way: that is, I have used and interrogated them at the same time. The optimistic and pessimistic moments for democracy do not lie parallel to each other but intersect in a continually contesting way. This book has, I hope, reflected the postmodern condition of South Africa. It is undecided. The future path looks uncertain and politics keep changing. The world of the media itself is undecided, open, and split, lacking a unified identity, but the ANC desires unity with it, as though it was one entity whereas pluralistic and agonistic spaces can only flourish in a lack of unity and a radical ambiguity, intrinsic to the deepening of democracy, the final realisation of which is imperfect and unending.

Political hyenas or paranoia

> We're headed for a full-blown predator state where a powerful, corrupt and demagogic elite of political hyenas is increasing controlling the state as a vehicle for accumulation.[2]

Even though the independent media understood its role as that of a watchdog, holding power to account to prevent the graphic and dramatic scenario that Vavi painted of a corrupt predator state full of political hyenas; and even though the media understood it should remain separate from the ruling party, the state, and the government, it nevertheless, under the auspices of Sanef, believed in engagement with the ANC-led government. It gave the ANC the benefit of the doubt. On 15 and 16 October 2010, government representatives and Sanef met at the Mount Grace hotel, in the Magaliesberg hills, to discuss problems with the media and how to defuse hostilities. After this two-day summit, the deputy president, Kgalema Motlanthe, announced that the ANC would give the media a chance to review and strengthen its self-regulatory mechanism before forging ahead – if it did at all – with a state regulated media appeals tribunal. This seemed to go directly against the ANC's NGC resolution of September 2010, less than a month earlier, which tasked Parliament with an investigation into setting up the tribunal. According to the deputy president, the government would also make submissions to the South African Press Council's review process about the functioning of the press ombudsman's office. Motlanthe said that 'a lot' depended on how the government's concerns would be addressed. The concerns he raised were the turnaround time for printing corrections and the commensurate importance of the prominence given to apologies. If these were put right it could remove the basis for disquiet (*Sunday Times*: 17 October 2010).

At first glance this appeared to be an about-turn from the NGC decision, but it is not necessarily the case. An about-turn would be a superficial interpretation. It should rather be seen as a classic example of the ANC alliance showing its many ideological strands, as well as its fractious and split nature. Some within the cabinet, such as Motlanthe, had stronger democratic tendencies, as did some within the alliance such as Vavi of Cosatu, who had spoken out against a media appeals tribunal and the Protection of State Information Bill. This stood in stark contrast to the Stalinist tendencies of Nzimande of the SACP, Malema of the ANC Youth League and Mthembu of the ANC. Sanef released a statement agreeing that 'improved relations between the government and the media were critical to the achievement of South Africa envisaged in the country's constitution' (Sanef 2010a). This agreement gave the independent print media some breathing space from possible foreclosures. But it remained to be seen which ideological tendency would win in the end. Ultimately, based on the fact that the government did not stipulate any timeframe for the review process of the self-regulatory mechanism of the media, it would seem that the ANC's 2012 policy conference would decide.

Two days after the government-Sanef summit, on 19 October 2010, campaigners from the Right2Know engaged in a silent march to Constitution Hill in Braamfontein to mark Black Wednesday. A further commemoration, on the same day, took the form of a seminar entitled 'Freedom of expression is every citizen's business', held jointly by Sanef, Wits University's Faculty of Humanities and the Institute for the Advancement of Journalism. It was held at Wits University and chaired by the faculty's dean, Professor Tawana Kupe. Professor Kader Asmal, the former minister of education in the Mbeki cabinet, was a keynote speaker on 'Free speech is life itself'. He openly declared himself a *persona non grata* in the ANC at this time because of his critical and dissenting voice on many issues – the latest was the Protection of State Information Bill.

Some striking issues emerged from the 2010 Black Wednesday commemoration.

First, some Sanef members who negotiated with government about the freedom of the press were enthusiastic afterwards (for example, Thabo Leshilo, who chaired the session said 'I left the meeting largely enthused. We seem to be going in the right direction', more than hinting that he believed the good faith of the meeting).

Second, the editor of the *Financial Mail*, Barney Mthombothi, felt that whether or not the media appeals tribunal was instituted 'the damage is done' and that some leaders in Africa were now saying 'look at what is happening in South Africa, yet you are complaining'. The proposed repressive measures to curb the media's freedom in South Africa were being used in other African states to justify their own lack of media freedom – if curbs on media freedom were happening in South Africa, a shining beacon of democracy and freedom of expression, how could citizens elsewhere protest? Kupe noted the same point in his opening remarks, when he observed that media freedom in South Africa had been an example to the rest of Africa, but if this changed to a repressive media environment it would 'negatively affect' the continent.

Third, one of the panellists, a former editor of the *Sowetan* and in 2012 Avusa ombudsman, Joe Latakgomo, drew on his experience from apartheid days to sketch parallels about press freedom in the democratic era. He remembered how his newspaper *The World* was closed down in 1977 and how, prior to this, journalists were not allowed to tell the truth. He made direct links with the ANC's attempted subjections of 2010. He asked: should Sanef be meeting with the government about media freedom? Would it really make a difference? Latakgomo felt the government and the ANC would, in the end, simply do what they wanted to do. He considered that the proposals for the enactment of the Protection of State Information Bill and for instituting the media appeals tribunal were intended to intimidate journalists and to make them feel guilty about their legitimate work. This raised the following questions: would journalists start to turn towards the voice of power? Would they begin to self-censor? Would they feel that they were doing something wrong by reporting corruption and the abuse of power? Latakgomo hinted that this stepping backwards could already be happening, given the numerous advertisements in the newspapers calling for the review of self-regulation. Latakgomo thought that the self-regulation system worked well as it was. He was convinced that these repressive moves by the ANC and the ruling alliance were repeated patterns of the past, that this was a case of an insecure government shutting down the dissenting voices of civil society. *En passant*, after a civil society conference organised by Cosatu (for representatives of sixty-six organisations, ranging from trade unions, churches and communities to street traders, traditional leaders and taxi associations) on 27 and 28 October 2010 in Boksburg, to discuss poverty, service delivery, corruption and nepotism, and to which the ANC, the government and the SACP were not invited, the ANC's secretary general, Gwede Mantashe, accused the union federation of being 'oppositionist' and wanting to unseat the ruling party. Vavi's response was apposite: 'The ANC is paranoid' (*The Times*: 3 November 2010).[3] What this showed, then, was that the ANC's anti-media stance was part of a wider and broader antipathy related to any criticism and dissension which highlighted the ruling party's own insecurity. It was an insecurity bordering on hysteria in the last few months of 2010.

So it was within this context, the all-pervasive fear, hysteria, insecurity and paranoia of the ruling party, that Latakgomo's analysis made sense. He warned that the ruling bloc would continue to 'swing the sword above the heads' of journalists and editors, and it was not going to stop, even after the review process of the self-regulatory mechanism was completed. He predicted, at the Black Wednesday commemorative seminar, that 'it is inevitable that we will get to a point when they will say this is not enough'.

Barely a week after Latakgomo's predictions, a front page lead in *The Times* of 25 October 2010 broke the story that police had threatened to arrest two journalists from the Eastern Cape on 22 October in connection with an anonymous letter threatening the safety of a cabinet minister. The journalists said they felt threatened when police warned them that what had happened in Mpumalanga could happen in the Eastern Cape (in Mpumalanga there was a hit list of those who uncovered corruption and reported unfavourably about politicians, the newspaper report said, and the arrest on 4 August of the *Sunday Times* investigative journalist, Mzilikazi wa Afrika, who uncovered corruption in that province, had made international headlines). After the intimidation of the two Eastern Cape journalists, Sanef's chairperson, Mondli Makhanya, observed that the behaviour of the police appeared to violate the agreement reached between the government and the media that prior consultation between the government and Sanef was necessary before a subpoena was issued for a journalist to give evidence (*The Times:* 25 October 2010). It could be argued by a cynic that the incident vindicated the view that Sanef might have been naïve in putting so much faith in its negotiations with the government, or turning towards the voice of power. The damage was already done when the ANC first began its strident calls for the media appeals tribunal and when Wa Afrika was arrested. The arrest seemed to have given the green light to the police to clamp down on journalists.

Had the green light also been given to the courts that secrecy was already the order of the day, even though the enactment of the Protection of State Information Bill had not yet occurred? In a further incident, after the government-media summit, a North Gauteng High Court judge, Judge Ephraim Makgoba, granted an interdict to the SAPS to stop the publication of details of corruption in the police's crime intelligence unit in the *Sunday Independent* of 31 October 2010. The court backed the police to interdict Independent Newspapers from publishing the full story of nepotism and corruption by keeping names secret (*Saturday Star*: 30 October 2010; *Sunday Times* and *Sunday Independent*: 31 October 2010). If the independent media continued to pursue openness, the codes of the profession, and remained loyal to their task of holding power to account, as in the case of the *Sunday Independent*, whose editor, Makhadu Sefara, stated that he intended fighting the gagging in the Constitutional Court, it would be unlikely that the ANC alliance or the government would accept the self-regulation review process by the media. It was more likely that they would continue to be unhappy with the uncovering of corruption, using ideological labels and obfuscation that this was 'anti-transformation'

Two more turns took place after the Sanef-government summit. First, Zuma announced during a rally to mark the 66th anniversary of the ANC Youth League on 30 October 2010 in Stellenbosch that he was still committed to the media appeals tribunal, and this emerged a mere two weeks after the government-Sanef summit at which his deputy president had announced that the tribunal was on ice until the self-regulatory review process had taken place.

Second, the government announced a plan to channel advertising to 'patriotic media' (*Mail & Guardian*: 29 October-4 November 2010) and aimed to allocate sixty per cent of spending to the SABC and thirty per cent to *The New Age*.

Vavi, on corruption and political hyenas, captured some of the issues in the then sixteen year-old democracy: the need to fight patronage, corruption and greed. Implicit in this is the need for an independent, robust media which should be steadfast in holding power to account. The fight between the ANC and the media for democracy, a fight internal to democracy itself, was characterised by contradictions and unpredictable twists and turns. Foucault's famous reflection said, 'Don't ask me who I am, I am constantly changing'. So it is with South Africa's zeitgeist. It changes day by day.

NOTES

1   Mouffe C (2005) *The Return of the Political*. London: Verso; 137.
2   Zwelinzima Vavi, at a Cosatu press conference held in Johannesburg in 26 August 2010, cited in *The Times*: 26 August 2010.
3   Gwede Mantashe said Cosatu should convince the ANC that it had no intention of forming an alternative party, adding that the ANC-led government had been prosecuted and found guilty in absentia at the conference, to which Vavi responded: 'I honestly don't know what informs this paranoia ... ' (*The Times*: 3 November 2010).

EPILOGUE

After the tensions and battles between the ANC and media since democracy which have been captured in this book's chapters, the year 2012 did not follow the same pattern. It was unpredictable, so typical of the postmodern condition. First, the much anticipated Press Freedom Commission report was released in April and this was welcomed very quickly by some of the most serious critics of the media – namely Gwede Mantashe and Jackson Mthembu, who attended the launch of the report on 25 April. They were once, and not so long ago, big proponents of the media appeals tribunal, which then seemed as if it would be put to bed – either for good or for now (there is no way of telling) but the matter would be sure to arise at the ANC elective conference at the end of 2012.

Second, the National Council of Provinces, in a surprise move, announced fairly substantial concessions, which in effect granted a public interest defence amendment to the Protection of State Information Bill. But just as quickly these were rejected by the State Security Agency.

There are a few ways to view the progressive developments. One is that the ANC had seen that it had enough bad publicity, locally and internationally, over these twin issues – the Secrecy Bill and the media appeals tribunal – which cut straight through the freedoms of journalism in a democracy. The ANC decided it needed to make amends, as this was seriously embarrassing. Then, civil society actions, as in the protests by the Right2Know campaign,[1] had an impact. At every turn in parliament the R2K engaged in protest action and made constructive legal feedback. And, further, the ANC was afraid it could be losing support, not only among the intelligentsia and middle classes, but also on the ground. It had witnessed, during the NCOP public hearings in the townships, how dissatisfied people were with service delivery and how they felt that secrecy would just make things worse. The recent developments are probably a combination of all these reasons. However, the gains made lasted a short while before the State Security Agency rejected the amendments to the Secrecy Bill and it was back to square one.

In keeping with the optimistic and pessimistic moments for democracy lying side by side, and the unpredictability in South African politics, another blast waltzed in, at the end of May 2012, to unsettle the most recent picture I have painted (that things might be settling down and the ANC might be back-tracking on curtailing freedoms). A painting called *The Spear*, by the artist Brett Murray, a former anti-apartheid activist, caused a huge storm because it depicted Zuma as a Leninist figure – that was no big deal – but with his penis exposed. The ANC went to court to order the art gallery in which it was displayed to remove the painting, declare it illegal, and ban it from the public eye – but not before two members of the public had defaced it. The unpredict-ability of South Africa reared its head in this scene too. A middle aged white man entered the art gallery and painted crosses over the painting and then declared in court that he did it to defuse the tension and prevent a race war. That's possibly rather presumptuous, but definitely unpredictable. The young black taxi driver who went in seconds later and smeared black paint all over *The Spear* was then captured on television being head butted and thrown on the floor in a violent manner by a security guard. This raised eyebrows too. Was there so much self-hatred in that black security guard that he had violently to arrest the young black man yet allow a polite arrest of the elderly white man? But back to the main contention. The matter of the dignity and privacy provid-ed by the Constitution versus freedom of expression had reared its head again.

This clash is not going to go away soon. All sorts of matters were invoked in the privacy and dignity argument in defence of Zuma and outrage at his exposed penis: culture, tradition, humiliation, apartheid, and racism. And this was how race, again, appeared as a Master-Signifier. Was it yet another case of being passionately attached to the past, to victimhood? The ANC asked the public to boycott the *City Press* newspaper, which had placed the painting on its website and refused to remove it. The point is that Zuma is a public figure, open to scrutiny but also to ridicule, and his right to privacy is curtailed by the fact that he is more than an ordinary private individual.

But let's pause for a moment with the artist, and get this out of the way quickly. As an artist his right to freedom of expression is undeniable. But could there be some *jouissance* in that particular work of art, as in something more than enjoyment, a surplus, and excess, some orgasmic delight, coupled with suffering and persecution? It is worth a questioning note and, after all, this book has used psychoanalytical concepts to understand tensions.

City Press sold out on Sunday 27 May 2012, despite the ANC's calling for a boycott of the newspaper a few days before (Ferial Haffajee apologised to members of the Zuma family for hurting them, but refused to remove the paint-ing from the *City Press* website). On the same Sunday, the newspaper received support from an unlikely ally – one whose dirty linen and shenanigans for tenderpreneurship, tax dodging and other allegedly corrupt dealings had been hung up for all to read in the *City Press*: the former Youth League leader Julius Malema, who said that in support of freedom of expression he would buy two newspapers instead of one. In a public letter published in *City Press*, he wrote: 'Of all the freedoms in the Bill of Rights, the right we should defend with our lives is the right to hold different opinions on how we view society and how we think certain matters should be handled. Banning newspapers simply because we disagree with them, and boycotting them on the basis that our conception of truth is absolute, poses a real threat to our democracy' (*City Press*: 27 May 2012). I did not predict when I started my research that I would end on a glowing note in praise of Malema, notwithstanding my awareness that if Malema had still been within the powerful fold of the ANC he would most probably not have said what he did. He might well have been as outraged in a typical populist sort of way as the rest of the ruling elite were about a mere painting that should have been laughed at. After all, doesn't democracy have a sense of humour? And, shouldn't public figures be robust enough to handle criticism?

Further demonstrating how quickly things change and how unpredictable politics are in South Africa, there was a further unexpected twist, arguably a turn towards the voice of power, when on Monday morning Haffajee announced on Twitter that she would remove the image of Zuma from her website. Her reasons? 'Out of care and fear.' She explained: 'Anger and rage is never the role of the media in society. We are robust and independent, yes, but divisive and deaf, no.'

Well and good, but what worries and disturbs me is the 'fear'. Haffajee reportedly received death threats. What does it all mean? Will this set a precedent for the future, when the ANC gets upset about some work of art, or some critique of power, or criticism of patriarchy, or corruption? When it clamps down on freedom of expression in a book, a website or an art gallery, in an article, or in a speech, will we then succumb to the ideologically interpellating voice (or bullying voice)?

Meanwhile, Zuma received generous lashings of sympathy and this would probably hold him in good stead for the ANC's elective conference to be held in Mangaung in December. Supporters of the Bill of Rights clause on freedom of expression were left confused and worried about the future. The important point is that politics in South Africa is unpredictable: as quickly as you had to get used to the idea that press freedom was under serious threat, you had as quickly to get used to the idea that it may not be under threat after all and that concessions and compromises were being reached. Then, just as quickly, a furor such as was brought on by *The Spear* arises, and we are left gasping. It is difficult to know what will happen next. The Secrecy Bill still had no public interest defence at the time of publication but the dreaded media appeals tribunal seems to be in abeyance, but who knows whether this Polokwane resolution will be resurrected at Mangaung in December, citing newspapers who stick to their right to publish in the public interest?

The black and white issue that the *Spear* story became in May 2012 was not literally a black and white issue. People seem to be called racists if they are not following the master narrative of the ANC. And, in this book we have seen how black journalists were also labelled racists, or coconuts, and one was even called a colonial creature.

The twist and turns with the Secrecy Bill signified the postmodern condition of South African politics sprinkled with healthy doses of uncertainty and chaos. On 6 June 2012, the State Security Agency rejected the ANC's recommendations to limit the powers of the ministry to delegate classification powers, to reduce penalties and to remove the burden of proof. In essence, journalists and whistleblowers still faced criminalisation if the amendments were not finally to be accepted. It was essential to keep up the pressure for reform. Murray Hunter, the Right2Know coordinator, said in a press release on 7 June, 2012: 'The Secrecy Bill has united people across the boundaries of space, race, class and ideology – from leafy suburbs to townships and informal settlements, shop floors and office blocks, university campuses and old-age homes. We can't stop pushing now; in fact, now's the time to start.'

And so the one step forwards, two steps backwards dance continued. Puzzling paradoxes? Twists and turns? Anxiety, ambivalence, or simply unpredictability and uncertainty? What best describes the future path in the fight for democracy between the ANC and the media in South Africa?

NOTES

1   I served as a member of R2K's national working group, Gauteng Working Group and Media Freedom and Diversity committee from February 2011 to February 2012. My views here, however, are not representative of R2K.

APPENDICES

Appendix 1

THE SOUTH AFRICAN PRESS CODE 1996

Preamble
WHEREAS:
Section 16 of the Constitution of the Republic of South Africa enshrines the right to freedom of expression as follows:

(1) Everyone has the right to freedom of expression, which includes:
(a) Freedom of the press and other media;
(b) Freedom to receive or impart information or ideas;
(c) Freedom of artistic creativity; and
(d) Academic freedom and freedom of scientific research.

(2) The right in subsection (1) does not extend to
(a) Propaganda for war;
(b) Incitement of imminent violence; or
(c) Advocacy of hatred that is based on race, ethnicity, gender or religion, and that constitutes incitement to cause harm.

The basic principle to be upheld is that the freedom of the press is indivisible from and subject to the same rights and duties as that of the individual and rests on the public's fundamental right to be informed and freely to receive and to disseminate opinions; and

The primary purpose of gathering and distributing news and opinion is to serve society by informing citizens and enabling them to make informed judgments on the issues of the time; and

The freedom of the press allows for an independent scrutiny to bear on the forces that shape society.

NOW THEREFORE:
The Press Council of South Africa accepts the following Code which will guide the South African Press Ombudsman and the South African Press Appeals Panel to reach decisions on complaints from the public after publication of the elevant material.

Furthermore, the Press Council of South Africa is hereby constituted as a self-regulatory mechanism to provide impartial, expeditious and cost-effective arbitration to settle complaints based on and arising from this Code.

Definition

For purposes of this Code, "child pornography" shall mean: "Any image or any description of a person, real or simulated, who is or who is depicted or described as being, under the age of 18 years, engaged in sexual conduct; participating in or assisting another person to participate in sexual conduct; or showing or describing the body or parts of the body of the person in a manner or circumstances which, in context, amounts to sexual exploitation, or in a manner capable of being used for purposes of sexual exploitation."

1. Reporting of News

1.1 The press shall be obliged to report news truthfully, accurately and fairly.

1.2 News shall be presented in context and in a balanced manner, without any intentional or negligent departure from the facts whether by:

1.2.1 Distortion, exaggeration or misrepresentation;

1.2.2 Material omissions; or

1.2.3 Summarisation.

1.3 Only what may reasonably be true, having regard to the sources of the news, may be presented as fact, and such facts shall be published fairly with due regard to context and importance. Where a report is not based on facts or is founded on opinions, allegation, rumour or supposition, it shall be presented in such manner as to indicate this clearly.

1.4 Where there is reason to doubt the accuracy of a report and it is practicable to verify the accuracy thereof, it shall be verified. Where it has not been practicable to verify the accuracy of a report, this shall be mentioned in such report.

1.5 A publication should usually seek the views of the subject of serious critical reportage in advance of publication; provided that this need not be done where the publication has reasonable grounds for believing that by doing so it would be prevented from publishing the report or where evidence might be destroyed or witnesses intimidated.

1.6 A publication should make amends for publishing information or comment that is found to be inaccurate by printing, promptly and with appropriate prominence, a retraction, correction or explanation.

1.7 Reports, photographs or sketches relative to matters involving indecency or obscenity shall be presented with due sensitivity towards the prevailing moral climate.

1.7.1 A visual presentation of sexual conduct may not be published, unless a legitimate public interest dictates otherwise.

1.7.2 Child pornography shall not be published.

1.8 The identity of rape victims and victims of sexual violence shall not be published without the consent of the victim.

1.9 News obtained by dishonest or unfair means, or the publication of which would involve a breach of confidence, should not be published unless a legitimate public interest dictates otherwise.

1.10 In both news and comment the press shall exercise exceptional care and consideration in matters involving the private lives and concerns of individuals, bearing in mind that any right to privacy may be overridden only by a legitimate public interest.

2. Discrimination and Hate Speech

2.1 The press should avoid discriminatory or denigratory references to people's race, colour, ethnicity, religion, gender, sexual orientation or preference, physical or mental disability or illness, or age.

2.2 The press should not refer to a person's race, colour, ethnicity, religion, gender, sexual orientation or preference, physical or mental illness in a prejudicial or pejorative context except where it is strictly relevant to the matter reported or adds significantly to readers' understanding of that matter.

2.3 The press has the right and indeed the duty to report and comment on all matters of legitimate public interest. This right and duty must, however, be balanced against the obligation not to publish material which amounts to hate speech.

3. Advocacy

A publication is justified in strongly advocating its own views on controversial topics provided that it treats its readers fairly by:

3.1 Making fact and opinion clearly distinguishable;

3.2 Not misrepresenting or suppressing relevant facts;

3.4 Not distorting the facts in text or headlines.

4. Comment

4.1 The press shall be entitled to comment upon or criticise any actions or events of public importance provided such comments or criticisms are fairly and honestly made.

4.2 Comment by the press shall be presented in such manner that it appears clearly that it is comment, and shall be made on facts truly stated or fairly indicated and referred to.

4.3 Comment by the press shall be an honest expression of opinion, without malice or dishonest motives, and shall take fair account of all available facts which are material to the matter commented upon.

5. Headlines, Posters, Pictures and Captions

5.1 Headlines and captions to pictures shall give a reasonable reflection of the contents of the report or picture in question.

5.2 Posters shall not mislead the public and shall give a reasonable reflection of the contents of the reports in question.

5.3 Pictures shall not misrepresent or mislead nor be manipulated to do so.

6. Confidential Sources

The press has an obligation to protect confidential sources of information.

7. Payment for Articles

No payment shall be made for feature articles to persons engaged in crime or other notorious misbehaviour, or to convicted persons or their associates, including family, friends, neighbours and colleagues, except where the material concerned ought to be published in the public interest and the payment is necessary for this to be done.

8. Violence

Due care and responsibility shall be exercised by the press with regard to the presentation of brutality, violence and atrocities.

THE SOUTH AFRICAN PRESS CODE 2011

In operation from 15 October 2011

Preamble

The press exists to serve society. Its freedom provides for independent scrutiny of the forces that shape society, and is essential to realising the promise of democracy. It enables citizens to make informed judgments on the issues of the time, a role whose centrality is recognised in the South African Constitution.

Section 16 of the Bill of Rights sets out that:

"Everyone has the right to freedom of expression, which includes:
a) Freedom of the press and other media;
b) Freedom to receive and impart information or ideas;
c) Freedom of artistic creativity; and
d) Academic freedom and freedom of scientific research.

"The right in subsection (1) does not extend to
a) Propaganda for war;
b) Incitement of imminent violence; or
c) Advocacy of hatred that is based on race, ethnicity, gender or religion, and that constitutes incitement to cause harm."

The press holds these rights in trust for the country's citizens; and it is subject to the same rights and duties as the individual. Everyone has the duty to defend and further these rights, in recognition of the struggles that created them: the media, the public and government, who all make up the democratic state. Our work is guided at all times by the public interest, understood to describe information of legitimate interest or importance to citizens.

As journalists, we commit ourselves to the highest standards of excellence, to maintain credibility and keep the trust of our readers. This means striving for the maximum truth, avoiding unnecessary harm and acting independently.

We adopt the following Code:

1. Reporting of News

1.1 The press shall be obliged to report news truthfully, accurately and fairly.

1.2 News shall be presented in context and in a balanced manner, without any intentional or negligent departure from the facts whether by distortion, exaggeration or misrepresentation, material omissions, or summarisation.

1.3 Only what may reasonably be true, having regard to the sources of the news, may be presented as fact, and such facts shall be published fairly with due regard to context and importance. Where a report is not based on facts or is founded on opinions, allegation, rumour or supposition, it shall be presented in such manner as to indicate this clearly.

1.4 Where there is reason to doubt the accuracy of a report and it is practicable to verify the accuracy thereof, it shall be verified. Where it has not been practicable to verify the accuracy of a report, this shall be mentioned in such report.

1.5 A publication should seek the views of the subject of serious critical reportage in advance of publication; provided that this need not be done where the publication has reasonable grounds for believing that by doing so it would be prevented from publishing the report or where evidence might be destroyed or sources intimidated. If the publication is unable to obtain such comment, this shall be stated in the report.

1.6 A publication should make amends for publishing information or comment that is found to be inaccurate by printing, promptly and with appropriate prominence, a retraction, correction or explanation.

1.7 Reports, photographs or sketches relating to indecency or obscenity shall be presented with due sensitivity to the prevailing moral climate. A visual presentation of sexual conduct should not be published, unless public interest dictates otherwise.

1.8 Journalists shall not plagiarise.

2. Gathering of news

2.1 News should be obtained legally, honestly and fairly unless public interest dictates otherwise.

2.2 Press representatives shall identify themselves as such, unless public interest dictates otherwise.

3. Independence & conflicts of interest

3.1 The press shall not allow commercial, political, personal or other non-professional considerations to influence or slant reporting. Conflicts of interest must be avoided, as well as arrangements or practices that could lead audiences to doubt the press's independence and professionalism.

3.2 Journalists shall not accept a bribe, gift or any other benefit where this is intended or likely to influence coverage.

3.3 The press shall indicate clearly when an outside organisation has contributed to the cost of newsgathering.

3.4 Editorial material shall be kept clearly distinct from advertising.

4. Privacy

4.1 The press shall exercise exceptional care and consideration in matters involving the private lives and concerns of individuals, bearing in mind that any right to privacy may be overridden only by a legitimate public interest.

4.2 The identity of rape victims and victims of sexual violence shall not be published without the consent of the victim or in the case of children, without the consent of their legal guardians.

4.3 The HIV/AIDS status of people should not be disclosed without their consent, or in the case of children, without the consent of their legal guardians.

5. Dignity & Reputation

The press shall exercise exceptional care and consideration in matters involving dignity and reputation, bearing in mind that any right to privacy may be overridden only by a legitimate public interest.

6. Discrimination and Hate Speech

6.1 The press should avoid discriminatory or denigratory references to people's race, colour, ethnicity, religion, gender, sexual orientation or preference, physical or mental disability or illness, age, or other status except where it is strictly relevant to the matter reported.

6.2 The press should not refer to a person's race, colour, ethnicity, religion, gender, sexual orientation or preference, physical or mental disability or other status in a prejudicial or pejorative context except where it is strictly relevant to the matter reported.

6.3 The press has the right and indeed the duty to report and comment on all matters of legitimate public interest. This right and duty must, however, be balanced against the obligation not to publish material which amounts to hate speech.

7. Advocacy

A publication is justified in strongly advocating its own views on controversial topics provided that it treats its readers fairly by

7.1 Making fact and opinion clearly distinguishable;

7.2 Not misrepresenting or suppressing relevant facts;

7.3 Not distorting the facts.

8. Comment

8.1 The press shall be entitled to comment upon or criticise any actions or events of public interest provided such comments or criticisms are fairly and honestly made.

8.2 Comment by the press shall be presented in such manner that it appears clearly that it is comment, and shall be made on facts truly stated or fairly indicated and referred to.

8.3 Comment by the press shall be an honest expression of opinion, without malice or dishonest motives, and shall take fair account of all available facts which are material to the matter commented upon.

9. Children

Definition of Child Pornography
For purposes of this Code, "child pornography" shall mean: "Any image or any description of a person, real or simulated, who is or who is depicted or described as being, under the age of 18 years, engaged in sexual conduct; participating in or assisting another person to participate in sexual conduct; or showing or describing the body or parts of the body of the person in a manner or circumstances which, in context, amounts to sexual exploitation, or in a manner capable of being used for purposes of sexual exploitation."

9.1 Child pornography shall not be published.

9.2 Exceptional care and consideration must be exercised when reporting on matters where children under the age of 18 are involved. If there is any chance that coverage might cause harm of any kind to a child, he or she should not be interviewed, photographed or identified unless a custodial parent or similarly responsible adult consents or a public interest is evident.

9.3 The press shall not identify children who have been victims of abuse or exploitation, or have been charged with or convicted of a crime

10. Violence

Due care and responsibility shall be exercised by the press with regard to the presentation of brutality, violence and atrocities.

11. Headlines, Posters, Pictures and Captions

11.1 Headlines and captions to pictures shall give a reasonable reflection of the contents of the report or picture in question.

11.2 Posters shall not mislead the public and shall give a reasonable reflection of the contents of the reports in question.

11.3 Pictures shall not misrepresent or mislead nor be manipulated to do so.

12. Confidential & Anonymous sources

12.1 The press has an obligation to protect confidential sources of information.

12.2 The press shall avoid the use of anonymous sources unless there is no other way to handle a story. Care should be taken to corroborate the information.

12.3 The press shall not publish information that constitutes a breach of confidence unless a legitimate public interest dictates otherwise.

13. Payment for Articles

The press shall avoid chequebook journalism where informants are paid, particularly when criminals are involved, except where the material concerned ought to be published in the public interest and the payment is necessary for this to be done.

Appendix 2

Interview questionnaire

1. Is an independent media needed in SA?
2. If so, why?
3. What does the term "developmental journalism" mean to you?
4. What does the ANC mean when it advocates "transformation of the media"?
5. How free do you find the media in SA?
6. Is independence of the media a principle to you, or is it contingent on politics, the state of the nation?
7. How do you view the *Sunday Times* vs Manto Tshabalala-Msimang argument in 2007?
8. Do you think the media appeals tribunal will be instituted?
9. What is your view of the future of the media in SA ... in terms of being free and independent?
10. Is an independent media intrinsic to democracy?

Appendix 3

The Media Appeals Tribunal Resolution adopted at the ANC National General Council in Durban, 20-24 September 2010.

The existing self-regulatory system (Press Ombudsman and Press Council) is ineffective and needs to be strengthened to balance the rights of the media and those of other citizens, guided by the values enshrined in our bill of rights, for example human dignity, equality and freedom. The commission affirmed the call for Parliament to conduct a public enquiry on:

a) balancing the rights enshrined in the Constitution, like rights to dignity, freedom of expression and media, guided by the values enshrined in our bill of rights, human dignity, equality and freedom.

b) enquiry on transformation of the print media in respect of a [black economic empowerment] media charter, ownership and control, advertising and marketing and the desirability of the establishment of a media accountability mechanism, for example the media appeals tribunal.

c) the media accountability mechanism [should be] in the public interest including the investigations into the best international practices, without compromising the values enshrined in our Constitution

d) what regulatory mechanisms can be put in place to ensure the effective balancing of rights, this may include self-regulation, co-regulation and independent regulation. Any media accountability mechanism, should be independent of commercial and party political interests, should act without fear, favour and prejudice, should be empowered to impose appropriate sanctions and must not be pre-publication censorship.

In preparation for this enquiry, the ANC will itself submit to Parliament its own submissions. (Source: The Daily Maverick: 27 September 2010: www.thedailymaverick.co.za)

REFERENCES

Adam H and K Moodley (2000) Race and nation in post-apartheid South Africa, *Current Sociology* 48 (3).

African National Congress: Submission to the Press Freedom Commission, January 2012. (Document accessed in hard copy at the attendance of the PFC hearings in Braamfontein, Johannesburg on January 31, 2012)

All Media and Products Survey (AMPs) (2009) www.mediaclubsouthafrica.com. Accessed: 24 March 2010.

Althusser L (1984) Ideology and ideological state apparatuses: Essays on ideology. In Žižek S (ed.) (1994) *Mapping Ideology*. London and New York: Verso, pp 100-140.

ANC (1991) Draft Workers Charter. www.anc.org.za/ancdocs/history/wcharter. Accessed: 20 July 2010.

ANC (2002) Media in a Democratic South Africa. Discussion Document, ANC National Conference, Stellenbosch, December 2002. www.anc.org.za/doc/discus/2002/media. Accessed: 7 April 2008

ANC (2010) Media, Transformation, Ownership and Diversity. www.anc.org.za/ancdocs/ngcouncil/2010/media/pdf. Accessed: 2 August 2010.

ANC Media Statement (2010) 'Zuma child no big deal'. 1 February 2010. www.polity.org.za/anc-statement/by-jackson-mthembu-2010-02-01. Accessed: 10 February 2010

ANC Media statement (2006) 'Zuma's 2006 apology following rape acquittal'. 9 May 2006. www.politicsweb.co.za. Accessed: 24 March 2010

ANC NEC (2008) 'Media and the battle of ideas'. Statement of the ANC National Executive Committee (NEC). 20 January 2008. www.anc.org.za/ancdocs/anctoday/2008. Accessed: 28 January 2009.

ANC Today. 2001. 'Letter from the President: Welcome to ANC Today'. *ANC Today* 1 (1). 26 January-1 February 2001. www.anc.org.za/ancdocs/2001. Accessed: 6 April 2008.

ANC Today. 2006. 'Letter from the President: What the media says: Trying to prove the people wrong … again'. *ANC Today* 6 (46). 24-30 November 2006. www.anc.org.za/ancdocs/anctoday/2006. Accessed: 6 April 2008.

ANC Today (2007) 'Who are our heroes and heroines?' *ANC Today* 7 (32): 17-23 August 2007. www.anc.org.za/ancdocs/anctoday/2007. Accessed: 4 October 2008.

ANC Today. 2007. 'The Media Speaks'. *ANC Today* 7 (33). 24-30 August 2007. www.anc.org.za/ancdocs/anctoday/2007. Accessed: 4 October 2008.

ANC Today (2008) 'The Voice of the ANC must be heard'. *ANC Today* 8 (2). 18-24 January 2008. www.anc.org.za/ancdocs/anctoday/2008. Accessed: 28 January 2009.

ANC Today. 2010. 'The ANC has not and shall not wilt under criticism or close scrutiny'. *ANC Today* 10 (31). 20-26 August 2010. www.anc.org.za/ancdocs/anctoday/2010 Accessed: 5 September 2010.

ANC Today. 2010. 'Differentiate between Media Freedom and Commercial Agenda'. *ANC Today* 10 (28). 30 July-5 August 2010. www.anc.org.za/ancdocs/anctoday/2010. Accessed: 24 April 2011.

Asmal K (2010) 'Free Speech is Life itself': Speech made on Black Wednesday, 19 October 2010, Graduate School of Humanities, University of the Witwatersrand, Johannesburg. Seminar organised by Wits Graduate School, Sanef, and the Institute for the Advancement of Journalism.

Barrett M (1994) 'Ideology, Politics, Hegemony: From Gramsci to Laclau and Mouffe' in Žižek, S. (ed.). *Mapping Ideology.* London and New York: Verso, pp 235-264.

Berger G (1998) Media and democracy in Southern Africa, *Review of African Economy* 78, pp 599-610.

Berger G (1999) Towards an analysis of South African media. Transformation 1994-1999. *Transformation* 38, pp 84-115.

Berger G (2000) Deracialisation, democracy and development: Transformation of the South African media 1994-2000. Paper prepared for the Political Economy of the Media in Southern Africa, Durban, pp 24-29.

Berger G (2002) Theorising the media democracy relationship in Southern Africa. *International Communication Gazette* 64 (1), pp 21-45.

Biko S (1978) *Black Consciousness in South Africa.* New York: Random House.

Biz Community 'Will *ThisDay* live to fight another day?' October 2004 www.bizcommunity.com/article/196/90/4987. Accessed: 24 November 2010.

Biz Community. 2010. 'Power without responsibility'. 30 July 2010 www.bizcommunity.com Accessed: 5 August 2010.

Boloka G (2003) 'Perspectives on Economic Conduct in South African Media: A case study'. ISSN 0256 – 0054 Ecquid Novi 24 (1), pp 55-68.

Brand, R. 2008. 'The Price of Freedom: South Africa's Media'. *Rhodes Journalism Review* 28, September 2008

Bruce P (2009) Goodbye to The Weekender. 6 November 2009. *http://blogs.businessday.co.za/peterbruce/2009/11/06/goodbye-to-the-weekender/.*Accessed:9November2009.

Butler J (1997) *The Psychic Life of Power: Theories in Subjection.* Stanford: Stanford University Press.

Butler J (2000) Dynamic conclusions. In Butler J, A Laclau and S Žižek (eds). *Contingency, Hegemony and Universality: Contemporary Dialogues of the Left.* London and New York: Verso.

Carpentier N and B Cammaerts (2006) Hegemony, Democracy, Agonism and Journalism: An interview with Chantal Mouffe'. Theory Review. *Journalism Studies* 7, pp 964-965.

Civil Society Statement. 2010. 'Let the truth be told: Stop the Secrecy Bill'. Statement received via email. 2 August 2010.

Cosatu Submission on the Protection of Information Bill [B6-2010]: Submitted to the Ad Hoc Committee of Information Legislation: 25 June 2010.

Cosatu Press Statement on the first birthday of the Daily Maverick, 4 November 2010, Nelson Mandela Square, Sandton http://groups-beta.google.com/group/COSATU-press

Cowling L (2010) Media and production of public debate, *Social Dynamics.* 36 (1), pp 78-84.

Cowling L and C Hamilton (2010). Thinking aloud/allowed, *Social Dynamics* 36 (1), pp 85-98.

Da Silva IS (2009) Journey to transformation: Portfolio Black Business South Africa 2009'. *The Triple BEE Review*, pp 183-185.

Dahl R (2000) *On Democracy*. New Haven: Yale University Press.

Daniels G (2006) What is the role of race in Thabo Mbeki's discourse? Unpublished MA thesis. Johannesburg: University of the Witwatersrand.

Davies N (2009) *Flat Earth News*. London: Vintage Books.

Dawes N (2011) *Facing down the new authoritarians*. *Mail & Guardian* 23 December 2012

Derrida J (1967) *Of Grammatology*. Maryland: The John Hopkins University Press. First American Edition: 1976.

Derrida J (2004) 'The last of the Rogue States: the Democracy to come'. *The South Atlantic Quarterly* 103 (2/3). Maryland: The John Hopkins University Press, pp 323-341.

De Waal M (2008) 'Media Conspiracy'. Moneyweb. 3 September 2008. http://bit.ly/aJ8HYT. Accessed: 28 November 2010.

Dugmore H (2009) Meeting democracy's challenge. *Rhodes Journalism Review* 29, September 2009, pp 30-31.

Duncan J (2009) The uses and abuses of political economy: the ANC's media policy, *Transformation: Critical Perspectives on Southern Africa* 70, pp 1-30.

Durrheim K, M Quayle, K Whitehead and A Kriel (2005) Denying racism: Discursive strategies used by the South African media. *Critical Arts* 19 (1 & 2), pp 167-186.

Eagleton T (1991) *Ideology: An Introduction*. London: Verso.

Fallon I (1996) The 1996 Freedom of the Press Lecture. *Rhodes Journalism Review* 12, October 1996, pp 41-43.

Ford H (2009) Freeing the Future, *Rhodes Journalism Review* 29, September 2009, p 35.

Foucault M (ed.) (1969) *The Archaeology of Knowledge*. London and New York: Routledge 1972.

Freedom of Expression Institute (2008) *The Media and the Law: a Handbook for Community Journalists*. Johannesburg: Freedom of Expression Institute.

Gauteng Provincial Government. 1998. 'Allegations Against Public Security MEC Jessie Duarte'. 9 February 1998 www.info.gov.za/speeches/1998 Accessed: 28 November 2010.

Gevisser M (2007) *Thabo Mbeki: The Dream Deferred*. Cape Town: Jonathan Ball.

Giddens A (1990) *The Consequences of Modernity*. Palo Alto: Stanford University Press.

Gumede W (2005) Democracy, Transformation and the Media: The Role of the Media in Strengthening Democracy'. www.caribank.org/events.nsf/forum1. Accessed: 25 June 2008.

Hadland A (2007a) The SA Print Media 1994-2004: an application and critique of comparative media systems. Unpublished PhD thesis: University of Cape Town.

Hadland A (2007b) State media relations in post-apartheid South Africa: An application of comparative media systems theory, *Communicare* 26 (2).

Haffajee F (2008) Is the media free in South Africa to report what it wants? Panel discussion at the Second International Media Forum South Africa, Johannesburg, 21-22 May 2008.

Harber A (2004) Report from SA: Reflections on journalism in the transition to democracy, *Ethics and International Affairs* 18 (3), pp 79-87.

Harber A (2009) 'Rags'. Unpublished paper delivered at the Politics and Media Discussion Group, May 2009, Johannesburg.

Harber A and M Renn (2010) *Troublemakers: The Best of South Africa's Investigative Journalism*. Johannesburg: Jacana.

Held D (1994) *Prospects for Democracy.* Oxford: Polity Press.

Held D (2006) *Models of Democracy.* Stanford: Stanford University Press.

Hudson P (2005) 'Psychoanalytical Concepts: Comprehensibility for the Social Sciences'. Unpublished Paper presented at a symposium entitled 'Rethinking the Social: Psychoanalytical Approaches' at Wits University, 25 August 2005, Wiser Seminar Room, Richard Ward Building.

Huffington A (2009) 'It's the consumer Stupid!' www.huffingtonpost.com/ariannahuffington/the-the-debate-over-online. Accessed: 1 December 2009.

Jacobs S (1999) Tensions of a Free Press: South Africa after Apartheid. Research paper: John F Kennedy School of Government, Harvard University, pp 1-14.

Johannsen RC (1994) Military policies and the state system. In Held D (ed.) *Prospects for Democracy: North South, East, West.* Cambridge: Polity Press.

Kay S (2003) *Žižek: A Critical Introduction.* Cambridge: Polity Press.

Kupe T (2004) Notes towards critical reflections on media transformation and ten years of media freedom: Theory matters and matters of theory. Wits Institute for Social and Economic Research (Wiser). 2004 – inferred date. http://wiserweb.wits.ac.za. Accessed: 26 January 2009.

Laclau E (2000) Constructing Universality in Butler, J, A Laclau, and S Žižek. (eds). *Contingency, Hegemony and Universality: Contemporary Dialogues of the Left.* London and New York: Verso.

Lacan, J. 2008. *My Teaching.* London, New York: Verso.

Laclau E 1996. *Emancipation(s).* London: Verso.

Laclau E (2005) *On Populist Reason.* London and New York: Verso.

Laclau E and C Mouffe (eds) (1985) *Hegemony and Socialist Strategy: Towards a Radical Democratic Politics.* London: Verso.

LaMay C (2004) 'Civil Society and Media Freedom: Problems of Purpose and Sustainability in Democratic Transition'. *The International Journal of Not for Profit Law* 7 (1), Nov 2004.

Leader D and J Groves (1995). *Lacan for Beginners.* Cambridge: Icon Books.

Little A and M Lloyd (eds) (2009) *The Politics of Radical Democracy.* Edinburgh: Edinburgh University Press.

Lloyd L (1990) Shut up, shut out and blown up, *The Free Press*, Volume 1 Number 4, June-August.

Macdonell D (1986) *Theories of Discourse: An Introduction.* New York: Basil Blackwell.

Mandela N (1994) Address to the International Press Institute Congress. 14 February 1994. (http://blogs.businessday.co.za/peterbruce/2010/08/01/Nelson-Mandela's-view-of-press-freedom-read-before-you-leap. Accessed: 26 November 2009.

Manoim I (2009) 'The newspaper may be dying: Long live the news. In Chang D (ed.) *The State We're In: The 2010 Flux Trend Review.* Johannesburg: Macmillan, pp 51-62.

Mason A (2008) Cartooning in a time of calamity. *Rhodes Journalism Review* 28, September 2008, pp 54-55.

Mbeki T (2001) The way forward: Closing remarks at the Cabinet-Sanef Indaba. www.info.gov.za/speeches/2001. Accessed 26 January 2009.

Mcleod D (2009) 'The Shock of the New', *Rhodes Journalism Review* 29, September 2009, p 42.

Media Institute of Southern Africa (Misa). 2008. *So is this democracy? State of Media Freedom in Southern Africa in 2008.* Windhoek: Media Institute of Southern Africa.

Media Monitoring Africa (MMA) (2010) State of South Africa's media: A media monitors perspective. Presentation by William Bird, Sanef's Media Summit, 30 August 2010.

Mouffe C (1999) *The Challenge of Carl Schmitt: The Essence of Politics is Struggle.* London and New York: Verso.

Mouffe C (2000) *The Democratic Paradox.* London: Verso.

Mouffe C (2005) *The Return of the Political.* London: Verso.

Mouffe C (2006) *On the Political: Thinking in Action.* London and New York: Routledge.

Moyo D (2009) Citizen journalism as political praxis: The parallel market of information in Zimbabwe's 2008 election. *Routledge Journalism Studies* 10 (4), pp 551-567.

Mthembu J (2010) Media under siege, Critical Thinkers Forum. *Mail & Guardian,* Johannesburg, 11 August 2010.

Norval AJ (1996) *Deconstructing Apartheid Discourse.* London: Verso.

Nzimande B (2010a) Tenderpreneurs of a special type? South African media on trial, *Red Alert,* newsletter of the SACP. Umsebenzi online 9 (13). 7 July 2010.

Nzimande B (2010b) Media Appeals Tribunal, *Red Alert,* newsletter of the SACP. Umsebenzi online 9 (17), September.

Open Society Foundation for South Africa (2007) *Meeting their Mandates? A critical analysis of SA Media Statutory Bodies.* Open Society Foundation.

Pahad, E. 2001. *Communicating in a Changing society – A News Agenda for Development.* The Government Paper. Communication in Social Transformation. Cabinet/ Government/Sanef Indaba.

Pecheux M (1982) *Language, Semantics and Ideology.* Basingstoke: Macmillan.

Posetti, J. 2009. 'Transforming Journalism 140 characters at a time', *Rhodes Journalism Review* 29, September 2009, pp 38-40.

Quinlan T and S Willan (2005) HIV/AIDS: Finding ways to contain the pandemic. In Daniel J, R Southall and J Lutchman (eds) *South Africa 2004-2005: State of the Nation.* Cape Town: HSRC Press.

Rabinow P (ed.) (1994) *The Subject and Power in Ethics: Subjectivity and Truth,* Volume One. London: Penguin Books.

Reber A (1985) *The Penguin Dictionary of Psychology.* London: Penguin.

Redman E (2009) Circulation falls for UK quality press. World Association of Newspapers. www.editorsweblog.org/newspaper/2009/12/circulationfallsforUkquality_press. Accessed: 2 April 2010.

Rhodes Journalism Review. 1996.'Media on the Menu'. *Rhodes Journalism Review* (13). December 1996. www.rjr.ru.ac.za/no13 Accessed: 22 July 2009.

Rhodes Journalism Review. 1997. 'Tough Talk from the President'. *Rhodes Journalism Review* (15). November 1997. www.rjr.ru.ac.za/no15. Accessed: 22 July 2009.

Right2Know. 2010. Press statement issued by Coordinator of the Right2Know Coalition, Mark Weinberg. Received via email. 10 November 2010.

Ruiters T (2008) 'Zapiro's Zuma rape cartoon furor'. 30 September 2008. www.south-africa. suite101.com/article.cfm/zapiros_suma_rapecartoon_furor. Accessed: 23 September 2009.

Sandbrook, R. 1996. 'Transitions without Consolidation: Democratisation in Six African Cases'. *Third World Quarterly* 17 (1), pp 69-87.

Schippers B (2009) Judith Butler, radical democracy and micro politics. In Little A and M Lloyd (eds) *The Politics of Radical Democracy.* Edinburgh: Edinburgh University Press.

Segal, H. 1988. *Introduction to the work of Melanie Klein.* London: Karnac.

Serino K (2010) Setting the agenda: the production of opinion at the Sunday Times, *Social Dynamics* 36 (1), pp 99 – 111.

Shirky C (2009) Newspapers and thinking the unthinkable. www.shirky.com/weblog/2009/03/newspapers-and-thinking-the-unthinkable/. Accessed: 1 December 2009.

South African National Editors Forum (Sanef) (2010a) Media statement following Sanef and government meeting, 15-16 October 2010, Magaliesberg.

Sanef/Government workshop (2001). Briefing document for delegates to the Government/SANEF Indaba, Journalism Development in South Africa: 29-30 June 2001.

Steenveld L (2007) The SAHRC's enquiry into racism in the media: Problematising state-media relations. *Ecquid Novi* 28 (1&2).

Stokes P (2003) *Philosophy 100 Essential Thinkers*. London: Arcturus Publishing.

Taylor P (2007) Why Žižek, Why Now?, *International Journal of Žižek Studies* 1 (1) 1-10.

Thonjeni K and H Dugmore (2009) Calls across the divide, *Rhodes Journalism Review* 29, September 2009, pp 32-33.

Tomaselli R (1994) Militancy and pragmatism: The genesis of the ANC's media policy, *Africa Media Review* 8 (2), pp 73-85.

Tomaselli R, K Tomaselli and J Muller (1989) Currents of Power: State Broadcasting in SA. Belville: Anthropos Publishers.

Torfing J (1999) *New Theories of Discourse: Laclau, Mouffe, Žižek*. Oxford: Blackwell.

Wertheim-Aymes G (2009) On the future of newspapers. www.bizcommunity.com/article. Accessed: 26 November 2009.

West D (1996) *An introduction to Continental Philosophy*. Cambridge: Polity Press and Blackwell.

Young IM (2009) Inclusion and democracy. In Little A and M Lloyd (eds) *The Politics of Radical Democracy*. Edinburgh: Edinburgh University Press.

Žižek S (1989) *The Sublime Object of Ideology*. London: Verso.

Žižek S (1994) *Mapping Ideology*. London: Verso.

Žižek S (1999) 'Subjectivity, Multiculturalism, Sex and Unfreedom after 11 September: Interview with Slavoj Žižek', *London Review of Books*. California State University.

Žižek S (2000a) *The Ticklish Subject: The Absent Centre of Political Ontology*. London: Verso.

Žižek S (2000b) in Butler, J, Laclau, E and Žižek, S (eds). *Contingency, Hegemony and Universality: Contemporary Dialogues of the Left*. London and New York: Verso.

Žižek S (2002a) *Did Somebody say Totalitarianism?* London: Verso.

Žižek S (2002b) 'I am a fighting atheist: Interview by Doug Henwood: editor of the Left Observer', *Left Observer* Issue no 59, February 2002.

Žižek S (2004) *Iraq the Borrowed Kettle*. London: Verso.

Žižek S (2006a) *Interrogating the Real*. New York: Continuum.

Žižek S (2006b) *How to Read Lacan*. London: Granta Books.

Žižek S (2006c) *The Parallax View*. Cambridge, Massachusetts: MIT Press.

Žižek S (2007) *The Indivisible Remainder: On Schelling and Related Matters*. London: Verso.

Žižek S (2007) 'A conversation with Paul A Taylor', *International Journal of Žižek Studies* 4.

INDEX

Hegel, Georg Friedrich 101, 117, 132, 172
Heywood, Mark 167–168, 172
Huffington, Arianna 68, 73

I

Independent Newspaper Group 33–34,
    44–47, 62, 111, 130, 133–134, 220
Institute for Democracy in South
    Africa (Idasa) 6, 169
Inter Press Service News
    Agency (IPS) 189–190
Internet *see* new media

J

Johncom 34, 176–178, *181n7*
Jones, Jim 133–134
Jordan, Pallo 6–7, 28, 177

K

Katopodis, Katy 78, 82
Kay, Sarah 3, 13, 17, 28, 101, 126, 149
Khumalo, Fred 142
Khoza, Irwin 195–196
Kruger, Franz 7–8, 64, 105–
    106, 125, 145, 207

L

Lacan's psychoanalytical tools
    divided/split subject 17–18, 78,
    84, 95, 108, 120, *124n5*, 126,
    150–151, 170, 202, 211, 216–217
    hysteria x, 4, 12–13, 17, 19, 85,
    138, 149–151, *153n11*, 157,
    165, 186–188, 202, 204, 219
    jouissance 17, 157, 183, 187,
    196, 202, 213–214, 223
    rigid designator 12–13, 17, 88
    social fantasy/gaze x, 3, 9,
    12–13, 17–18, 58–59, 106,
    125–126, 142, 144, 149, 170
    surplus and excess x, 12–13,
    17–18, 36–37, 58, 104, 149,
    151–152, 154, 157, 167, 173,
    179, 183, 188, 213–214, 223

Laclau, Ernesto 2, 11, 14–15, 20, 29, 36,
    86, 115, 126, 183, 185, 201–202
LaMay, Craig 184, 194
Langa, Pius 53, 140, 144
Latakgomo, Joe 218–219
Leader, Darien 12, 17, 213
Leshilo, Thabo 48–49, 64–65, 72,
    165–167, 172, *180n1*, 218
Louw, Raymond 52, 129, 134, 176
Lowe Morna, Colleen 200

M

Macdonell, Diane 15, 19
Madlala-Routledge, Nozizwe
    154–156, 161–162, 167–171,
    179–180, 211–212
Mafube publishing 33, 164
Mail & Guardian x, 4–7, 27, 33, 45,
    48, 58, 64, 78, 81–84, 87, 93,
    95–96, 103, 105–107, 109, 112,
    114–115, 129–130, 135, 145,
    149, *152n4*, 155–156, 163, 165,
    168–169, 171, 178–179, 187, 199,
    201–*202n2*, 206, 208, 216, 221
M&G Centre for Investigative
    Journalism (amaBhungane)
    viii, 65, 67, *74n5*, 207
Maker, Jocelyn 158, 162, 164
Makhanya, Mondli 3, 6, 38, 49,
    88–89, 92, 97–98, 105, 119,
    143–144, 148, 151, *153n7*, 158,
    162, 164, 173–174, 179–180,
    191–192, 209, 211–212, 220
Makoe, Abbey 14, 79–80, 82–85,
    87–88, 92, 96–98
Malala, Justice 14, 80–81, 83, 86,
    111–112, 143–144, 151–*152n5*,
    173, 191–193, 209
Malema, Julius 4–5, 7, 39–40,
    102, 104–105, 113, 120,
    185–186, 194, 217, 224
Mandela, Nelson 11, 18, 35, 37, 61, 111,
    125, 127–136, 138, 140–141, *152n4*
Mangcu, Xolela 90, 103, 106
Manoim, Irwin 50–51, 69
Mantashe, Gwede viii, 102, 119,
    1238, 150, 219, *221n3*–222